797,885 Books
are available to read at

www.ForgottenBooks.com

Forgotten Books' App
Available for mobile, tablet & eReader

ISBN 978-1-331-20727-6
PIBN 10158416

This book is a reproduction of an important historical work. Forgotten Books uses state-of-the-art technology to digitally reconstruct the work, preserving the original format whilst repairing imperfections present in the aged copy. In rare cases, an imperfection in the original, such as a blemish or missing page, may be replicated in our edition. We do, however, repair the vast majority of imperfections successfully; any imperfections that remain are intentionally left to preserve the state of such historical works.

Forgotten Books is a registered trademark of FB &c Ltd.
Copyright © 2015 FB &c Ltd.
FB &c Ltd, Dalton House, 60 Windsor Avenue, London, SW19 2RR.
Company number 08720141. Registered in England and Wales.

For support please visit www.forgottenbooks.com

1 MONTH OF FREE READING

at

www.ForgottenBooks.com

By purchasing this book you are eligible for one month membership to ForgottenBooks.com, giving you unlimited access to our entire collection of over 700,000 titles via our web site and mobile apps.

To claim your free month visit:

www.forgottenbooks.com/free158416

* Offer is valid for 45 days from date of purchase. Terms and conditions apply.

English
Français
Deutsche
Italiano
Español
Português

www.forgottenbooks.com

Mythology Photography **Fiction** Fishing Christianity **Art** Cooking Essays **Buddhism** Freemasonry Medicine **Biology** Music **Ancient Egypt** Evolution Carpentry Physics Dance Geology **Mathematics** Fitness Shakespeare **Folklore** Yoga Marketing **Confidence** Immortality Biographies Poetry **Psychology** Witchcraft Electronics Chemistry History **Law** Accounting **Philosophy** Anthropology Alchemy Drama Quantum Mechanics Atheism Sexual Health **Ancient History Entrepreneurship** Languages Sport Paleontology Needlework Islam **Metaphysics** Investment Archaeology Parenting Statistics Criminology **Motivational**

Camden Society, n.s. 20

A CHRONICLE OF ENGLAND

DURING THE REIGNS OF THE TUDORS,

FROM A.D. 1485 TO 1559.

BY

CHARLES WRIOTHESLEY, WINDSOR HERALD.

EDITED,

FROM A MS. IN THE POSSESSION OF

LIEUT.-GENERAL LORD HENRY H. M. PERCY K.C.B., V.C., F.R.G.S.

BY

WILLIAM DOUGLAS HAMILTON, F.S.A.

VOLUME II.

PRINTED FOR THE CAMDEN SOCIETY.

M.DCCC.LXXVII.

WESTMINSTER:
PRINTED BY J. B. NICHOLS AND SONS,
25, PARLIAMENT STREET.

[NEW SERIES XX.]

COUNCIL OF THE CAMDEN SOCIETY

FOR THE YEAR 1877-78.

President,

THE RIGHT HON. THE EARL OF VERULAM, F.R.G.S.
REV. J. S. BREWER, M.A.
WILLIAM CHAPPELL, ESQ., F.S.A., *Treasurer.*
HENRY CHARLES COOTE, ESQ., F.S.A.
JAMES GAIRDNER, ESQ.
SAMUEL RAWSON GARDINER, ESQ., *Director.*
WILLIAM GILBERT, ESQ.
JOHN W. HALES, ESQ., M.A.
WILLIAM OXENHAM HEWLETT, ESQ., F.S.A.
ALFRED KINGSTON, ESQ., *Secretary.*
FREDERIC OUVRY, ESQ. Pres. S.A.
THE EARL OF POWIS, LL.D.
REV. W. SPARROW SIMPSON, D.D. F.S.A.
JAMES SPEDDING, ESQ.
WILLIAM JOHN THOMS, ESQ., F.S.A.
J. R. DANIEL-TYSSEN, ESQ., F.S.A.

The COUNCIL of the CAMDEN SOCIETY desire it to be understood that they are not answerable for any opinions or observations that may appear in the Society's publications; the Editors of the several works being alone responsible for the same.

WRIOTHESLEY'S CHRONICLE.

Anno Edwardi Sexti primo.

The sixtenth daie of Nouember the Kinges Maiesties visitors[a] beganne that night to take downe the roode with all the images in Poules Church, which were clene taken awaie, and by negligence of the laborers certaine persons were hurt and one slaine in the falling downe of the great crosse in the rode loft, which the papish priestes said was the will of God for the pulling downe of the said idolls. Likwise all images in euerie parish church in London were pulled downe and broken by the commandment of the said visitors. [A.D. 1547.] *Images pulled downe and broken throwe England.*

The xxvii[th] daie of November, being the first Soundaie of Aduent, preched at Poules Crosse Doctor Barlowe, Bishopp of Sainct Davides, where he shewed a picture of the resurrection of our Lord made with vices,[b] which putt out his legges of sepulchree and blessed with his hand, and turned his heade; and their stoode afore the pilpitt the imag of our Ladie which they of Poules had lapped in seerecloth, which was hid in a corner of Poules Church, and found by the visitors in their visitation. And in his sermon he declared the great abhomination of idolatrie in images, with other fayned ceremonies contrarie to scripture, to the extolling of Godes glorie, and to the great compfort of the awdience. After the sermon the boyes brooke the idolls in peaces. *An idoll made of vices and shewed at Poules crosse.*

[a] The kingdom was divided into six circuits, to each of which were appointed three or four visitors, in most cases partly clergymen, partly laymen. They began their visitation in August.—Burnet, ii. pp. 26, 31.

[b] Moveable joints.

A.D. 1547. The sacrament of the aulter receaued under booth kindes.	The xxiiii[th] daie of December the Perliament was proroged, in the which Parliament was granted to the Kinges Maiestie all chauntres, free chapelles, and brotherhoodes, and another act for receavinge the sacrament of the aulter under booth kindes of breade and wyne.
[Anno Reg. 2.] [A.D. 1548.] Spirituall landes surveyed by the Kinges commission.	Memorandum: in the beginning of March the Kinge sent his Commissioners into euerie shire in England, to survey all colleges, free chappells, and chantres.
A proclamation for receuing the sacrament at Easter.	The said moneth of March the Kinges Maiestie sent his proclamation with a booke for the [order of] [a] receaving of the holie communion of the bodie and bloude of Christ under booth kindes of bread and wyne, which shal be ministred by the priest to all persons at Easter, and at all tymes after when the people will require the same.
The seruise song in English.	Memorandum: in Maye Poules quire with diners other parishes in London song all the service in English, both mattens, masse, and even-songe; and kept no masse, without some receaued the communion with the priest.
King Henrie the Seauenthe aniversary.	The xii[th] daie of Maie, 1548, King Henrie the seauenth aniversarie was kept at Westminster, the masse song all in English, with the consecration of the sacrament also spoken in English, the priest leauing out all the canon after the creede saue the "Pater noster," and then ministering the communion after the Kinges booke;[b] at which masse was a sermon made by Mr. Tong, the Kinges chaplaine.
Sermons for the sensinge.	This yeare in the Whitson holidaies my Lord Maior [c] caused three notable sermons to be made at Sainct Marie Spittell, according as they are kept at Easter. The Moundaie preached

---

[a] Supplied from Stow.

[b] The Reformed Communion Service was printed in 1547 before the rest of the Liturgy had been drawn up by the Committee of selected bishops and divines. It was first published 8 March, 1547-8, and may be seen in its original form in Sparrow's Collection of Canons, &c., and Collier's Eccles. Hist., Appen. of Records, No. 59.

[c] Sir John Gresham.

Doctor Tonge, the Kinges chaplaine. Twesdaie Doctor Taylor, parson of Hadley, the Archbishopp of Canterberies chaplaine. Wednesdaie Mr. Cardmaker,[a] vicar of Sainct Brides in Fleete Streete, and reader of Poules in the lecture. And the sensing in Poules cleene putt downe.

A.D. 1548.

This month of Maie also the Kinges Maiestie sent letters under his priuie signett to the Maior and Aldermen with diners other head Comyners, to find men of armes with demilances and horses and light horsemen, some to finde sixe, some foure, some three, and some tow, after their sessing in the Kinges bookes, to the subsedie which should be readie the xiith daie of June next for the defence of this realme.

London to finde horsmen for the Kinges warrs.

This yeare their was a great watch kept on Midsomer eaven[b] and Sainct Peeters caven,[c] by the Kinges counsells commandement, which had in it all the horsemen that should goe into Scotland[d] which were three hundred and more, and seaven hundreth gonners and Morris pikes all in one lyuerie with drummes and standerds, and thirtene hundreth armed men of the Lorde Maiors watch, the Kinges trumpeters blowing afore him booth nightes, and he had sixtene gentlemen of the mercers riding in veluett cotes and chaines of gold afore him, euerie man having three in a lyverie to wayte on them, which was at their owne charges, the sheriffes watch following after my Lord Maior; it was the goodliest sight.

A watche at Midsomer.

On Sainct Peters[e] daie in the afternonne the Bishopp of Wynchester[f] preached at Westminster in the Court[g] afore the Kinge, and the morrow after he was sent to the Towre of London.

The Bishopp ot Winchester sent to the Towre.

[a] John Cardmaker, afterwards burnt in 1555.
[b] Midsummer or St. John's Eve, June 23.
[c] St. Peter's Eve, June 28.
[d] "Which watch was greatly beautified by the number of more than 300 demilances and light horsemen that were prepared by the citizens, to be sent into Scotland for the rescue of the town of Haddington" Stow, p. 595.
[e] June 29.
[f] As Stephen Gardiner was not in the Tower when the Parliament ended, he enjoyed the benefit of the general pardon then proclaimed.—Strype.
[g] In the palace of Whitehall.—Stow.

A.D. 1548.
A single woman sett on the pillorie.

The sixth daie of Julie, 1548, their was a single woman called Founsing Besse, which was a whore of the stewes, and, after the putting downe of them, was taken and banished out of diuers wardes of this cittie. And now taken in a garden by Fynesburie Court with one of the Kinges trumpeters. which for her vicious livinge not yet amended was had to the counter in Bread Streete, and from thence was lead with bassons tynged afore her into Cheepe afore the standard, and their sett on the pillorie, her heare cutt of by the cares and a paper sett on her breast declaring her vicious livinge, and so stoode from tenne of the clocke till eleuen, which punishment hath bene an old auncient lawe in this citie of longe tyme and now putt in vse againe.

A priest hanged and quartered in Smithfield.

Also the seuenth daie of Julie a priest was drawen from the Towre of London into Smythfield and their hanged, headed, and quartered, and his membres and bowells brent, which was one of the causes of a commotion in Cornewall, where one Bodie,[a] a gentleman and one of the Kinges commissioners, was slaine, and other of the said traytors were putt to death in diners other partes of this realme. His head was sett one London Bridge and his quarters on fower gates of this cittie.

Doctor Coxe rehersing the Bishopp of Wynchester's sermon and articles at Paules cross.

The eight daie of Julie, being Reliques Sondaie, Doctor Coxe, the Kinges almoner and schoolemaster,[b] preached at Paules Crosse, where he rehersed the Bishopp of Wynchesters sermon made before the Kinge one Sainct Peters daie last. And declared and read the articles that he promised to the Kinges counsell to haue shewed his conscience in according to the truth of scripture, which he contemptuouslie and obstinatlie did contrarie to his promise, wherfore he was committed to ward as is afore-wrytten. Exhorting all the audience to pray for his conuersion to the truth, and not to reioyce of this his troble, which was godlie donne.

[a] William Body.
[b] Dr. Cox was preceptor to King Edward VI. See Burnet's account of him, ii. 453.

This yeare in Julie the Citizens of London sett out to Scotland [a] one hundred light-horses and one hundred demilances well apparayled and horsed in blewe cottes garded yellow, Mr. Jakes Granado captaine of them under my Lord John Gray,[b] brother to my Lord Marques Dorsett.

<small>A.D. 1548. Horsemen sent out of London into Scotland.</small>

This yeare the first daie of August, being the daie of election of the sherive, which my Lord Maior chose for sheriffe at the Mercers supper, the comens chose to him Mr. John Ayliffe, Barbor surgeon, and Mr of Blackwell.[c] And the same daie was chosen for chamberleine of the Cittie of London Mr. Thomas Haies gouldsmith, which was done of evill will they ought to Mr. Georg Medley, now chamberline.

<small>The ellection of a sherif and a chamberlaine.</small>

This sommer was a great drought for lacke of raine, and in Julie the plage raigned sore in London with great death of people, wherfore tearme and Perliament were adiorned from *Octavis Michaelis*[d] to the third daie of Nouember.

This yeare in September[e] died Queene Katherin,[f] dowager, late wief to King Henrie the eight, and after maried to Sir Thomas Seymor, Lord Admirall and brother to the Lord Protectors grace, which queene died in childbed,[g] the child living, which is a daughter.[h]

<small>Death of the Queene.</small>

---

[a] A journal of this invasion of Scotland is extant, written by W. Patten, a Londoner, who served in the Protector's army. This narrative, which was first published at London in 1548, and reprinted in 1798 in Dalyell's Fragments of Scottish History, is not only one of the most minutely curious records of that age, but one of the most vivid pictures of the realities of war ever drawn. Patten's Diary is still a tract of great rarity.

[b] Severely wounded at the battle of Pinkie.

[c] Master of Bakewell Hall.

[d] 7th of October.   [e] 30 September.

[f] Catherine Parr, widow of Lord Latimer, became the sixth queen of Henry VIII. in 1543.

[g] It is noteworthy that the text gives no countenance to the suspicion of poison administered by her husband, that he might be at liberty to renew his addresses to the Princess Elizabeth.—See Strype, notes on Hayward, p. 301.

[h] In March, 1549, the infant was committed to the charge of the Duchess of Suffolk, but survived her parents only a few months.

A.D. 1548.

A mervale.

A maruaile.

Preachers inhibited generallie.

Memorandum, on Michaelmas daie was chosen for Lord Maior of the Citie of London Mr. Henrie Amcottes, alderman and fishmonger of London.

This yeare in Octobre was a cow about Highgate that had a calfe with tow neckes and heades with white faces, and eight feete, fower on euery side, and two tailes, which cowe died, and the calf taken out of her bellie and bought of a butcher, which had taken out all her inwardes and tooke much money with the sight of the dead calf in the Bell in Newgate markett, till my Lord Maior commanded the calf to be cutt in peeces and buried in the fieldes without the gates.

Also this yeare in Julie, in Amstredame, their was a woman had a chield with two bodies ioyned togeether at the bellie, with hedes, armes, and leggs, and the shape of tow weomen, which were christened in the mothers wombe, and the print brought into Englande.

This yeare, the xxviiith daie of September, proclamation was made to inhibite all preachers generallie till the kinges further pleasure. After which daie all sermons seasede at Poules Crosse, and in all other places.

Anno Edwardi Sexti secundo.

The Maior tooke his othe at the Tower.

The Maiors feast.

Sainct Annes church brent.

This yeare, the morrowe after Simon and Judes daie,[a] the Lord Maior tooke his oth at the Towre bacause the terme was proroged till Crastino Animarum.[b]

This yeare the Maiors feast at the Guilde hall was serued with one course. The higher tables for the Lord Maior and Ladies with uyne dishes, and seauen dishes throughe the hall.

This yeare, the sixteenth daie of Nouember, at eleuen of the clocke at night, was Sainct Annes[c] church without Aldersgate Streete brent by casualtie of fire, being Fridaie.

[a] 29th October.   [b] The 2nd of November.
[c] St. Ann's-in-the-Willows.

The xxi daie of Nouember, one of the great towres next the draw bridge within the Towre of London was thorowen downe by fire that fell in a vessell of gone pouder.[a] A French man being prisoner in the same chamber for quoyning of testornes[b] lying sicke in his bed was slaine with the fall of the stones in his bed, and tow or three persons more hurt, which thing happened about seuen of the clocke at night, the which ward or towre Haukins the under porter had in his custodie, and great fauld laid to him by reason he kept powdre their, and having a prisoner in that warde; the said Hawkins was comitted for the same.

A.D. 1548.
Fire in the Tower of London.

[A.D. 1549.]

Memorandum: the seavententh daie of Januarie, 1548[-9], Sir Thomas Seymor, Lord Sidley,[c] and High Admirall of Englande, and brother to my Lord Protector, was sent to ward to the Towre of London for treason.

Lord Admirall sent to the Tower.
[Anno Reg. 3.]

Memorandum: the xiiii[th] daie of Februarie their was an Oir Determyner kept in the Guildhall by the kynges commission for the enditement and arraignement of Sir William Sherington, knight, and treasorer of the kinges mynte of Bristowe, for suspition of treason[d] against the king. Wherupon this daie he was endited for counterfetting the kinges coyne to his owne proper use at the said cittie of Bristow, the sixtenth daie of Julie last past, to the some of two thousand poundes[e] in siluer in testornes, upon which enditement he was arraigned, and without any further triall he confessed his treason, wherupon he had judgement to be had to the Towre of London from whence he came, and from thence to be drawen on an hirdell to the place of execution at the kinges pleasure, and

The arraignment of Sir William Sherington, knight, at the Guildhall.

---

[a] "By the menes of a Frenchman that sette a barrelle of gounepoder a fyere."—Grey Friars' Chronicle, p. 57.

[b] Testoon or teston, an old coin made of brass covered with silver, which from 1s. 6d. the original value, came down to 6d.—a tester.

[c] Baron of Sudley.

[d] He was accused of conspiring against the government, with the Lord Admiral, whom he was to have supplied with 10,000l. a month.

[e] Other authorities state that he had already coined about 12,000l. of false money and had clipped a great deal more, to the value of 40,000l. in all.—See Strype, ii. p. 122; and Burnet, Hist. ii. p. 97.

their to be hanged till he died. The Commissioners that sate on him [were] my Lord Maior cheiffe, M^r of the Rolls, my Lord Montague Cheiffe Justice of the Common Place, my Lord Cheiffe Baron, Justice Hynde, Sir Thomas Pope,[a] Sir Raffe Warreyne, Sir Richard Gressam, Sir John Gressam, Mr. Recorder.

<small>A.D. 1549.</small>

<small>A butcher punished for adoultrie and conspiring a mans death.</small>

Memorandum: the first daie of March, 1548[-9], being Fridaie, John Abram, botcher in Sainct Nicholas Shambles, was had from the Counter in Bread Streete, and sett on a horse with his face to the horsetaile and so leed up Cheepe to the Newgate on one side of the streete and coming downe Sainct Nicholas Shambles on the other side of the streete, and so through Cheepe, the Pultrie, Stockes, Cornehill, Gracious Streat, Fishe Streat, and along Thames Streete to Queenehith, and their turned up to Bread Streete, and so to the Standard in Cheepeside, where he was sett on the pillorie with a paper pynned over his heade and another pynned on his backe, upon which papers was wrytten in great lettres as followeth " for the keepinge of an other mans wiefe and hiringe a man to kill her husband." And thus he stoode on the pillorie from eight of the clocke in the forenonne till half an hower after aleuen, and then he was taken downe and sent to warde againe. This Abram kept one Woodshawes wief, a botcher against his owne dore, in Sainct Nicholas Shambles, and should haue killed him by her procuremente. And he hired one Head, of the Kinges garde, to doe the deede because his hert serued him not, and gaue him at tymes fortie poundes in money to kill him, which Heade opened this conspiracie in Sir John Gresshames tyme, and by fauor and sute to the Kinges counsell and rewardes geuen punishment was differred till now that my Lord Maior had commandment to punish him as he and his brethren should thincke best. And so he was sodenlie taken on the Thursdaie afore selling fleshe at his shopp and sent to ward not knowing the cause, and commandment geauen to the keeper that no person should speake with him, so that when he came to doe his pennance no person knewe it till he rode aboute.

<small>[a] The founder of Trinity College, Oxford.</small>

The third daie of March, being Shroue Sondaie, Mr. Henry Amcottes, Lord Maior of London, was presented to the Kinges Maiestie at his pallace at Westminster. And after the oration made by Mr. Recorder to his Maiestie and aunswere againe by my Lord Chauncelor unto the maior and aldermen, the Kinges Maiestie made my Lord Maior, knight, and Mr. William Locke, alderman, and Mr. John Ayliffe, barbar surgeon, sheriffes of London for this yeare, weare made knightes also in the Chambre of Presens, the Kinges Maiestie standing under his cloath of estate.

A.D. 1549.
My Lord Maior and booth the sheriffes made knightes.

Memorandum: the xiiii[th] daie of March the Parliament was proroged which had be[en] kept at Westminster since the [twenty[a]] fourth daie of Nouember last past, in which session diuers godlie actes were made.[b] And the Kinges Majestie gaue a generall free pardon, certaine persons in the Towre of London excepted.[c]

A generall pardon by Act of Perliament.

Memorandum: at this session of Perliamente one uniforme booke was sett fourth of one sort of seruice with the ministration of the holie communion and other sacramentes to be used in this realme of Englande and other the Kinges dominions whatsoeauer. To be obserued after the feast of Pentecost next coming, as by an Act of Perliment against the transgressors of the same doeth appeare. Howbeit Poules quire, with divers parishes in London and other places in England, begane the use after the said booke in the beginning of Lent, and putt downe the priuate masses as by the acte is ordayned.

The new seruice begonne and priuat masses put downe.

Also at this Perliament the cleargie granted to the Kinges Maiestie a subsedie of vi s. in the pounde, to be paid in three yeares next ensuing, that is to say, of all benefices and spirituall promotions from aboue fortie shillinges upwardes yearelie during the said three yeares ii s. of the pounde, as by the said Act more at larg appeareth.

A subsedie granted by the spiritualtie.

[a] The Parliament reassembled at Westminster on the 24th of November, 1548, having been prorogued to that day from the 25th October in consequence of the plagne then being in London.

[b] A very accurate and full account of the Acts passed in this Parliament will be found in Burnet's History of the Reformation.

[c] As also all those who had absented themselves out of the kingdom.

A.D. 1549.
A reliefe of moueables, goodes, sheepe, and cloth granted to the kinges majestic.

All the Lordes and Commons of the temporalltie granted to the Kinges Maiestie at this Perliament a relief of xii d. of the pounde of all moueable goodes from x l. upwardes, to be paid cuerie yeare for three yeares next ensuing, and of strangers every of the three yeares tow shillinges of the pounde, and of euerie stranger under tenne poundes in goodes xii d. yearelie during the said three yeares, and of euerie other stranger of the age of xii yeares and upwardes not payable by this Act of their goodes viii d. yearelie, weomen couert excepted, and an other relief granted to be paide of sheepe, and another of cloth, as by the Act more at large [appeareth.[a]]

The Lord Admirall beheaded.

Memorandum: the xx[th] daie of March, 1548-[9], Sir Thomas Seymor, Lord of Sidley [b] and High Admirall of England, and brother to my Lord Protector, was beheaded at the Towrehill, which said Lord Admirall was condemned of high treason by the hole Perliament,[c] as by an Act made by the same more plainelie appeareth.[d]

Fire at Broken wharfe.

The twentie third daie of Aprill, being Saint Georges daie, and the Twesdaie in Easter weeke, was a fire at Broken wharfe among the hayhowses, which appeared at fower of the clocke in the morninge, and brent and perished aboue six howses.

One bearing a fagott at Poules Cross.

The xxviii[th] daie of Aprill, being the first Soundaie after Easter, one Champnes, of Stratford, bare a fagott at Poules Crosse, which was an Anabaptist, whose opinion was, that after man was regenerate by baptisme and the Holic Ghost that he could not sine, which

[a] Omitted in MS.
[b] Baron of Sudley.
[c] On the 4th of March a message came from the King to the Commons stating that "he thought it was not necessary to send for the Admiral, but that the Lords should come down and renew before them the evidence they had given in their own House;" and thereupon the Bill of Attainder was agreed to in a House of about four hundred members, not more than ten or twelve voting in the negative.—See Burnet, ii. p. 99.
[d] Strype, in his notes to Hayward, pp. 301-3, has given a full account of these proceedings from the Journals of the two Houses, to prove "how fairly the admiral was judged and dealt with in the Parliament." The journals notice that the Lord Protector was present at each reading of the Bill.

damnable opinion he abiured the daie before at Poules before my Lord of Canterburie, and was sorie for his error.

Memorandum: on Maie daie at night 1549, a certaine armie of Frenchmen to the number of vii thousand came priuelie to assault Bulleine Barke,[a] which was the M^r[b] of the Horse camp at the wynninge of Bulleyne, in the which fort was not fower hundred soldiors that kept it, which persons hauing knowledge not tow howres afore the assalt by one Carter ane Inglish man, a soldier in the French campe, and fleed out of Bulleyne for a felonie committed by him their, which said Carter pricked forward from the French campe to the fort and called for Mr. Arnolde the captaine, and their shewed to him how they were betrayed. By his aduise the captaine sett and made all thinges readie to defende the assalt. The French men to the number of three thousand marching to assalt him, and shooting of vii hundred shott att ones with hakes[c] and hagebuttes,[d] some men keeping them close and not seene and a great number scaling the forte, some of them, shooting haileshott out of the fort and casting out stones and other artillerie on the Frenchmen, ouerthrew and bete them of. So that by the purveyance[e] of Almightie God, after long fight and seaven assaltes geauen by the Frenchmen with gonne shott and otherwise, a great number of Frenchmen were slaine[f] and hurt, and fiftene waggons of their dead bodies caried awaie by the Frenchmen and so fleed, and not an hundred Englishmen slaine and hurt. The captaine of the fort sore hurt

A.D. 1549.

An assalt geauen to Bullenbarke by the Frenchmen, with their ouerthrowe.

---

[a] By an article of the treaty of peace, concluded at London in March 1547, the English were allowed to continue the fortifications of Bullenberg, but Henry II. sent so rough a message by his ambassador, when these were resumed, that the Protector, rather than hazard a quarrel with France, ordered the works to be discontinued before the fort was finished.

[b] Probably "the camp of the Master of the Horse."

[c] Hake or haque, a hand-gun (three quarters of a yard long).—See "Egerton Papers," p. 17.

[d] Haguebut is only another form of arquebuse, which ancient species of fire-arm was cocked with a wheel and supported on a rest. One of those used at the siege of Boulogne may still be seen in the Museum there.

[e] The French word pourvoyance, providence.

[f] In King Edward's Journal, p. 6, it is said, that the French lost 1,000 men.

A.D. 1549.

and Carter that gaue them knowledge first. But the said Carter slewe the said French captaine himself and fought very valiantlie against the Frenchmen till he was so sore hurt that he could no more.

A Anabaptist bearinge a fagott at Poules Crosse.

Memorandum: the fifth daie of Maie, being the second Soundaie after Easter, one Puttoe, a tanner in Collchester in Essex, bare a faggott at Poules Crosse, which was an Anabaptist and was abiured the xxx[th] daie of Aprill at Poules, before my Lorde of Canterburie; his opynion was, he denied that Christ descended not[a] into hell, which damnable opinion he now lamentith.

An oir determiner kept by my Lord Maior in Southwark.

Memorandum: the sixth daie of Maie their was an Oyer Deter myner[b] kept at the justice court at Southwarke for the enditement and arraignment of William Pate, of Islington, in the countie of Middlesex, monyer, which said Pate had coyned in the Kinges mynte in Sothwarke, in the countie of Surrey, tow hundred plates of siluer, being the grote plate of iiii d. and had sett the stampe and coyne of the new shyling of xii d. the peece on them. And this daie was endited of the same by a quest of enquirie of certaine persons of the county of Surrey, and upon his enditement was arraigned, and confessed his fact himself without further triall, and had judgment to be drawen and hanged, and so was committed to the Kinges Bench; Sir Henry Amcottes, knight, Lord Maior of London, being the Cheiffe Commissioner, Sir Roger Cholmeley, Lord Cheiffe Baron, Sir Humphrey Browne, Lord Cheiffe Justice of the Comen Place, Sir William Curson, one of the Barons of the Exchequer, Serieant Morgan, Mr. Recorder, Mr. Chidley, Sir Martin Bowes, Sir John Gressame, with other aldermen knightes in the commission, and they all dined at the Bridghouse at the costes of the Chambre of London.

A Anabaptist beringe a fagott at Poules Cross.

Memorandum: the xii[th] daie of Maie, the third Soundaie after Easter, their was a bucher dwelling by Ould Fish Streeto which bare a faggott at Poules Crosse, which was an Anabaptist, denying

---

[a] Sic MS.

[b] A clerical error for "Oyer et termyner;" the writer would appear to have mistaken the contracted "et" employed in the original for "de," here and throughout.

that Christ tooke no nature of the Virgin Marie, which damnable **A.D. 1549.**
opinion he did abiure the daie before, before my Lord of Canterburie, at Lambeth, and now lamenteth the same.

 Memorandum: the xiiith daie of Maie at tow of the clocke in the **Pate, monier, put to death at St. Thomas of Wattringes.**
afternoune William Pate, monyer, which was condemned the sixth
daie of Maie afore, was drawen from the Kinges Bench on a hirdell
in Southwarke to the bridge foote, and so by Sainct Olaue's Church
through Barnesey^a Streete to Sainct Thomas Wattringes, where he
was hanged for treason.

 Memorandum: the nynetenth daie of Maie, being the fourth **Putto an Anabaptist doinge penance the second tyme.**
Soundaie after Easter, Puttoe, which bare a fagott the second
Soundaie after Easter at Poules Crosse because he stoode that tyme
with his capp on his head all sermon tyme, to the peoples esty-
mation unpenitent for his offence, was sent for to my Lorde of
Canterburie, who had further ioyned him in pennanee to stand this
daie againe at Poules Crosse with a faggott on his sholdre bare-
headed, which he did. And after confessed his error and shewing
himself to be penitent for his offence, which the awdience well
accepted, praying for his reconciliation.

 Memorandum: in the moneth of Maie their was a commotion of **Commotion of Rebells.**
the commens in Somersetshire and Lyncolneshire concerning a
proclymation for enclosures, and they broke downe certaine parkes
of Sir William Harbertes and Lord Stourtons, which said Sir
William Harberd was sent into Wales for reskewe, and slewe and
putt to death diuers of the rebells. Also at Bristowe^b and diuers
other shires likewise the commons arose and pulled downe parkes,
but by good pollicie of the Counsell and other noblemen of the
countrey they were pacified.

 Memorandum: the xxiiiith daie of Maie their was two oyrs and **Coyners arraigned.**
determyners keept at the guildhall in the afternoune for the French-
men coyners at Dirham^c mynt, which had made the counterfeite
new money named shillinges. And this daie after their enditementes
confessed their treason and had judgment to be drawen and hanged,

^a Bermondsey Street.   ^b Bristol.   ^c Durham.

14   WRIOTHESLEY'S CHRONICLE.

A.D. 1549.

my Lord Maior cheiffe in commission; they had after the Kinges pardon.

For Whit Sondaie.

Memorandum: on Whit Soundaie, being the nynth of June, my Lord Maior and his brethren the Aldermen assembled at Poules for a sermon which was apoynted by my Lord of Canterburie. Mr. Lydall should haue preached, who came not, so that they were disapoynted of the sermon. On Whitsoundaie the cannons and petie cannons in Poules left of their gray and calabre amises,[a] and the cannons wore hoodes on their surpleses after the degrees of the universities, and the petie cannons tipittes like other priestes; and all the chauntre priestes were putt to their pencions and to be at libertie.

Sermons kept at Poules Cross in Whitson week.

Also on Mundaie and Tuesdaie my lord maior had apoynted tow sermons to be made at Poules Crosse, the Aldermen coming in their scarlettes on foote thither, as they doe everie other soundaie. Mr. Miles Couerdale[b] preached on Mundaie, and Mr. Bill of Cambridge[c] preached on Tuesdaie. And on Wednesdaie should haue bene another sermon, but because they stoode in doubt that it shold be holidaie because their was no proper service for that daie in the Kinges booke their was no sermon. And such gestes of the aldermen and their wifes as was of old custome to dine with my lord maior and the sheriffes was putt of for that daie to Trinitie Soundaie,

[a] Mr. Way, in the Promptorium (p. 11), remarks that the amice for a canon, which was made of fur or calaber, was a vestment perfectly distinct from the more ancient ecclesiastical vestment of the same name, which was of linen. In the inventory of church ornaments in Westminster Abbey at the Dissolution is the item, "Oon good graye Amyes not moche worne." And in the "Traditions and Customs of Cathedrals, p. 120," the amice is described as an ornament of grey fur, worn by dignitaries, as in the well known portraits of Warham and Cranmer; and the inventories of St. Alban's have the entry, "iii Almicia quorum duo de griseo et tercium de serico." Brit. Mus. Claud. E. IV. fol. 351. See also "Stow's Survey," ed. 1633, p. 660, and Brit. B. ii. 401.

[b] Miles Coverdale, who completed the first English version of the Bible. He was appointed Bishop of Exeter, August 14, 1551, but was deprived and imprisoned by Queen Mary, 1553, and afterwards banished. On Mary's death he refused to return to his bishopric, and lived privately until he attained his 81st year.

[c] William Bill, S.T.P., was Master of St. John's College, Cambridge, and in 1551 was translated to the mastership of Trinity College.

which was done by the consent of a court of aldermen the Twes- A.D. 1549.
daie afore Whitsoundaie.

Also on Whitson Moundaie my lord maior did elect and chuse at The sheriffe chosen.
his table after dynner Mr. Richard Turke, alderman and fishmonger,
for one of the sheriffes for the next yeare, according to the prero-
gative of the Maior of London.

This yeare in the moneth of Julie the commons of Essex and
Kent, Sufforke and Norfolke made ensurrections against enclosures,
and pulled downe diuers parkes and howses in diners places, and
did much hurte.

Also in Devonshire about Exceter the Devonshire men and Cornish Commotions of the
men made insurrections against the Kinges proceedinges to mayn Commons.
tayne the masse and other ceremonies of the Popes law, which were
a great number, and camped about the citie of Exceter.

Memorandum: the third daie of Julie, 1549, my lord maior The Lord Maior and
beganne to watch at night, riding about the citie to peruse the Aldermen wachinge
constables with their watches, and to see that they keepe the howres weeklie.
apoynted at the last court of aldermen holden at the guildhall, for
the preseruation and savegard of the citie because of the rebellion
in diuers places of this realme.

And so after him euerie alderman in their courses to keepe like
order till Michaelmas next, without their be other commandement
to the contrarie. The xith daie of Julie a commen counsell was
keept in the guildhall; Mr. Goodyere, alderman of the warde of
Portsokin, gaue up his cloake, and his fine to be sett by my lord
maior and aldermen, which was five hundreth poundes, to buy
wheate for the use of the cittie, which he paid out of hande.

And the same daie Mr. Kirton, alderman, had licence for iiii
yeares to be spared from the office of shivaltie.

The eighteenth daie of Julie was a proclamation made in the cittie Proclamation for
of London for mershall lawe, booth the sheriffes riding and the Marshall Law.
knight mershall with them in the middle with the trumpett and
the common cryer afore them with one of the clarkes of the papers
with him, which proclamation was made within the citie in diuers

A.D. 1549.

places in the forenonne, and at afternonne without the gates of the cittie, which proclamation was for rebells and upsterrers without any enditement or arraignment [to be apprehended.] [a]

The twentith daie of Julie Mr. Thomas Offley, marchant taylor, was sworne alderman for Mr. Goodyer for the warde of Portesokin, which daie was Satterdaie, and a court keept in the Guildhàll for diuers affaires for the King and preserving of his chambre and cittie of London.

Watching the gates of London on the day tyme.

Also the same daie euerie gate of the cittie beganne to be watched with certaine commyners [b] of the craftes of the cittie of London, and so to be contynued dailie from fiue of the clocke in the morning till eight of the clocke in the night till contrarie commandement be prouided in that behalf.

Ordynance and other wepons for the defence of the cittie.

Also the same daie preceptes were sent to euerie alderman and all the companies of the citie to be in a redines with harnis, gonns, bowes, and other wepons for the defence of the same, and also diuers great peeces of ordinance of brasse of the Kinges was had from the Towre and sett at euerie gate of the cittie, and all the walls of the citie from Criplegate to Bevis Markes, by Christ Church,[c] were sett with ordenance on the walls, which was the cities ordenance, and gonners apoynted to cuerie gate and for the walls, having wages at the cities charges.[d]

The one and twentith daie of Julie, the sixth daie after Trinitie Soundaie, the Archbishopp of Canterburie [e] came to Poules, and their in the quire after mattens in a cope with an aulble under it, and his crosse borne afore him with two priestes of Poules for deakin

---

[a] Omitted in MS.

[b] Commoners or liverymen.

[c] Christ Church or Creechurch within Aldgate; it formerly belonged to the Augustinian Canons of the Holy Trinity, and a neighbouring church in Leadenhall Street is still named St. Katharine Creechurch.

[d] " Every daye from the xx day of July satte at every gatte viii of the comyneres and ii gonners every day from vi in the mornynge unto it was [late] atte nyght unto the x day of September."—Grey Friars' Chronicle, p. 61.

[e] Thomas Cranmer.

and sub-decon with aulbles and tuniceles,[a] the deane of Poules followinge him in his surples, came into the quire,[b] my lord Maior with most part of the aldermen sitting their with him. And after certaine assembly of people gathered into the quire the said Bishopp made a certaine exhortation to the people to pray to almightie God for his grace and mercy to be shewed unto us. In the which exhortation he admonished the people of the great plague of God reigning ouer us now in this realme of Englande for our great sins and neglecting his worde and commandments, which plage is the commotion of the people in most parts of this realme now raigning among us speciallie against Godes commandmente and the true obedience to our most Christen king Edwarde the sixt, naturall, christian,[c] and supream head of this realme of Englande and other his domynions, which plage of sedition and divicion amonge ourselues is the greatest plage, and not like heard of since the passion of Christ, which is come on us by the instigation of the Devill for our miserable sinnes and trespasses in that we have shewed us to be the professors and diligent hearers of his worde by his true preachers and our lives not amended, which godlie exhortation was so godlie sett fourth to the hearers with the true obedience also to our kinge and superiors and also to the confutation of the rebellors, with also monition geauen to the people to fast and pray, putting all pride aside with other sinns and vices raigning amonge us, as delicious and superfluous feedinge and sumptuous apparell, that it would haue moued and stirred any christian hart to lament their offences and call to Almightie God for mercy and grace.

This daie procession was song according to the Kinges booke,[d] my lord [archbishop][e] and the quire kneling, my lord singing the

A.D. 1549.

The Archbishop of Canterbury ministeringe the communion in Paules.

---

[a] Albs and tunicles.

[b] "And soo the Byshoppe of Caunterbery was there at procession, and dyd the offes hymselfe in a cope and no vestment, nor mytter, nor crosse, but a crose staffe; and soo dyd alle the offes, and hys sattene cappe on hys hede alle the tyme of the offes; and soo gave the communione hymselfe unto viii persons of the sayd church." —Grey Friars' Chronicle, p. 60.   [c] By the law of nature and Christianity.

[d] This is the same the Church of England makes use of at this day, excepting a few alterations.   [e] Archbishop Cranmer.

collectes and praying and adding one other prayer which he had written for this plage. This donne he went to the highe aulter with deacon and subdeacon, and their to celebrate the holie communion of the bodie and bloud of Christ, according to the Kinges booke last sett fourth by Act of Parliament[a] for the service and sacrafice of the church, he ministring the sacrament of the bodie of Christ himself to the deane and vii other, the deacons following with the chalice of the bloud of Christ.[b]

The communion donne, Mr. Joseph,[c] his chaplaine, went to Poules Crosse and made a sermon of the gospell of this Soundaie, breiflie and shortlie declaring in the same sermon parte of my lordes exhortation to the people, because all herde him not before, and so committed the people to God.

Tow hanged by marshall law.

Mondaie, the twentie-second daie of Julie and Marie Magdalens daie, their was tow jebettes sett up in London, [one] at the bridg foote in Southwarke, and another within Algate by the well, upon which jebetts their was hanged tow of the rebells of Kent and Essex, the knight marshall with booth the sheriffes seing the execution,

---

[a] This Act confirming the new Liturgy sanctioned the preface concerning ceremonies, and gave the whole a turn favourable to the Reformation. It is said in the preamble of the Act, "That there might be an uniform way of worship all over the Kingdom; the King, by the advice of the Protector and his council, had appointed the Archbishop of Canterbury and other Bishops and Divines named to draw an Order of divine worship, &c. which they, by the aid of the Holy Ghost, had with one uniform agreement concluded on. Wherefore the Parliament, having considered the Book, did enact, &c." This Act was variously criticised at the time. Some thought it too much that it was said the book was drawn by "the aid of the Holy Ghost." Others censured it because it was said to be done "by uniform agreement," though eight of the bishops employed in drawing it up protested against its being published in its present form, viz. the bishops of London, Durham, Carlisle, Worcester, Norwich, Hereford, Chichester, and Westminster, as also the Earl of Derby and the Lords Dacres and Windsor.—See Journals of Parl.; Burnet, Hist. Ref. ii. p. 61-95; and Collier Ecclesiastical Hist. ii. p. 255-9.

[b] The sacrament of the Eucharist was to be made of bread and of wine mixed with water. In the Consecration Prayer were these words, since left out, "With thy Holy Spirit vouchsafe to ble+ss and sanc+tify these thy Gifts of Bread and Wine, that they may be unto us the Body and Blood of thy most dearly beloved Son, &c."

[c] John Joseph, S.T.P. rector of St. Mary-le-Bow.

which was by marshall lawe; he that honge at Algate was a taylor at Raynesford,[a] in Essex, and the other a Bullenor.[b] A.D. 1549.

The xxiii[rd] daie of Julie in the afternoune the Kinges Majestic came from Greenewych and rode from his place in Southwarke throwe the cittie of London to his palace at Westminster, aecompanied with his lordes, knightes, and gentlemen richlie appayrayled, the lord maior riding in a *gowne* of crymoysin veluett with his mace afore the Kinges Majestic, with my Lord of Oxford which bare the Kinges sworde, my Lord Protectors grace following the Kinge, the aldermen followinge the knightes, riding in scarlett, and before the lordes; the maior and the aldermen receauing the King at Sainct Margaretts Church that was in Southwarke; and so riding before his maiestie in their places till they came to Charing Crosse, where the aldermen stoode in aray till the Kinges Majestic passed by them, which saluted them, putting of his capp to euerie of them; my lord maior riding still before his majestic to his palace of Westminster, where the Kinges Majestic with hartie thankesgeuing to him tooke his leaue, my Lord Protectors grace likewise, thanking him after the Kinge. The kinge ridinge thronghe the cittie of London.

The last daie of Julie the Lord Marques of Northampton entred the Citie of Norwych,[c] and that night the enimies entred the towne and tooke it and burned part of it and putt the Lord Marques to flight and slew the Lord Sheiffeld[d] with other.[e] Norwiche taken by the rebells.

[a] Romford—*See* Grey Friars' Chronicle, p. 60. [b] A man of Boulogne.

[c] With only 1,060 horsemen, (King Edward's Journal, p. 7,) or according to Holingshead (p. 1033) and Hayward (p. 297) with 1,500 horse and a small band of Italian mercenaries.

[d] Edmund, first Lord Sheffield (created baron 1 Edward VI.) His horse falling into a ditch he was slain by a butcher with a club. *See* Dugdale, Baronage, ii. p. 336.

[e] Neither Blackstone nor Hallam give the exact date of the first commissions of lieutenancy, but both refer to the statute 4 and 5 Phil. and Mary, c. 3, in which lords-lieutenant are mentioned as known officers. It would appear, however, that these officers were first instituted in the reign of Edward VI. the more readily to repress these insurrections. Their commissions are dated 24th July, and run, " that they should enquire of all treasons, misprisions of treason, insurrections, riots, and all other breaches of the King's peace, with authority to levy men and fight against the King's enemies." *See* Strype's Memorials, ii. p. 178.

A.D. 1549.

The towne diche was taken and new made.

The third daie of August the Towne dych betwene Aldersgate and Newgate that had bene long closed upp in gardens was begone to be made dych new againe, and seauen score workemen sett a worke at the cost of the chambre with certaine of the Companie[s] of the Cittie.

A defiaunce from the Frenche Kinge.

The 8 of August in the afternoone the embassadour of the French Kinge gaue my Lord Protector defyance from the French Kinge at the Kinges pallace of Whitehall at Westminster. And at midnight lettres were sent to the Mayor of London to make a privie watch ymmediately and to apprehende all Frenchmen and theyr goodes which were not denizons, which thinge was done, for the Lord Mayor sent for all the Aldermen to his house, and they ymmediately made search in theyr wardes, and all shippes and passyges were restrayned likewise.

The victory of the Lord Privie Seale against the rebelles in Devonshire.

The tenth of August, beinge Saterday, the Archbishop of Canterbury made a colation in Pawles quire for the victory that the Lord Russell,[a] Lord Privie Seale, had on Monday last past against the rebells in Devonshire, which had beseeged Exeter, and lyen in campe afore yt by the space of 3 weeks [b] and like to have famished them in the towne,[c] but the sayd monday the Lord Privye Seale entred the city and slewe, hurte, and tooke prisoners of the sayd rebells aboue iiii M.[d] and after hanged divers of them in the towne and about the countrye.

Rebelles put to death.

The 16 of August there were two rebelles put to execution by marshall lawe, one called Church, which was hanged without Bishopsgate, and another called Payne, which was sent to Waltham and there hanged.

---

[a] John, Lord Russell.

[b] The rebels, finding they could not take the city of Exeter by force, as they had no artillery, at length turned the siege into a blockade, in hopes that the want of provisions would compel the besieged to surrender.

[c] The citizens, who were the sole defenders, endured extreme famine for twelve days, eating their horses and the horses' bran. *See* Hayward, p. 294.

[d] The rebels lost 600 men.—Hayward, p. 294.

The sayd day in the afternoone was araigned at the Guildhall   A.D. 1549.
one John Allen, of Southwarke, pedler, William Gates, of Hampton, Rebelles araigned.
in the county of Willshire, shepeard, Roger Baker, of Southfeld, in
the county of Suffolke, fawconer, and James Webbe, of Barford, in
the county of Oxford, clark and vicar of the same towne; which
foure persons were this afternoone indyted and condempned of
high treason, for rebelles and captaines of Norfolke, Suffolke, and
Oxfordshire, and had judgment for the same.

The 22 of August, James Webbe, vicar of Barford, was sent to Rebelles put to death.
Alisbury, there to be drawne, hanged, and quartered, and the same
day John Allen was drawne to Tyburne and there hanged, headed,
and quartered, and his bowelles and members burnt; and Roger
Baker was drawne to Tower Hill, where he had lyke execution;
and William Gates, sheepheard, was drawne to Totnam, and there
put to lyke execution; the sheriffes of London rydinge and scinge
the execution of all iii persons one after another, their heades and
quarters were set at divers gates of London.

Memorandum: yt was ordeyned at a Court of Aldermen that Wrestlinge left.
the wrestlinge should be put downe and left for this yeare, because
of the commotions of Norfolke and other partes of this realme.

The 24 of August, beinge Bartholomewe daye, my Lord Mayor For Bartholomewe
and aldermen rode after dinner in theyr scarlet to Bartholomewe daye.
fayre and brought my lord [Mayor]ᵃ home againe to his house,
where they had frutes, wafers, and ipocras, which order was taken
at theyr assembly the even afore at the Guildhall before they rode
to the fayre, because there was noe wrestlinge kept.

The 28 of August tydinges was brought to the Kinges Majestic The victory of the
and the Lord Protectors grace that the rebelles in Norfolke were against the rebelles
subdued, and that the Earle of Warwicke had entred the citie of in Norfolke.
Norwiche the 27 of August, and had slayne v M. of the rebelles,ᵇ
and had taken theyr cheife captaine, which was called Robert Kett
of Windam,ᶜ tanner, which might dispend in landes l𝑙 and aboue,

---

ᵃ Omitted in MS.   ᵇ Other authorities say 2,000, but Stow follows our text.
ᶜ Wymondham or Windham, in Norfolk, about eight miles from Norwich.

A.D. 1549.

and worth in moveables before his rebellion above a M. markes;[a] and the sayd Earle put to execution divers of the rebelles after in divers places about Norwich.

Certeine houldes lost by Bulleine.

Allso the same daye tydinges came to the Kinge that the Frenchmen had taken Blacknesse, Hamylkewe, and Newe Haven, by Bulleyne,[b] and had slayne all the Englishmen, and taken the Kinges ordinaunce and victualls; which was reported beganne by one Sturton, a bastard sonne of the Lord Sturtons, which had betrayed Newehaven and went to the French Kinges servis.

A pollicye.

Allso in the beginninge of the moneth of September the captaine of Bulleine Barke,[c] by Bulleine, for feare of the French army, which was great, conveyed all the ordinance, victualles, goods, and men of that forte to the high towne of Bulleine, and after theyr departinge with gunpowder destroyed the forte.[d]

Frenchmen slayne.

Allso the French army assaulted the Ould-man,[e] but they within shot soe sore with ordinaunce at them that they slewe aboue 3 M. Frenchmen, and made them recule backe againe.[f]

[a] Ket, though a tanner, was wealthy, and the owner of several manors in the county of Norfolk. See Strype, Eccles. Mem. ii. 281.

[b] The forts of Blackness, Ambleteuse, and Newcastle, situated in the Boulonnais.

[c] Boulognebourg or Bullenberg, a fort in the Boulonnais constructed by the English.

[d] The remains of the ancient fortifications of Boulogne are easily discovered in many places along the ramparts and in the gardens of the Petits Arbres. All these fortifications were pulled down in 1687, under the ministry of Louvois, except the chateau or citadel, for many ages the residence of the captains or governors of Boulogne.

[e] "The Old Man of Boulogne" was the English name for the Tour d'Ordre, originally built by Caius Caligula, the Roman Emperor, as a triumphal monument, and on the top of which was placed a light, to serve as a beacon during the night to vessels navigating the Channel. When the English gained possession of Boulogne in 1544, they constructed considerable works round this ancient tower, the curtains of which were 600 feet in length, and the flank of each bastion 200. At the time of its construction the tower was more than a bow-shot from the sea, and in 1544 stood about 400 yards from the edge of the cliff. The encroachment of the sea in later times however gradually gained so much on the land that the hill on which the Tour d'Ordre was built became undermined, and slipped down on the 29th of July, 1744.

[f] This defence was conducted by the valiant Sir Nicholas Arnold.

Memorandum: the 10 of September the wardinge of the gates of London by the commoners was discharged, and the Kinges ordinaunce allso that stoode at the gates of the Citye, and sent to the Tower againe.

{A.D. 1549. Watchinge the gates discharged.}

Allso the same day, at a court of aldermen yt was ordeyned that certeyne of the commoners should be appointed to peruse the fleshe shambles and fishe markets weekly; the fishmongers to beginne to morrowe; viii persons to devide them in foure partes, and to see and peruse the shambles on the fleshe daye, that the people may haue reasonable peniworthes for their mony, and not to pay above theise prices followinge, that is to saye:

{Citizens keeping the fleshe markets.}

The best beefe to be sould not above iii. qd. et di. le lb.

The best mutton not above i d. qd. le lb.

All other mutton not above i d. di. qd. le lb.

The best veale to be sould not above, the carkasse ready dressed, vi s. viii d.

And so euery quarter and other peces after the same rate, or better cheape as the parties can agree; this order to continewe till the feast of All Sainctes[a] next comminge.

The 11 of September my Lord Mayor and the Aldermen satt in theyr wardes for the two last paymentes of the release graunted to the kinge, and called afore them the people of theyr wardes which were seassed at xx l. and upward, and by theyr good informations to desyre them to pay the sayd payments out of hand towardes the kinges affayres, which at this present had great need thereof.

{Sittinge for the release.}

The xvi of September the Aldermen were discharged of theyr watchinge at nightes for perusinge of constables watches for the saffegard of the citie.

Memorandum; on Michaellmas day this yeare, beinge the day for the election of the Lord Mayor, Sir Henry Amcottes, knight, Lord Mayor, Sir William Laxton, knight, Sir Martin Bowes, knight, and Mr. Richard Turck, Aldermen, received the holy comunion at the Guildhall chappell, the service songe in Englishe, accordinge to the Kinges booke; my Lord Mayors chapleine executinge at the aulter and ministringe the communion in a cope, with certeine of

{The Mayor received the comunion the day of the election of the Mayor in the Guildhall Chappell.}

[a] November 1.

24   WRIOTHESLEY'S CHRONICLE.

A.D. 1549.

the parishes clarkes, which songe the service in the quire, which was a goodly ensample for all the citizens to followe. And this daye was chosen for Lord Mayor for the next yeare Sir Rowland Hill, knight and alderman.

The Bishop of London deposed and sent to the Marshalsea.

Memorandum: the first of October Doctor Edmunde Bonner, Bishop of London, was depriued from his Bishoppricke and dignity at Lambheth by the sentence of th'Archbishop of Canterbury, which with other persons appointed in commission by the Kinge and the Lord Protector to haue the examination of him for a sermon that he had made at Pawles Crosse the 8 of September last,[a] and should in his sermon haue set forth the prerogatiue of the Kinge in his nonage, and did not, whereupon he after was diuers times examined, and would make noe directe aunswere, and for his contumacye allso he after was comitted to warde to the Marshallsea, and there remayned a x dayes before this day, and after sentence giuen this daye he was committed to warde againe as the Kinges prisoner, there to remaine at the Kinges Maiesties pleasure.

The Mayor and Aldermen sent for to the Counsaill.

Sonday, the 6 of October, in the morninge, the Earle of Warwicke with other Lordes of the Counsaill[b] sent for my Lord Mayor and th'Aldermen to his place[c] in Holborne, where was declared to them, by the Lord Chauncellor and other of the Kinges Maiesties counsaill, diners abuses of the Lord Protector concerninge the Kinges Maiesties person and other his affayres, both in England, and allso in Scotland, and other his perts beyonde the seas. And that afternoone was kept a court of th'Aldermen in the Guyldhall, where was shewed a lettre from the Kinge and my Lord Protector, for to haue a M men of the city well harnissed with weapons for the defence and surety of

[a] Stow adds: "For the which he was accused unto the Councell by William Latimer, parson of Saint Laurence Pountney, and John Hooper, sometime a white monke, and so convented before the Archbishop of Canterbury and other Commissioners at Lambheath."—Chronicle, ed. Howes, 1631, p. 597.

[b] Viz. Lord St. John, President of the Council and Lord Great Master of the Household, the Earls of Southampton and Arundel, Sir Edward North, Sir Richard Southwell, Sir Edmund Peckham, Sir Edward Wotton, and Dr. Wotton, Dean of Canterbury. They met there privately, armed.—Hollinshead, p. 1057.

[c] Ely House, then the residence of the Earl of Warwick.

the Kinges Maiesties person. And another lettre allso from the Lordes to haue ij M men to ayde them for the defence and surety of the Kinges person allso. And allso that the citye should be well kept with watches both day and night; whereupon the sayd Aldermen agreed that precepts should be sent forth to euery Alderman in his warde, and allso other precepts to certeine of the cheife companies of the citye, to haue xvi persons to watch at euery gate of the city of euery of theyr companies, and euery person one seruaunt with him in harnis all the daye, and a double watch of the constables euery night from ix of the clocke till v in the morninge, which was begunne the morrowe after. And allso that 2 of the Aldermen should ryde euery night about the city to peruse the sayd watches.

This daye allso, the Kinges Maiestie lyinge a[t] Hampton Court, the Lord Protector caused proclamations to be made in diuers townes nere the court for men to ayde the Kinge against the Lordes, and sent lettres likewise to divers townes, whereupon great assembly of people gathered to Hampton Courte; and in the night he conveighed the Kinges Maiestie to Windsore, with a great nomber of horsmen and footemen. Lord Protector caused proclamations nere the courte.

Monday, the 7 of October, was kept a common counsell in the Guyldhall, where was read both the lettres of the Kinge and the Lordes afore mentioned. And this daye all the Lordes of the Counsayll sat in the forenoone at the Mercers Hall, and dyned at my Lord Mayors, and sat there in counsail till night. And this day the wardinge of the gates beganne their watch in harnis, and all the Lordes lodged within the citye, and set Mr. Chamberlaine, Mr. Domer, and another, to be aydinge with the leyftenaunte of the Tower[a] for the safegard of the same to the use of the Kinge. Common Counsaill, and wardinge of the gates in harnis.

Tuesday the 8 of October was kept another common counsell in the Guyldhall, whether all the lordes came, and there by the mouth of the Lord Chauncellor[b] and other of the lords was declared the A Common Counsaill.

[a] Sir Leonard Chamberlaine.
[b] Baron Rich of Lecze, co. Essex.

A.D. 1549.

great abuses of the sayd Lord Protector, desyringe all the citizens to be aydinge and assistinge with the lordes for the preseruation of the Kinges maiesties person, which they greatly feared beinge in his aduersaries handes, and this day they dined at Mr. Yorkes, sheriffe.

The Lord Protector proclaymed traytor.

This daye in the afternoone about iiii a clocke a proclamation was made in the citye of London in diuers places with two trumpets, iiii haroulds, and 2 kinges of armes, Norey and Clarentius, with theyr coates of armes, the sergeaunt of the trumpetters and the commen cryer rydinge with their maces afore them.

Mr. Turcke, sheriffe, and Mr. Chaliner, one of the clarkes of the counsaill, which read the proclamation, which proclamation conteyned the very truth of the Duke of Somersettes evill gouernment, false and detestable proceedinges.

A Common Counsaill.

The 9 of October was kept another commen counsell, where was graunted v C men of the city to be sett forth to ayde the lordes for the safegard of the Kinges maiesties person.

A Common Counsaill.

The 10 of October was kept another commen counsell in the forenoone, where was read a letter to haue of the v C. men ii C. to be horsemen, but they graunted to i C. which should be ready on the morrowe by two of the clocke in the afternoone in Morefeilde.

A generall assembly of the Commons in the Guilde hall.

Allso this daye in the afternoone was an assembly of all the commons of the citie havinge lyveries, where was read in the Guilde hall a letter sent from the lordes concerninge the castinge abroad of divers libelles touchinge the lordes, my Lord Mayor, and the aldermen, and all the citye of London, exhortinge all the citizens to be circumspect to search and finde out such persons as wrote and endyted them. And this daye all the lordes dyned at Mr. Turkes, sheriffe, and satt in his house in counsaill from vii of the clocke in the morninge till iiii in the afternoone, and then went to supper to my lord Great Masters[a] house by London Wall.

Piue hundred men graunted to ayde the Kinge.

The 11 of October in the afternoone the sayd v C. persons well armed all in white coates mustered in Morefeildes, whereof diuers were bowemen, gunners, and i C. horsemen, which after they had

[a] Lord Saint John.

mustered went in at Moregate, iii in a ranke, euery sort of weapons by themselves, and so through Coleman Streat, through Cheape, and out at Newegate and so into Smithfeilde, the sword bearer rydinge afore them as captaine, with a trumpett and a drume in the middest of them, and there they brake of and were discharged by the commaundment of the counsaill for this tyme.

This day the lordes of the counsaill satt in my Lord Great Masters house. And Sir Anthony Wingfeild, captaine of the Guarde,[a] was sent to Windsore to the Kinge, and seuered my Lord Protector from his grace, and caused the Guard to watch him till the lordes cominge. *The Lord Protector put in warde at Windsore.*

The 12 of October my Lord Chaunceller, with the rest of the lordes of the counsaill, rode to Windsore to the Kinge,[b] and this night the Lord Protector was put in warde within the castle of Windesore in Bewechampes tower, and there was watched by the Garde and other.[c] *The Lords of the Counsaill.*

The 14 of October, in the afternoone, the Duke of Somersett was brought from Windsore to the Tower of London, rydinge through Holborne and in at Newegate, and so through all the high streates to the Tower, accompanied with diuers Lordes, knightes, and gentlemen with iii c horsemen, euery bande in their Masters' livery, my Lord Mayor, Sir Raufe Warreine, Sir John Gresham, Mr. Recorder, Sir William Lock, and both the sheriffs, Sir John Baker, Chauncellor of the Tenthes,[d] Sir [Richard] Southwell, Sir Edmunde Candishe,[e] and Sir Thomas Pope, knightes, sitting all on their horses against Sooper-lane, with all the officers of the sheriffes standinge by them with billes and holberdes in theyr handes; and from Holborne-bridge to the Tower certaine Aldermen or theyr deputies sitting on horsebacke in euery streat, with a *The Duke of Somersett sent to the Tower.*

---

[a] Accompanied by Sir Anthony St. Leiger and Sir John Williams.—Burnet, ii. p. 137.

[b] Who received them graciously and assured them he took all they had done in good part.

[c] Next day they proceeded to the examination of the duke's friends, who were all sent to the Tower, except Cecill, who had his liberty.

[d] Chancellor of the First Fruits and Tenths.   [e] Cavendish.

28   WRIOTHESLEY'S CHRONICLE.

A.D. 1549.   nomber of househoulders standinge by them with billes in their
handes, in euery quarter, as he passed through the streates to the
Tower hill, where he was deliuered to the Constable of the Tower [a]
with theise persons followinge.

Names of the prisoners.

The Duke of Somersett.
[Sir Michael[b]] Stanope, knight of the Privie Chamber.
[Sir Thomas[b]] Smyth, Secretarye.
Sir John Thynne, knight.
[Edward] [c] Wolfe of the Privye Chamber.
[William] [d] Grey of Reedinge.

Watches at the gates in harneis discharged.
The 17 of October at a court of aldermen the watches at the gates of the citizens in harneis were discharged and also the watches of the aldermen at nights.

Mr. Yorke, one of the sheriffes, made knight.
And this daye the Kinges Maiestie came from Hampton Court to his place in Southwarke[e] and there dyned, and after dinner he made Mr. John Yorke, sheriffe, knight in the garden there: And then his Maiestie set forewarde to ryde through the City of London, with all his nobles, Lordes, knightes, and gentlemen richly apparrelled and their horses allso, the Lord Mayor bearinge the Scepter before his Maiestie and rydinge with Garter Kinge of Armes, the Earle of Warwicke as High Chamberlaine of England followinge them, then the Lord Grey bearinge the sworde before ye Kinges

The Kinges Maiestie rydinge throughe the City of London.
Maiestie, his Maiestie richly apparrelled in a coate of cloth of Tyshewe, and his horse trapped of the same, and then his Privie Chamber[f] followinge with the Master of his Horse, the guard fol-

[a] Sir John Gage.   [b] Supplied from Stow.
[c] See Burnet, ii. p. 138.   [d] See Burnet, ii. p. 149.
[e] Southwark Place, situated almost directly over against St. George's church. It is described by Stow as a large and most sumptuous house, built by Charles Brandon, late Duke of Suffolk, in the reign of Henry VIII., which was called Suffolk House, but coming afterwards into the King's hands, the same was called Southwarke Place, and a mint of coinage was there kept for the king. To this place came King Edward VI. in the second year of his reign, from Hampton Court, and dined in it.— Stow's Survey of London, ed. 1842, p. 153.
[f] A clerical error for "his Privy Council."

lowinge after and about a M. horse of the Lordes and knightes yeomen, euery one in their Masters' liveries, all the streates of the City of London beinge gravelled, and the houses from the bridge foote to Temple Barre richlye hanged with clothes of Arras, silkes, vellvets and clothes of gould, with diuers melodies of instruments and singinge men standinge in diuers places of the citye; which was to the great rejoycinge of his Maiestie; and so he was brought to his pallace of Whitehall at Westminster, where they tooke leave of his Maiestie and so departed.

This yeare the 24 of October beinge the Mayors feast, there dyned at the Guildhall divers of the Lordes of the Counsell, where they had great chere, and were served but with one course, which was great. And in the afternoone the Lord Mayor[a] rydinge to Pawles after the ould custome, when he came into Pawles church, entringe at the north dore next Pawles Churchyarde, he tooke his waye up the steppes of the quire of the same syde, and so rounde about the quire and downe the stepps on the south syde, and soe alonge that yle of the church to the West dore, and then turned up the middle yle to the Bishops stone accustomed, and sayd the Psalme of "de profundis" as he passed by, which they of ould tyme used to say about the stone. All the craftes of the Citye standing in there order all the sayd compasse of the church. And this order was taken because the clostre called Pardon churchyard was dissolved and broken downe the last yere,[b] so that they had noe passage more that way.

A newe order for the Mayor to passe in Pawles on bighe feastes.

Edwardi VI. Anno 3.

The fourth day of November the Session of the Parliament beganne againe at Westminster, which afore was proroged to that daye.[c]

---

[a] Sir Andrew Judde, skinner.

[b] "Item the x day of April [1549] was pullyd downe the clowster in Powlles that was callyd the Pardon churcheyerd wyth the chappelle that stode in the myddes, to bylde the Protectores place withalle."—Grey Friars' Chronicle, p. 58.

[c] It was still the same Parliament the Duke of Somerset had called, and the Council had still the same maxims with respect to the Reformation.

A.D. 1549.
Corne waxed deare.

In the begininge of this mayors^a tyme corne beganne to waxe very dere in England, so that wheat was sold for xvi. xvii. xviii s. the quarter, and meale at ii s. viii d. the bushell, which caused the syse of bread to be smale, so that the bakers of the City did bake after xxvi ounces the penny wheaten loafe; wherefor the mayor and his brethren called diuers merchantes of the Stillyard and other Englishe merchauntes before them, and bargayned with them for x or xii quarters of wheate to be had out of Bremberland and Danske,^b to give xvi s. for the quarter, to be deliuered here before midsommer next comminge, beinge good and sweete.

The prices of fleshe waxed better cheape then yt had bene theise two yeares.

Rebelles arraigned.

The 25 of November, 1549, Robert Kett, of Windame^c in the countye of Norfolke, tanner, and William Kett, his brother, which were captaines of the rebelles in Norfolke, and Humphrey Arundell, Bery, Wyneslowe, and Holmes, Captaines of the Rebelles in Devonshire, were all araigned in the Kinges Bench in Westminster-hall, and there confessed theyr treasons, and so had judgement to be drawne, hanged, and quartered in such places where the Kinge should appointe, which persons had lyen in the Tower of London since September last past that they were taken.

Sir William Shirington pardoned.

Allso this moneth Sir William Shirington, knight, which was condempned the last yeare for high treason, had his pardon, and was released out of prison in the Tower, and admitted to be one of the Comon House of the Parliament againe.

Captaine Kette sent to execution.

The 29 of November, Robert Kett, and William Kett his brother, were deliuered out of the Tower to Sir Edmund Windham, knight and sheriffe of Norfolke, to be conveyed to Mount Surrey by Norwich, where the rebelles kept their campe,^d and there to have

---

^a Sir Andrew Judde, skinner.
^b Bremen and Danzig.
^c Wymondham.
^d The Rebels' camp was at Monshold, near Mount-Surrey.—Baker's Chronicle, p. 325.

execution of death on Monday next, which shall be the 2ᵈ day of December, to be hanged in chaynes.ᵃ

This moneth of November and December the Scottes tooke Burthecragge ᵇ in Scotland, and other holdes, and slewe man, woman, and childe, except Sir John Luttrell the Captaine, whom they tooke prisoner. Allso the Frenchmen gate Newehaven by Bulleine, and had all the Kinges ordinaunce there, which was much. And the Scots allso had great store of ordinaunce that they wanne at the houldes in Scotland, so that fortune fell from the Englishmen this yere.

Sonday, the 19 of January, 1549 [-50], Sir John Russell, Lord Privie Seale, was created Earle of Bedford at the court at Whitehall in Westminster. And Lord St. John, Lord Great Master of the Kinges householde, was created Earle of Willshire. And Sir William Paget, Comptroller of the Kinges house, was made Lord Pagett. And 2 dayes after the Earle of Bedford, Lord Pagett, Sir [William]ᶜ Peter, one of the Kinges secretaries, Mr. Masson,ᵈ knight, cheife cleark of the Counsaill, were sent into Fraunce for Embassadours to the French Kinge.ᵉ

Allso the sayd 19 of Januarye at night was a foule murther done by St. Pulchers church by the Kinges Head without Newgate, where were slayne two straungers, one called Sir Peter Gambo,ᶠ

A.D. 1549.

Holdes lost in Scotland and Fraunce.

[A.D. 1550.]
Earles created.

ᵃ Robert Ket was hanged in chaines on the top of Norwich Castle, and William Ket likewise hanged on the top of Windham steeple.—Stow.

ᵇ Brochty-Crag, called by the English Broughty Castle, was situated on the Frith of Tay, near Broughty Ferry, in Monifieth parish, four miles east of Dundee. It was taken by the English after the battle of Pinkie, and garrisoned by the Protector with 200 men, but was afterwards recaptured by De Thermes, who had succeeded Dessé d'Espanvilliers in command of the French contingent.

ᶜ Supplied from Stow.　　　　ᵈ Sir John Mason.

ᵉ Notwithstanding all his greatness, the Earl of Warwick was not a little embarrassed concerning the affair of Boulogne. He had himself most exclaimed against the Duke of Somerset for proposing to resign that place to the French, and ridiculed all his reasons, and yet for these same reasons he resolved at length to do what he so much blamed in another.—Rapin, Hist. Engl. vol. ii. p. 19.

ᶠ Captain Gambolde, a valyant man, a Spanyerd.—Grey Friars' Chronicle, p. 65.

A.D. 1550.

knight, Captaine, and another Captaine, an Italian[a] allso, which murther was done by straungers,[b] and on the morrowe after 4 of them were taken in Smithfeild by the Lord Pagett and sent to Newgate. And the 23 of January there was an oyer determiner kept in the Guildhall for the sayd murthers, where they were first endyted by the coroners enquest. And after endyted by another enquest allso, and then araigned on the same, and so wear condemned to death. And on the morrowe, beinge Fryday and the 24 of January, the sayd 4 persons, called Charles Degavaro, Balthazar Degavaro, Michaell Desaluaron, and Frauncis Desalvasto,[c] were had in a carre from Newegate into Smythfeild, and by the way, as they went at the place where the murther was done, Charles Degavaro, which was the cheife Captaine and did the murther, had his right hand stryken of on the cart whele with an axe by the executioner, and then all foure were had to the place of execution in the middest of Smythfeild, and there hanged to death.

Execution of 4 straungers for murther.

The 27 of January Humphrey Arundell, esquire, Thomas Holmes, Wynslowe, and Bery, 4 of the captains of the rebelles in Devonshire and Cornewall, which were brought up by the Lord Grey the 8 of September last, and had lyen prisoners in the Tower of London ever since, were this day drawne from the Tower of London to Tyburne and there hanged and quartered lyke traytors, and theyr heades and quarters set on the gates about the City of London.

Captaines of Devonshire put to deathe.

[Anno Reg. 4.]

The first day of February the Parliament brake up and was proroged to the xxi of Aprill next cominge.

Newe officers made by the Kinges counsaill.

This yeare, on Candlemas day,[d] Lord St. John, Earle of Willshire, Lord Great Master and President of the Counsell, was made Lord High Treasurer of England, and Sir John Dudley, Earle of Warwicke and Lord Great Chamberleyne, was made Lord Great Master of the Kinges Househould, and the Lord William Parre, Marques of

---

[a] Filicirga.—Stow, Annales, ed. 1631, p. 603.
[b] By hys own country-men.—Grey Friars' Chronicle, p. 65.
[c] These names are spelt in Stow, Charles Ganaro, Balthasar Ganaro, Nicholas Disalueton, and Francis Deualesco.   [d] February 2.

Northampton,[a] was made Lord Great Chamberlaine of England, and the Lord Wentworth was made Lord Chamberlaine of the Household, and Sir Anthony Wingfeild, Captaine of the Guard, was made Comptroller of the Kinges House, and Sir Thomas Darcye, knight, was made Vice-Chamberlaine and Captaine of the Guard.

A.D. 1550.

The Earle of Arundell, late Lord Chamberlaine, and the Earle of Southampton, banished from the Counsell and commaunded to keep their houses in London and not departe thence.

The 6 of February, in the afternoone, about 3 of the clock, the Duke of Somersett was brought out of the Tower of London by the Leiftenant and the Knight-Marshall and tooke his barge at the Tower wharfe, and from thence went by water to the Crane in the Vintre, where he landed, and there tooke his horse and so rode to the Kinges Counsell to Mr. Yorkes house[b] in Walbroke, one of the Sheriffes of London, where the Earle of Warwyck laye, and after a litle taryinge there with the Counsell the sayd Duke of Somersett was discharged of his ymprisonment,[c] and then was brought by the Lord Wentworth and Sir William Harbert to his barge againe at the Crane, where they left him, and from thence he went to his place by Savoye, where he lay that night, and on the morrowe he went to his place at Shene.[d]

The Duke of Somersett discharged out of the Tower.

The 7 of February Doctor Bonner, Bishop of London, was sent for by the Knight Marshall from the prison of the Marshallsea[e] to the Kinges Counsell, which satt in the Starr Chamber at Westminster, where he had all his demeanour and proceedinges declared unto

---

[a] William Parr was created Earl of Essex 1543, and Marquis of Northampton 1546.

[b] " And that night he supped at Sir John York's."—Stow, p. 603.

[c] On the 16th of the same month he received the King's pardon.

[d] Thus his fall was not so great as his enemies expected, and on the 10th April following he was restored into favour and sworn of the Privy Council. He, however, forfeited much of the esteem he had acquired among the people, who, not diving into the reasons of his conduct, could not help thinking him guilty, since he had confessed all.—Rapin, Hist. Engl. ii. p. 19.

[e] He had been deprived and committed to prison in September 1549.

A.D. 1550.

Doctor Bonner, late Bishop of London, committed to perpetuall prison.

him that he had used in his sermon[a] and examination at Lambheth afore my Lord of Canterbury, which he coulde not deny,[b] and for his contempt deprived by the Bishop of Canterbury from his bishopricke, which sentence this day all the Counsaill by the mouth of the Lord Chauncellor of England confirmed, and so my Lord Chauncellor commanded him to be had from thence to the place he came from, there to remaine in perpetuall prison at the Kinges pleasure, and to loose all his spirituall promotions and dignities for ever.

Bonvise House and others seased to the King.

This daye allso the houses of Anthony Bonvise, Doctor Clement, phisition, Balthasar, surgeon, and Rastall, which maryed Doctor Clementes daughter, were seassed by the sheriffes of London to the Kinges use because they had fled the realme and conveyed theyr cheife substance and goodes out of the realme, which persons were ranke Papistes.

Prisoners released out of the Tower.

Allso this moneth the rest of the prisoners that were sent to the Tower with the Duke of Somerset, as Mr. Stanope, Thomas Smyth, secretary, Wollfe,[c] and Grey, were discharged out of the Tower and lost all their offices and fees, and allso were set at diuers fynes to the Kinge.

A proclamation for peace with England and Fraunce.

This yeare, the xxix day of Marche, 1550, there was a proclamation made in London with 4 harroldes of armes, a trumpetter, and the common cryer, for a perpetuall peace[d] betwene the Kinges

[a] He was summoned before the council, and after a declaration of the causes of complaint against him he was ordered to preach on a Sunday at St. Paul's Cross, and to prove in his sermon certain points, whereof this was one of the principal, "That the authority of a king was the same when he was in minority as when of full age." He preached on the 1st of September before a numerous audience, and touched upon all the points that were enjoined him, except the last. Besides, he brought in some things which gave offence to the Court.

[b] Dr. Burnet says, he behaved before the judges more like a madman than a bishop.

[c] In MS. the names "Smyth" and "Wollfe" have been accidentally transposed.

[d] The principal condition of this peace was the surrender to France of Boulogne upon a money payment of 400,000 crowns.

Maiestie and the French Kinge, theyr heires and successors for ever. In the which peace is allso comprehended Charles the Emperor; and moreover is comprehended in the said peace the Quene and realme of Scotland and the subiectes of the same.

A.D. 1550.

Allso this night were bonfires made in every parishe within the City of London, and drinkinges by my Lord Mayors and the Counsells commaundement, for ioy of the sayd peace.[a]

The 30 of March, beinge Palme Sonday, was a sermon made at Pawles Crosse to giue laude to God for the peace, and, the sermon ended, the canons and clarkes of Pawles quire songe Te Deum in Englishe in partes, standinge before my Lord Mayor where he sitteth the sermon tymes in Pawles Churchyard, my Lord Mayor and all the aldermen wearinge scarlett this day to the sermon.[b]

Prayses to God for the peace.

And in the afternoone of this daye the sayd proclamation was proclaymed in the Court at Whitehall in the great court with harouldes of armes and trumpettes before the sermon beganne afore the Kinges Maiestie, and there was a great bonfire made in the same court, and that night were bonfires made in the Citie of Westminster and alonge to Temple Barre.

The peace proclaymed in the Court

Allso about the latter end of this moneth the cityzens of London of diuers mysteries and corporations which had chauntry landes suppressed into the Kinges handes for [priests'][c] wages, obites, and lightes by Acte of Parliament which amounted to the yerely valewe of M l. purchased all the sayd yerely quitrentes of the Kinges Maiestie after xx^{tie} yeres purchase, which amounted to xx M l. which was payd within viii dayes after the counsells commaundement came for makinge of the sayd payment. The sayde corporations were fayne to sell much of theyr landes that belonged to the sayd

The Citizens of London purchased quit-rents of the Kings Maiestie.

---

[a] The same members of the council who now assented to the peace had, when it was before proposed by the late Lord Protector, exclaimed against it as the consummation of national disgrace.

[b] " At these sermons the mayor and aldermen were wont to be present in their violets at Pauls on Good Friday, and in their scarlets at the Spittle in the holidays, except Wednesday, in their violets."—Stow's London.

[c] Supplied from Stow, p. 604.

A.D. 1550.

Southwark purchased by the Mayor.

The Duke of Somerset admitted of the Privie Counsell to the Kinge.

Execution for whoredome and scouldinge.

corporations.[a] Which mony was gathered toward the ayde of the Kinges Maiestie toward the payment of his debtes in his neede.

Allso this moneth my Lord Mayor and the aldermen purchased all the liberties of Southwarke which was in the Kinges handes, which cost the City a M. markes, so that nowe they shall have all the whole towne of Southwarke by Letters Patent as free as they haue the City of London; the Kinges place [b] and the two prison houses of the Kinges Bench and the Marshallsea excepted.

The 8 of Aprill, 1550, and beinge the Tuesday in Easter weeke, the Duke of Somersett came to the Court to the Kinges Maiestie at Grenewiche, where he was honorably receyved of the Kinges Maiestie and his counsell, and dyned with the Kinge, and was sworne of the Pryvie Counsell, and then departed to his house at Savoye.

This moneth of Aprill the Lord Mayor of London caused all the aldermen of London to cause there warde-mote inquestes in every warde, within the City of London, to sitt and enquire of all misrule done in their wardes since Candlemas last past, and presented newe inditements againe, upon which inditementes the Lord Mayor sate many tymes, and caused such persons to be arraigned by newe questes for the Kinge, for bawdry, whoredome, and scouldinge, and upon the araignment of such offenders which were found culpable he caused execution to be done ymediately by rydinge in cartes with ray [c] hoodes after the lawes of the Citie, so that he spared none ; for wher there was one Ferdinando Lopus a phisition which was a straunger dwellinge within St. Helines, which was cast for whoredome and condempned for the same, and at the sute of themperors embassador and other of the Kinges privie counsell spared for a tyme, yet within vi dayes after that he had declared to the counsell his abominable livinge, the counsell sent a letter to

---

[a] " Which caused the said corporations to sell much of their best lands, farre better cheape than they had bought their quit rents, as after sixteen or fourteen years purchase."—Stow, p. 604.

[b] Southwark Place, formerly called Suffolk House.

[c] Striped.

my Lord Mayor, with xiii of their handes at yt, to proceede to the A.D. 1550.
execution accordinge to the lawes of the City, which was done, and
further that he should be banished the realme of England for ever,
never to returne upon payne of death; this straunger was a Jewe
borne, by reporte, and should once have bene burnt in Portingale.

This yeare the 25 of Aprill, 1550, beinge Fryday and Saint Bulleine deliuered
Markes daye, the tower of Bulleine was deliuered to the possession unto the French
of the French Kinge and all the marches of the same, and all Kinge.
Englishmen clerely avoyded, which was done by composition for
great somes of mony [a] to be payd to the Kinges Maiestie at the last
peace making. And certeine lordes of Fraunce sent ouer into
England for pledges till the payment were all payd,[b] which delivery
was sore lamented of all Englishemen, but referringe that to the
will of God and the Kinges Maiestie.[c]

Allso this moneth of Aprill came great store of rye out of Great plentie of rye.
Holland and Zeland to the number of two M. quarters and more,
and was sould at Belingesgate at xviii d. the bushell, which the
people of the country in divers shires fetched some lx myles from
London, so that yt was better cheap here then for the most part of
all the shyres in England.

Memorandum: the 2 day of May, Joane Barne, alias Joane Joane of Kent burnt.
Bocher,[d] alias Joane of Kent, was burnt in Smythfeild, which sayd
woman was condempned the 29 of Aprill, 1549, befor the Arch-

[a] Upon the payment of 200,000 crowns of gold at the time of the delivery of the town, and of as much more in five months after, under the name of a compensation to the English for the cost of keeping up the fortifications while it had been in their possession.

[b] It was stipulated that France should give six hostages for payment of the 200,000 crowns in August, and England the like number of hostages for the security of the restitution of Boulogne to the French King.

[c] By this treaty all the pains taken by Henry VIII. to secure a pension or rather a yearly tribute in lieu of the title he pretended to have to the Crown of France were rendered fruitless, while in favour of England the treaty contained only an indeterminate reservation of the claim which had occasioned the effusion of so much blood since the reign of Edward III.

[d] Joane Knell alias Butcher, in Stow.

A.D. 1550.

bishop of Canterbury for heresy, denying that Christ tooke noe nature of the blessed Virgin Mary,[a] and she had lyen in Newegate euer since, and could neuer be converted by noe godly man.[b] Mr. Storye, a learned man, declared her opinion, standing in a pulpitt in Smythfeild at her death, to haue converted hir, but she dyed in her evill opinion like a wretch.[c]

A newe Bishop of London.

Allso this moneth Doctor Nicholas Ridley, late Bishop of Rochester, and nowe admitted to the Bishoppricke of London,[d] satt in visitation in Pawles Church, and in divers parishes within his diocese of the citye of London, having a sermon in everye place where he sat, some tyme preaching himselfe, and called all the parsons and curats of his dioces with vi. persons of euery parishe afore him, and gave them divers godly injunctions and instructions to be enquired of, and allso examininge euery parson and curate himselfe in his owne house privately of theyr learninge, and gave them 4 dayes to make theyr aunswere in Whitsonweeke next.

o o taken of Southwarke.

Memorandum: the 9 of May my Lord Mayor tooke possession of all the borough of Southwarke, and rode all the precinckt, and after the common cryer made a proclamation with a trumpett under the Kinges great seale in v. places, for the avoydinge of vagabondes out of the city of London and the borough of Southwarke, and the suburbes and liberties of the same.

[a] It would appear from the expressions attributed to her that she affirmed Christ's body was not really but only apparently of human flesh.

[b] It is supposed that, struck with some uncomfortable feelings consequent on the young King's solemn admonition, Cranmer would gladly have escaped from the execution of the sentence which he and his fellow commissioners had passed on her, and both he and Ridley took great pains to prevail upon Joan to save her life by the same abjuration which had already enabled them to dispense with the actual lighting of the fagots in several other cases. But the enthusiast, courting martyrdom, treated all their exhortations with contempt, and she was at last consigned to the flames.

[c] *i.e.* wretchedly or miserably. The passage in Stow runs thus, " but she, not regarding his (Dr. Story's) doctrine, said to him, he lied like, &c."

[d] The see of Westminster, vacant by the resignation of Thirleby, was united to that of London and given to Dr. Ridley, who was translated from Rochester 1 April, and installed in St. Paul's Cathedral on the 12th April.

Allso this moneth of May Mr. John Wyllford, alderman,[a] gaue over his cloke without payinge any fyne to the use of the citye, and so was clearly discharged for his aldermanship.

A.D. 1550.

Allso in the beginninge of this moneth of May watches were appointed in every warde of the citye of London, to beginne at ix of the clock at night and to continewe till iiii of the clocke in the morninge, for the preseruation of the citye; and, that the constables should keep theyr houres, yt was appointed by court of aldermen that every night two of the aldermen or their deputies should ryde every night the circuite of the city within and without, one the east parte and the other the west parte; and they to beginne theyr watches at ii of the clocke in the morninge, and to continue till iiii, to see that the watches might duely be obserued, and this order to continue till Michaellmas next cominge.

Watches in London.

Memorandum: the 23 of May, beinge Fryday, in the afternoone at the tyde, one Monsieur Satilian [b] came to Ratcliffe with vi gallyes and ii pinnaces out of Fraunce, and he and his companie shott London bridge in the Kinges barge and was brought to Durham Place, which was richly hanged and prepared for him to lodge, and had at his comminge ready sett in the court of the same, for present from the Kinges Maiestie, certeine fatt oxen, calues, sheepe, lambes, and all manner of wyld foule of every sort, a certein [number] all alive, and allso of all manner of freshe fyshe of the best that might be gotten, with wyne allso in his cellar. And the 24 of May he came to the Kinges presence in the afternoone to Whitehall, which was richly hanged; and after a bankett made to him he departed; and the morrowe, beinge Whitsonday, he came to the court againe, and there, at the comunion tyme, he received the Kinges Maiesties oath for the French Kinge, the Kinges Maiestie receivinge the holy sacrament upon the same, for the confirmation of certeine articles of the peace concerninge the deliuery of Bulleine,

Mounsier Satilians comminge into England from the French Kinge.

---

[a] He served, with Andrew Judde, the office of sheriff in 1544.

[b] Gaspard de Coligny, Seigneur de Châtillon, Admiral of France and Ambassador to England, died 1572.

A.D. 1550.

with other thinges conteyned in the sayd articles of the perpetuall peace betwixte the Kinges Majestie and the French Kinge. And that daye dyned at the Kinges measse, and had bankettinge and feastinge, with divers pastimes, all the holy dayes with the Kinge, and hunted in Hyde Parke. And on Thursday he went to Hampton Court and there hunted, and after [went to]^a see the Kinges place, where he had a bankett, and that night he came to the court, where he had a great banket and pastime on the water of Thames, and maskinge after, and that night tooke his leave of the Kinges Maiestie, havinge a rich cupbord of plate given him, with allso great giftes to the other noblemen and gentlemen of Fraunce that came with him; and the morrowe, beinge Fryday, he departed and had a banquett at Grenewich, and so tooke his galleis and departed, havinge to accompany him for his safe-conduite vi. of the Kinges shippes with the Kinges galley to see him passe the seas in safety into Fraunce againe.

An order at Whitsontyde.

Allso this yeare the sermons at Whitsontyde was kept at Pawles Crosse, the Bishop of London preachinge Whitsonday, Mr. Houper Monday, and Mr. Cottesfurth ^b Tuesday, my Lord Mayor and Sheriffes keepinge there dinners all iii dayes, having the aldermen and theyr wyues, and so Wednesday was broken this yeare.

irst Alderman in outhwarke.

Memorandum: Wednesday in the Whitsonweeke, at a court of the aldermen kept in the Guyldhall, Sir John Aliffe, knight, and master of Blackwell Hall, was sworne an alderman of the Bridg ward without, and to haue the jurisdiction of the borough of Southwark, and 2 deputies to be appointed there to assist him, which was the first alderman that ever was there, which was done by the advise of my Lord Mayor and th' Aldermen, for the better order to be kept there, and for the more quietnes of the Mayors hereafter to come, and the good order of the Kinges subjectes there, accordinge to the lawes of the city; and the Fryday after he rode with my Lord Mayor all the precinct of Southwarke, my Lord Mayor havinge a certeine nomber of the honest persons of the borough at the bridg-house, to whom he shewed theyr alderman, and appointed deputies

^a Omitted in MS.   ^b John Cottisford, S.T.P.

under him, and so hereafter to see a good order to be kept in the Borough, as in other wardes of the citye of London.

Tuesday, the 3 day of June, was a great mariadg at Sheine betwene the Lord Lysle, sonne and heyre to the Earle of Warwicke, and the Duke of Somersettes eldest daughter, the Kinges Maiestie beinge there present, where was made a great feast, with maskinge and diuers other pastimes.^a

This moneth of June, in Whitson weeke, the parsons and other of the parishe that were sworne in the last moneth of May afore the Bishop of London in his dioces,^b at his visitation, gaue up theyr verdyte. And all the aulters in euery parishe through London were taken away, and a table made in the quire for the receivinge of the communion. And the xiii of June the high aulter in Pawles Church was taken away, and a table sett in the quire where the aulter stode for the ministration of the holy communion.

This yeare was noe watch kept at Midsommer nor St. Peters tyde, neither with constables nor lightes, but a watch as is kept euery night, my Lord Mayor and the Sheriffs ryding priuilye at midnight with theyr officers to peruse the city and the constables in theyr wardes.

Memorandum: the 30 of July^c Sir Thomas Wryothesly, Lord Wryothesly, Earle of Southampton, and knight of the garter, and one of the executors of Kinge Henry the VIII. departed out of this transitorye lyfe at his place in Holborne, called Lincolnes place,^d about midnight; he had bene longe sicke,^e and the 3 of August in the forenone he was buryed in St. Andrewes Church in Holborne, at the right hand of the high aulter,^f Mr. Hooper, Bishopp of Glocester, preachinge there at the buryall.

A.D. 1550.

A marriadge.

All aulters put down in London.

Noe watche at Midsommer.

Death of the Lorde Wriotheslye.

^a On the 3rd June, John, the Earl of Warwick's eldest son, married Ann, daughter of the Duke of Somerset, and on the next day Robert, his third son, married Sir John Robsart's daughter.—Edw. Journal, pp. 14 and 15.

^b London and Westminster.

^c Stow gives the 30th, as in our text, but Strype says the Earl died on the 31st.

^d Afterwards Southampton House.

^e Dr. Burnet says he died with grief and vexation, but some asserted he poisoned himself. ^f Where a fair monument was erected to his memory.—Stow.

A.D. 1550.
Pillorye.

This yeare, the vi of August, was one set on the pillory in Cheape, which was the millers seruaunt at Battlebridge, which had spoken sedicious wordes of the Duke of Somersett, sayinge that he had proclaymed himselfe Kinge of England in his country, wherefore by the Connselles commaundement he was set on the pillory and had both his eares cut of.

Wrestlinge.

This yeare was a wrestlinge kept on Sonday after Bartlemewe daye and noe more; there should haue bene kept on Bartlemewe day wrestlinge, but when my Lord Mayor was rydinge thither yt rayned, and so he went into Christes Church at Newegate to here evensonge, and so departed home againe.

Grygge the false prophett.

The 8 of September, beinge the day of the Natiuity of Our Lady, there was one Gryg, a pulter in Surrey, which was taken amonge the people in London for a prophett in curinge diuers people but with speaking prayers on them, sayinge he tooke noe mony, so that people would followe him as yf he had bene a God. But, after he had bene examined by th' Earle of Warwycke and other of the Counsell, he was commaunded to be set first at Crowden in Surrey on a scaffold with a paper on his brest on Saterday last, which was the vi day of this moneth, and this day he was sett on a scaffold in Southwarke, on a scaffold before the pillorye in the afternoone, against my Lord Mayor and his brethren rode thorowe the fayre, and there desyred my Lord Mayor and all the people whom he had deceyved to forgiue him, which penaunce was enioyned him by the Counsell, for he was a very dissemblinge person, and toke mony of many, and coates, and other thinges, and had bene a very great deceiver of the people, in [a] sellinge of his ware as conies and other in the markett in Cheape.

The Keeper of the Counter.

This moneth my Lord Mayor, by th' assent of a court of Aldermen, sent one Richard Husband, keeper of the counter in Bread Streat, to the gayole of Newegate for cruelly handlinge of his prisoners, and commaunded the keeper to set a payre of yrons on his legges, which was called the wydowes almes, which he ware

[a] "and" in MS.

from Thursday to Sonday till 3 of the clock in the afternone, and then at great sute by th' assent of the Aldermen that day at Pawles he was released of his yrons, but he remayned there prisoner till Tuesday after, till he was sent for to the Court of Aldermen, and there bound in recognizance in c markes to obserue an Acte made by Common Counsell the first day of August last past, for the orderinge of prisoners in both the counters, and then he was released out of prison.

A.D. 1550.

Allso in this moneth of September my Lord Mayor, with both the sheriffes, rode to the bowlinge allyes and play-houses at Pawles wharfe and by Aldgate, and there findinge diuers simple persons and vagabondes playinge at tables and bowles, sent a lx. or more of them to warde to the Counters, and brake theyr playinge tables in peeces, and bound diuers of them by recognisance that they should neuer more haunt such places, ere he would release them.

The 18 of September, Mr. Christopher Aleyn, Alderman of the warde of Faringdon Extra, gaue up his cloake and was set to fyne at 2 c. markes, and payd 1 c. markes in hand, and should pay the other c. markes at midsommer next, and had 2 suretys bound with him for the payment thereof.

Memorandum: This year on Michaellmas day, Mr. Andrewe Judde, Alderman, was chosen Mayor of London for the yeare ensueynge, and afore the election there was a communion kept in the Guild hall chappell, Sir Rowland Hill knight, Lord Mayor, Sir William Laxton, Sir Martin Bowes, Sir Raufe Warreine, and Sir John Gresham, knightes and aldermen, receivinge the communion. The service songe lyke parishe clarkes accordinge to the Kinges proceedinges.

Edwardi VI. Anno 4.

Memorandum: The v. of November there were two persons punished for breakinge of lanthornes in Southwark, which persons rode from the Counter in Bredstreat, and so all the high streates into Southwarke, havinge 2 lanthornes hanginge about euery· of theyr neckes one afore and another at theyr back, with papers set

44   WRIOTHESLEY'S CHRONICLE.

A D. 1550.

Deathe of my Lady Mayres.

Death of the Chamberlaine of London.

The election of a newe Chamberlaine.

on theyr brestes, written, for breakinge of lanthornes, and allso they rode to St. Georges Church in Southwarke, and there sent them awaye.

Memorandum: The 14 of November my Lady Mayres departed out of this worlde, at ix. of the clock at night, and she was buryed the xx. day of November;[a] my Lord Mayor givinge for hir to euery [parish][b] of London, 2 gownes for 2 poore men and women, and xl. gownes for poore men and women of St. Bartlemew hospitall, which gownes were of Bristowe freese, so that the nomber he gaue was aboue xii^{xx} gownes, which was a godly act, for he gaue noe blacke to none of th' aldermen, but onely to his officers and the cheife mourners.

Allso the xv. of November, at noone, Thomas Hayes, goldsmith, Chamberlaine of the City of London, departed out of this world; and the 27 of November the Commons were assembled at the Guyld hall for the election of a Chamberlaine, and there were diuers persons that laboured to my Lord Mayor for the office and to the aldermen and the whole Commens; but, accordinge to an ould Act of Common Counsell made the vith yeare of King Henry the VIIth, which was that my Lord Mayor and his brethren should nominate 2 persons sad and wisemen, of which the Commons had free election to chose one of the 2 persons to be theyr Chamberlaine, which lawe was read to the whole Commens, and there was appointed by my Lord Mayor and th' aldermen John Sturgeon, haberdasher, and Henry Fisher, grocer, for the sayd election, but Henry Fisher had the Kinges Maiesties letter written to my Lord Mayor, Aldermen, and Commens, in his favour, which letter was read to the Commens, declaringe in the seyd letter that it was the first suyte that the Kinges Maiestie had required of them; but when they came to tryinge of handes quietly, without noyse or disturbance, th' election rested on John Sturgeon, haberdasher, to be theyr Chamber-

---

[a] "The xix day of November was bured my lade Jude, mayress of London, and wyff of Sir Andrew Jude, mayr of London, and bured in the parryche of Saynt Ellen, in Bysshope-gatt stret."—Diary of Henry Machyn, p. 2.

[b] Alderman in MS.

laine, which sayd Sturgeon was that tyme in Flanders. and gouernour of the Merchaunt Adventurers, and so at this tyme the Commons departed; and the 23rd of December, 1550, the sayd John Sturgeon was sworne Chamberlaine of London, in the Counsell Chamber, my Lord Mayor causinge a court of aldermen to be kept that day for the same purpose, and gaue him respyte to bringe vi. suertyes to be bound for him to make a true accompt yerely of the profittes of the City, which he did after Christmas, himselfe to be bound in 2 c^l. and euery one of his suerties in L^l. a peece.

A.D. 1550.

This moneth corne waxed very dere, for wheate was at xx s. and aboue, and malt at xv s. and xvi s. and all other corne rysinge after that rate; allso fleshe rose to excessiue prices, so that the counsell sent out commissioners through all England to knowe what plenty of grayne was within the realme; allso my Lord Mayor and his brethren made bargaine with divers merchauntes, both Englishe and straungers, for grayne for the city of London, to be had out of Danske and Hambrough.

The 15 of December Doctor Stephen Gardener, Bishopp of Wynchester, which had bene prisonner long in the Tower of London, was had from thence to Lambethe, to the Archbishopp of Canterburies place, where sate divers Commissioners, apoynted by the Kinges Maiesties commission under his great seale, for the examynation of the said Bishopp of Wynchester upon certeyne articles and interrogatories to them committed, for a contempt he made in his last sermon before the Kinges Maiestie, on Sainct Peeters daie, after Midsommer 1548, at his pallace at Westminster, against the Kinges Maiesties lawes, which articles were deliuered to him this daie, and he sworne to make a true answere to them the eighteenth daie of December next, at which daie he appeared their againe; and then he desired that he might haue learned counsell, which was granted him. And tho twentie-thirde daie of December he was commanded to appeare againe, on which daie he appeared, and then had daie to the eight of Januarie next, and so after he had diuers daies geuen him to the third of Februarie next. At which daie

The examynation of the Bishopp of Winchester and his depriuation of his title and dignitie.

[A.D. 1551.]

A.D. 1551.

he was brought from the Tower to Lambeth, going by land through Southwarke, with fortic of the Kinges garde with their halberdes going afore him, and threescore of the warders of the Tower with halberdes after him. And so came home againe after the same manner, and had divers other daies after to appeare thear till the fowertenth daie of Februarie;[a] and that daie, after longe pleadinge on his behalf, my Lord of Canterburie proceeded to judgement, which was that he should loose the name and dignitie of a bishopp, with all his spirituall promotions therunto belonginge; after which judgement he appealed to the Kings Maiestie, saying that the commissioners were not indifferent judges. And so he was committed to the Tower againe at the Kinges pleasure.

Mariadge of Mr. Judde, maior.

The seauenth daie of Februarie, being Saturdaie before Shroue Sundaie, my Lord Maior maried one Thomas Langton's widowe, a skinner, which died three daies before Tweluetide last past, which was a rich mariadge, the inventorie amounting to sixe thousand poundes and more, having five children by the said Langton, all orphans.

My Lorde Maior made knight.

The fifteenth daie of Februarie, being the first Soundaie of Lent, my Lord Maior was presented to the Kinges Maiestie at his pallace of Westminster; and, after the proposition made by the Recorder, the Kinges Maiestie made him knight.

New Bishoppes.

Memorandum: in the moneth of March Doctor Ponett,[b] Bishopp of Rochester, was made Bishopp of Wynchester, and Mr. Storie[c] was made Bishop of Rochester, which tow parsons preached before the Kinges Maiestie this Lent the Wednesdaies and Fridaies.

Vittailes deare and corne.

This yeare at Easter flesh was at excessiue prices, for beeffe was sold at three pence the pounde, a quarter of veale at fower shillinges,

---

[a] According to King Edward's Journal it was on February 13.

[b] John Poynet, who had succeeded Ridley at Rochester, was translated to Winchester the 23rd March, 1551, and resigned 1553.

[c] John Seory was appointed by the King 26th April, pursuant to statute 1 Edward VI., and the royal significavit to the Archbishop issued the next day; he was consecrated at Croydon 30th August following, and on the 23rd of May in the next year was translated to Chichester.

mutton, a quarter of the best at iii s. iiii d. so that my Lord Maior [and Aldermen] were greatlie exclamed of the people; but they cold not remedie it, for the grasiers sold their cattell at so high prices that the butcher could not sell it at meane prices. Also wheat was sold at xxvi s. viii d. the quarter, and other graine after the same rate. A.D. 1551.

Also in Easter weeke their came tenne or twelue shippes with rie and wheate out of Hollande, which marchantes of the Styliard and Englishmen brought thence, and some out of Brittanie, my Lord Maior setting the rie at ii s. and i d. the bushell, and wheate at xxii s. the quarter, to be sold at Billinsgate, which refreshed well the Cittie and the countrey neere London. Corne from beyond seas.

This yeare, against Easter, the Bishopp of London altered the Lordes table that stoode where the high aulter was, and he remoued the table beneth the steepps into the middes of the upper quire in Poules, and sett the endes east and west, the priest standing in the middest at the communion on the south side of the bord, and after the creed song he caused the vaile to be drawen, that no person shoulde see but those that receaued, and he closed the iron grates of the quire on the north and sowth side with bricke and plaister, that non might remaine in at the quire. Alteration in Poules.

Memorandum: in this moneth of Aprill, 1551, Mr. Robert Chersey, mercer, and alderman of the warde of Farringdon Within, gaue ouer his cloke, and gave a howse to the poore of the hospitall of St. Bartholomewes for the mayntenance of the poore, of the value of tenne poundes the yeare, and so was discharged. And Mr. Thomas Curteise, pewterer, was chosen *in loco eiusdem*, and sworne the twentie-eight daie of Aprill. Alderman gaue upp his clooke.

The twentie-fowerth daie of Aprill, 1551, their was a Dutchman[a] hanged[b] in Smithfield for heresie, denying the Godhead in Christ, the second person in the Trinitie, who was condemned before my Lorde of Cantorburie at Lambeth in March last past. A Duchman burnt.

---

[a] George Von Paris, a Dutchman, who resided in London in the practice of his profession of a surgeon, was burned in Smithfield for Arianism.

[b] A clerical error for "burnt." See margin, also Stow.

A.D. 1551.

This yeare, the viiith daie of Maie, was a proclamation made and sett fourth by the Kinges Maiestie and his Privie Councell for the deminishing of the coyne of shillinges and grotes, to go after the last daie of August next commyng, the shilling to go for ix d. and no more, and the grote at iii d. and no more.

After which proclamation made the people within the cittie of London murmured sore and sett upp booth their wares and victuales at higher prices, wherupon the Counsell sent for the Lord Maior to the Court at Greenewych the Soundaie, being the tenth daie of Maie, and gaue him sore words for the disobedience of the people, wheruppon the said Maior called a common Counsell, and also the wardens of euerie craft within the cittie of London to the Guildhall the xiith daie of Maie, and their, by the mouth of Mr. Recorder, was declared to the Commens that the Kinges Councell were so discontented with the citizens for the disobedience of the people by murmuringe at the proclamation, and for enhauncing of their wares and victuales, geving them straight charg and commandment on the King our soueraigne lordes behalf to call all their company afore them ymediatlie, and to admonish them that they keepe and sell their victuales and wares at no higher prices then they did before the proclamation was made, and declaring further unto them that they should also admonish all their companys that if they heard any person raile on any of the Kinges Counsell, that they should utter them to the Maior or some of the Councell. For the Erle of Warwicke declared to my Lord Maior at the Court, that, as he rode by Eastcheepe to the Court, he chepned a carcasse of mutton, and the butcher held it at xiii s. and he said that was to much; and another said xvi s. and then he answered that it were better he were hanged; wherupon their arose tales that the said Erle should saie that the daie should comme that a mutton should be worth xx s.; which slaunderous wordes, and also reporting by him that where we had one stranger wee should haue an hundred, with other slaunderous wordes, caused the Kinges Maiesties Councell to take high displeasure with the citizens of London, which by their good

obedience should geue ensample to all Englande; and now not so A.D. 1551.
stubborne as they were, wherefore Mr. Recorder exhorted them to
take heede from hensforth that such enormities and reportes might
be amended, as they tendered the Kinges Majesties high displeasure
and indignation, and, if they herd any such ill reportes, to bring
fourth the parties, or els it should be to the utter destruction of the
Cittie and people for euer, and cause all the whole realme to be
against them.

This moneth also diuers seditious bills were cast abroad in the For ringinge of bells.
streates in the night tyme against the high magistrates of the cittie,
and for diuers causes mouing the head of the cittie commandment
was geauen by the Lord Maior to the Wardens of the Clarkes that
no daie bells should be ronge in the morninges nor no curfors[a] in
the night from the feast of Pentecost next, untill they had further
warning from the Lord Maior, but onelie to ring to mattins and
eeavensong and burialls.

This yeare the xxvth daie of Maie was an earthquake in Surrey, An earthquake.
at Godston, Brenchingley,[b] Titsey, Rigate, Bedington, and Croydon, and a sixtene miles in length, about twelue of the clocke in
the forenoune, which lasted a quarter of an hower, so that the
howses, hills, and all the earth shaked that the people were in
great feare of God, but no hurt donne, praysed be God their-
fore.[c]

This yeare in the moneth of June was great tempest of weather Sore weather.
and signes in the element sene in many places in England, and in
Kent was haile stones of sixe, seaven, or nyne inches, and diuers
when they melted in ones hand were fashioned like a rose.

Also this month the sweating sicknes beganne to raigne in Eng- Sweatinge sicknes.
land, in Shropshire first, and so came from shire to shire, wherof

---

[a] Curfews.

[b] Stow reads, Bletchingly, which is in Surrey, and, therefore, most probably correct; but our text looks more like Brenchley in Kent.

[c] The writer of the Grey Friars' Chronicle, adds " and also at Westmyster and
dyvers other places in London, and abowte there."

A.D. 1551.

Marginal: The shilling at ix d. the grote at iii d.

Marginal: Brother and sister fornicators.

died verie many of yong men and weomen,[a] and it beganne in London, about the seaventh daie of Julie and contynued till the last daie therof,[b] wherof died many in the said cittie, booth of rich yong men and other.[c] Also the Duke of Suffolke. And Lord Charles his brother died in Cambridg of the sweete also.[d]

The nynth daie of Julie proclamation was made in London for the abatement of the coyne of the shilling to ix^d and the grote to iii^d, which tooke effect ymediatlie after the proclamation was made, which said proclamation was so sodenlie sett fourth that my Lord Maior saw yt not till hit was proclaymed, which was the Counsells commandment, and it was likewise the same daie proclaymed in all places of Englande.[e]

The thirtith daie of Julie at a court of Aldermen was presented to the said court one Richard Huise, tailor, and a batchlor, dwelling in Fleete streete, in Le Warde Farringdon, for committing fornication with his owne sister and having a cheild by her, which she confessed; and they booth before the said court for their pennance were committed to ward, and that the morrowe after, being Fridaie,

---

[a] "It is to be noted, that this mortality fell chiefly or rather on men and those also of the best age, as between 30 and 40 yeeres, fewe women, nor children, nor olde men died thereof."—Stow, p. 605. In King Edward's journal it is noticed that it raged chiefly among young men of a strong constitution, p. 30.

[b] "It began in London the 9th of July and the 12th of July it was most vehement."—Stow, p. 605.

[c] Some curious particulars of this epidemic are given by the late John Gough Nichols, in a note to Machyn's Diary, p. 319, and also in the Chronicle of the Grey Friars, p. 70. Stow's account is very circumstantial, p. 605.

[d] Henry Brandon, fifth Duke of Suffolk, son of Charles Brandon by his second wife, died of the sweating sickness, as did also two days after his brother, who had succeeded him, so that, the title having become extinct in the family of Brandon, the Earl of Warwick resolved to procure that honour for the Marquis of Dorset, father of Jane Grey, whom he designed for one of his sons.

[e] This abatement of the nominal value of the coinage would appear to have been made with the object of cheapening the high price of provisions, but completely failed in its object, as we read in the Chronicle of the Grey Friars of London that "the vitelles was as dere after as it was before and worser, [so] that the pepull cryde owte of it in every place thorrow alle the realme," p. 70.

they should be sett in a carr, the hear of their heades shaven over- A.D. 1551.
thwart for a deformitie and a paper sett on his backe of the offence,
and so to ride three markett daies about the Cittie, and proclamation to be made in euerie markett place of their offence, and then
to sett them without the gate at Temple Barre, but not be banished
the Cittie.[a]

The first daie of August, being the daie of election of the sheriffes The elextion of the sheriff Thomas Wilkes.
by the Comeus, one Mr. Thomas Wilkes, habardasher, was elect
sheriffe by the said Commens, which that daie was not in Towne,
but the third daie of August he came to my Lord Maior, laying his
excuse that he was not of abilitie nor substance for the said office,
and shewed a bill to my Lord Maior that he was in debt for a
purchase of landes aboue sixe thousand poundes, so that my Lord
Maior could not perswade him by no meanes to take the office on
him, wherupon my Lord Maior called a court of Aldermen the
morrow after, being the fourth daie of August, and their before
them he laid diuers causes for himself not of substance for the rome;
they causing diners lawes to be read unto him and other his freindes
that came with him conserning the refusing of the said rowme.
But all prevayled not; wherfore the court brooke upp and caused
the Commens to be assembled againe at the Guildhall the tenth of
August, at which daie he was called before the Commens, but first
before the aldermen, they reading an old lawe to him that he
should swere that he was not in substance of his moueable goodes,
as plate, jewells, money, ware, merchandies, booth in England and
elswhere beyonde the seas, with leases, one thousand markes his
debts paid, which he must swere preciselie, with six persons with
him, such as my Lord Maior and his brethren should apoynt.
After he declaring his mynde to the Commens, they would haue
licensed him, so that he would be bound in recognisance not to go
from the cittie, he laying diuers obiections for himself refusing it.
Then they would putt him to his oth. His oth being first read

[a] " And the 3rd day was bannyshyd the citte bothe ; but he would have gevyne
moch to be ascowsyd, but it wold not be tane."—Grey Friars' Chronicle, p. 70.

A.D. 1551.

before the Comens, he offred to swere, and presented to swere with him Mr. John Sadler, sometyme alderman, Raffe Davenett, marchant, Richard Owyn, George Tadlow, and Richard Grafton, grocer, with other, which said persons would not swere precisely. Then another act was reade that he and they refusinge the oth should pay for a fine iic[1] for refusing and to be elegible againe, he at last taking his oth, but then excepting his landes; wherupon he was putt of, and daie geuen him to bring in two hundred poundes on Twesdaie next, which is the eleventh daie of August, or els to take the office on him. And so the Commons departed.

Bawderye.

The said viii[th] daie of August was one Middleton, haberdasher, in Newe Fish Streete, and his wife, arraigned at the Guildhall, she for a common adoultrix with one Nicholas Ballard, gentleman, booth with her owne bodie and also bawde to him for her owne daughter also, and a maide of tenne or eleven yeares of age, her seruant, which the said Ballard occupied all three carnallie, proued by six substantiall and honest persons of the said warde, putting in a booke in wryting to my Lord Maior of five sheetes of paper of their said factes that daie and tyme, which said persons were endited the daie before by the wardens enquest, and this daie arraigned of the said cryme, which was most detestable to be hearde for the enormitie therof; wherfore they had judgement to be carted ymediatlie with raye hoodes and white roodes in their handes, according to the ould lawes of the cittie. The said Ballard after his pennance to remaine in Newgate for the rape of the maide till the next sessions at Newgate, the man and wife to be banished the citie.

Yet for the sheriffe.

The xi[th] daie of August, at a Court of Aldermen, the said Thomas Wilkes appeared againe at the said Courte, where was demanded of him whether he would take the office or els to pay tow hundreth poundes, which he yet stood stiffe in and refused. Butt yet would haue the Commens assembled againe, trusting that they would be good unto him; wherupon the Aldermen consulted among themselues, that they could not dispence against the lawes before ministered unto him. But that either he must take the office on him, or els pay his tow hundreth poundes, which he refusing was committed to warde to Mr. Augustine Hinde, one of the sheriffes, their to remaine in his howse till Satterdaie next, being the xvth daie of August. At which daie the Commens shal be assembled againe for a new election. Hee then to declare further of his mynde. And so the Court departed for this tyme.

A.D. 1551.

The xviiith daie of August, the Commons were assembled for a new election, my Lord Maior calling the said Wilkes afore him and his bretheren in the counsell chamber, first opening unto him whether he would take the office on him, or els whether he had brought his tow hundreth poundes; he still standing stiffe as he did before, refusing booth the office and fine, was putt apart twise or thrise and yett called againe; but he standing still in his old opinion disembling himself, and seing that he was sworne himself, thought it sufficient to be discharged without fine. My Lord Maior declaring unto him, that if he would not take the office nor paie his fine, that he must committ him to warde till he had paid his fine, further offring him that it was the Courtes minde he should pay an hundreth poundes on Michaelmas daie next, which the new sheriffe his fellow the successor must haue by the Act, and the other hundred poundes due to the Chamber he should paie at Easter next ensuing, finding suertie for the same. He yet refusing was comitted to warde to the counter in the Pultrey, the Commens seing when he went. After his departinge, my Lord Maior called upp a Common Counsell before the election, declaring to them how he had used the said Wilkes, axing them whether he should pay three hundred poundes and be discharged of all offices for euer, or els pay two hundreth poundes and haue respite for certaine yeares. They concluding that he should pay tow hundreth poundes for his fine according to lawe and haue respite for seaven yeares next after er' he should be called to the office of shrivaltie. And so my Lorde and his brethren departed to the election for a new sheriffe. After a proposition made by Mr. Recorder to the Commens, my Lord Maior and his

Yett for the sheriffe.

A.D. 1551.

bretheren being departed up to the Maires Court againe, after their ould aunciaent custome the Commens nominated five persons; that is to say, John Cowper, fishmonger, who was present at the ellection, Richard Grymes, chaundler, John Hobson, habardasher, Thomas Lee, mercer, and Barnard Jeninges, skinner. After triall by handes, the election rested on John Cowper, the said Cowper declaring his mind to the Commens that he was not of abilitie for the rome, the people crying God geue his ioy, and so accepted their election; and so the Commens departed.

Mr. Wilkes sett to his fine.

In the afternoune the Commons departed, and then my Lord Maior commond with Mr. Wilkes, who was sent for to dynner from the Counter, to know whether he would paie his tow hundreth poundes at the daies afore lymitted or not; he yet standinge still obstinate, would haue rather gonne to ward againe then paie it. But at last by the mediation of Mr. Knotting, one of his neighboures, he was content, and so the said Mr Wilkes and Knotting were bounde in recognisance in an hundreth poundes [to pay one hundred poundes]^a on Michaelmas even next, and the other hundreth poundes at Easter next ensuing, or any tyme before, and so he was discharged.

The alteration of siluer.

Memorandum: the seavententh daie of August, at seaven of the clocke in the morning, proclamation was made in Cheepe by the commen cryer for the abatement of the coyne, he first shewing the proclamation to the awdience vnder the Kinges seale that it was hole and not opened to witnes the same, which proclamation was that the peece of the Testor or shillinge should be currant from the said xviith daie of August for vi d. sterlinge and no more, the grote for ii d., the half grote for a peny, the peny for a half-penny, the ob for a farthing, and no more, as by the said proclamation doeth appeare.^{b}

Wrestlinge and showtinge.

This yeare, on Bartholomew daie, was kept a wrestling, and the Sundaie after a showting in Finsburie Fieldes by Mr. Sheriffes, booth

---

^{a} Omitted in MS.

^{b} "This was a terrible time in London, for many one lost, sodainly, his friends by the sweat, and their money by the proclamation."—Stow, p. 605.

in one daie, the best game of the standarde xiii s. iiii d. in money, A.D. 1551.
the second game x s., the iii^d game vi s. viii d., the iiiith game v s.
And the best game of the flight xiii s. iiii d., the second game x s., the
third game vi s. viii d., the fourth game vi s., summe 5*l.* which was
paid in money to the wynners at the costes of booth the sheriffes,
and no more daies after for this yeare.

 The iiiith daie of September, being Fridaie, was one Thomas, a A baker on the
baker in Sothwarke dwelling beyond Battell-bridge, sett on the pillorie.
pillorie in Sothwarke for lacking xiii^{en} ounces wyght in a tow penie
wheten loffe, which hath had diuers tymes this yeare warninge and
yett neauer kept his weight, wherfore this sentence was judged as
yesterdaie at a Court of Aldermen, which said baker stoode on the
pillorie from uyne of the clocke in the morninge till eleven, and had
his bread hanginge on nailes by him, and lay in ward the daie before
his pennance.

 The tenth daie of September, 1551, was burned in Finsburie Field Search for hopps.
xxxi sacke and pokettes of hopps in the afternoune, being nought
and not holsome for man's bodie, and condemned by an Act made
by my Lord Maior and his brethren th' aldermen the tenth daie of
September, at which court six comeners of the Cittie of London
were apoynted to be serchers for a hole yeare for the said hopps;
and they were sworne the fifth daie of this moneth and made search
ymediatlie for the same.

 This yeare, on Michaelmas daie, before the election of the Lord Election of the Maior.
Maior at the comunyon in the Guildhall chappell, my Lord Maior,
Sir Raffe Warrein, Sir William Laxston, Sir Martin Bowes, Sir
Henry Hobulthorne, Sir John Gressam, Sir Rowland Hill, receaued
the comunion; and all the Aldermen offred to the poore and receipt
of Mr. Chamberlaine for Sainct Bartholomewes hospitall; and after
the Commens went to the election of the Lord Maior, which was
Mr. Richard Dobbs, alderman.

 Memorandum: the tenth of October Doctor Daie,^a Bishopp of Bishopps deposed.

---

^a George Day, S.T.P. Provost of King's College 1538, and Bishop of Chichester 1543.

56   WRIOTHESLEY'S CHRONICLE.

A.D. 1551.   Chichester, which had bene long prisoner in the Fleete, and Doctor
Heath,[a] Bishopp of Worcestre, were deposed by the Bishopp of
London in Poules the said daie in the afternoune.[b]

Dukes and Erles   Memorandum: the xi[th] daie of October was a great solemnitie
created.   kept at the Kinges Maiesties Court at Hampton Court,[c] where that
daie Lord Gray,[d] Marques Dorsett, was created Duke of Suffolke;
Lord Dudley, Earle of Warwicke, was created Duke of Northumberlaunde;
Lord Sainct John, Earl of Wilshire, and Lord High
Treasorer of England, was created Marquis of Wynchester; and Sir
William Harbard, Master of the Kinges Horse, was first made Lord
of Karmarden,[e] and after was created Earl of Pembroke; also the
King made the same daie iiii knightes also [f]

Duke of Somersett   The sixtenth daie of October, 1551, the Duke of Somersett was
with other sent to   sent to the Tower of London by the Duke of Suffolke and the Lord
the Tower.   Marques of Wynchester. And the seventeenth daie the Lord Gray,[g]

---

[a] Nicholas Heath, S.T.P. Bishop of Rochester 1539, of Worcester 1544, and Archbishop of York 1555.

[b] Stow adds, " and sent again to the Fleet," p. 605.

[c] The Court had retired to Hampton Court on the sweating-sickness finding its way into the palace at Westminster, where it carried off one of the gentlemen of the bedchamber, and afterwards one of the King's grooms.

[d] Henry Lord Gray succeeded his father as 6th Marquis of Dorset in 1530, and was created Duke of Suffolk 11 Oct. 1551. He married Frances, daughter and coheir of Charles Brandon, Duke of Suffolk, by Mary, Queen Dowager of France and sister of King Henry VIII. K.G. attainted and beheaded 1554, when his honours became forfeited.

[e] Sir William Herbert was son and heir of Sir Richard Herbert, natural son of William Herbert, first Baron Herbert, of Chepstow, who was created Earl of Pembroke 27 May, 1468; he was knighted and made Chief Gentleman of the Privy Chamber by King Henry VIII. in 1546, and created Baron Herbert of Cardiff 10 October, 1551, and the day following made Earl of Pembroke.

[f] " The King also made William Cecil, his secretary, M. John Cheeke, one of his schoolmasters, M. Henry Dudley, and M. Henry Nevill, knights."—Stow, p. 605.

[g] William Lord Grey de Wilton was apprehended on a charge of participation in the Duke of Somerset's rebellion, but was afterwards released, and in 1560 assisted in blockading Leith.—Burnet, ii. p. 138.

Sir Thomas Palmer, Sir Thomas Arondell, latelie discharged thence, with other also,[a] were sent thither.   A.D. 1551.

The xvii[th] daie of October my Lord Maior and Aldermen were sent for to the Kinges Maiesties Counsell at Westminster to the Kinges place at Whitehall, and twelue of the head Comyners with them, which were of the Common Counsell. And this night watch begune with howseholders to be kept in euerie ward from nyne of the clocke at night till fiue in the morninge.   *The Maior and Alldermen sent for to the Cowrte.*

The eighteenth daie of October the Duches of Somerset[b] was sent to the Tower, and brought from Sion by water, and Mr. Crane and his wife, Sir Raffe Varne,[c] and one Handsome, one of the Duke of Somersettes men.   *Dutches of Somersett sent to the Tower.*

The xixth daie of October all the common councell and the wardens of euerie Company in the cittie of London were assembled in the Guildhall before my Lord Maior and Aldermen, where was read a letter directed to the Maior and Aldermen, which was sent them from the Kinges Maiesties Councell, how they should be greatlie circumspect to see good and substantiall watches and warding for the savegard and custodie of the Kinges Maiesties citie and chamber of London, and further Mr. Recorder declared by mouth to the said Commons assembled of the misdemeanor of the Duke of Somersett and his adherentes. How they had entended to haue taken the Tower of London, the Isle of Wyght, and haue destroyed the cittie of London, and the substantiall men of the same,[d] wherfore the counsells pleasure was that euerie cittizen in his owne howse   *A Common Councell.*

---

[a] Viz. Sir Ralph Vane, Sir Myles Partridge, Sir Michael Stanhope, and divers other gentlemen.—Stow, p. 605.

[b] Anne Stanhope, " a woman of a haughty stomack."— Baker's Chronicle, p. 326.

[c] Sir Ralph Vane or Fane.

[d] Upon these extravagant accusations, which were everywhere published with circumstances calculated to impose on the people, most ancient historians have, Dr. Burnet excepted, founded their accounts of this event. What is most probable is, that the Duke had projected to get himself declared Protector in the next Parliament, since the Earl of Rutland affirmed it upon oath. See Rapin's Hist. ii. p. 22.

CAMD. SOC.

58   WRIOTHESLEY'S CHRONICLE.

A.D. 1551.

should looke to his famelic and to see that vagabondes and idle persons might be auoyded out of the Cittie, and so the Comens departed.

Wardinge at the gates by daye.

Also the same daie the Maior and Aldermen directed preceiptes to certaine of the head companies for the warding of the gates of the cittie by daie, that is to say, that tow persons should waite at euerie gate of the Cittie from six of the clocke in the morning till seaven of the clocke at night to see that no suspect persons in maskes nor maisterles men should enter into the Cittie. But examyn them and send them to warde till the Kinges Conncell should discharg them. And that euerie night the constable that watched should haue the keies of euerie gate deliuered him and not open the gates till six of the clocke in the morning. And further that euerie alderman should apoynt tow of the councell to ride about the Cittie euerie night as their turnes came about, to see that the watches of the Cittie keepe their howres apoynted and that they should not beginne to ride about till tow of the clocke in the morninge, and euerie of them to haue one serieant and his yeoman to waite on them to lead the waie.

The said nynetenth daie Sir Michaell Stannopp, Mr. Banester, and Mr. Whalley were had to the Tower. And the twentie sixth daie of October Sir Nicholas Poynes,[a] Sir Miles Partridge, and Sir Thomas Holcroft were had to the Tower.

The xiii[th] [xxx] [b] ? daie of October the Kinges Maiestie sett fourth a proclamation for certaine newe coynes of siluer and gold to be made newe and currant within the realme, that is to saie, a peece of siluer of fiue shillings sterlinge, the second peece at iis. vid. sterling, the third peece of xiid. sterling, the fourth peece of vid. sterling, another peece called a peni of the doble rose,[c] the second an halfe penny of the single rose, the third peece a farthing with a port cullis.

[a] Sir Nicolas Poyntz.

[b] 30th October in Stow, which from the order in the text would appear to be correct.   [c] "not sterling but base."—Stow, p. 606.

The coines of gould, that is to saie, a whole soueraigne of fine gould of thirtie shillinges, another peece of fine goulde called a angell of tenne shillinges, the third peece called an angelett of fine gould of fiue shillinges, the half soueraigne of crowne gould of tenne shillinges, another peece of crowne gould called a soueraigne of twentie shillinges, the third peece of crowne goulde of fiue shillinges, the fourth peece of crowne goulde of tow shillinges six pence, and all other base moneies to go after the rate of the last proclamations.

A.D. 1551.

New coynes of fine gould and crowne gould.

The 31 of October the Kinges Maiesties Counsell sent a letter to my Lord Mayor of London, with a bill of provision for certeine kindes of victualles, as beefes, muttons, veales, swannes, and other kindes of poultry [and] meates, with allso for bread, fuell, wyne, and beere, waxe, and torches, for the provision of the Quene Dowager of Scotland, to be given by them as a present from [a] the citye of London to the sayd Quene; which Quene was lately aryued at Portesmouth, comminge out of Fraunce, and desyringe lycense of the Kinge to passe thorough England into Scotland; upon the readinge of which byll my Lord Mayor called a court of Aldermen in the afternone, and sent the commen sergeant and the towne clarke to the Kinges Maiesties Counsell to knowe theyr pleasures therein. And the first day of November, in the morninge, the aldermen assembled at my Lord Mayors house, and there was declared to them by the commen sergeant and towne clarke the aunswere of the Counsell, that the sayd provision should be provided by them to present her on the morrowe, at the Bishop of Londons place by Pawles. And in the afternone, as my Lord Mayor and his brethren the Aldermen were hearinge evensonge in the Guildhall chappell afore his goeinge to Pawles, a common counsell was called up into the Mayors Court, where after evensonge my Lord Mayor and his brethren declared the Counselles pleasure, and to knowe theyr mindes therein, which sayd yt should stand the City in iiii^{xx} l. or more, the sayd commen counsell affirminge the Counselles sute.

A prouision for the Lady Dowager, the ould Scottishe Quene, for a present by the City of London.

[a] "for" in MS.

A.D. 1551.   This yeare, in Mr. Juddes tyme, in October, the liberties of the Stiliard were seazed into the Kinges handes for diuers causes forfeited contrarie to the entercourse.[a]

EDWARDI VI. Anno 5. 1551.

The comminge of her to the Citie of London.

The 2 of November, beinge Monday, the sayd Quene came by water from the Kinges pallace of Hampton Court, and landed at Pawles Wharfe in the afternone, and so rode from thence to the Bishopes place, accompanied with divers noblemen and ladyes of England [sent][b] to receive her, where at her entry the Cities provision was ready with a bill of the same, and presented by the Chamberlaine of London.

The 4 of November the sayd Quene rode from the sayd place to the Kinges pallace at Whitehall by Westminster in hir charyot, accompanyed with diners knightes and gentlemen, earles and lordes, the Lady Margaret Dowglas, the Duches of Richmond, the Duches of Suffolke, the Duches of Northumberland, with diners other noble women of England and ladyes of Scotland followinge after them; the Dukes of Northumberland and Suffolke and the Lord Treasurer receivinge her within the Court gate, all the guard standinge on euery syde of the Court; and at her entringe in at the hall the Kinges Maiestie stode in the upper ende of the hall, the Earle

The comminge of her to the Kinges Majesties presence at the Courte.

of Warwicke houldinge the sworde afore the Kinge; she kneelinge downe, the Kinges Maiestie tooke her up and, kissinge her, he tooke her by the hand, she comminge with him, he led her up into the chamber of presence, and so from thence to the Quenes chamber of presence, where he kissed all the ladyes of Scotland, and so departed for a while; and that daye she dyned on the Quenes syde with the Kinges Maiestie, the Kinges service and hers comminge both togeather, richely serued in gylt plate; the Kinges seruice on the right hand of the table, and the Quenes on the left hand, she sit-

---

[a] This passage has been accidentally transposed in MS.
[b] Omitted in MS.

tinge by the Kinge apart by his cloth of estate; the goodly cupbord A.D. 1551.
of plate of gould and gylte that day there occupyed, with the rich
hanginges and costly meates, was wondrous to see. All the ladyes
of England and Scotland dyned in the Quenes great chamber, and
were serued in siluer all theyr meates; dinner ended, the Kinges
Maiestie shewed her his galleries and gardens, with other com-
modityes of that place; and about foure of the clocke he brought
her downe againe by the hand into the hall, where he received her
and there kissed hir, and so she departed to the Bishops house
againe to Pawles in lyke manner as she went thither.

The 6 of November the sayd Scottishe Quene departed toward The goinge away of the Scottishe Quene
Scotland, and rode from Pawles through all the high streates of and her passage into Scotland.
London and out at Bishops-gate, accompanyed with diuers noble
men and women, to bringe her through the Citye to Shordich
Church; the Duke of Northumberlande havinge standinge of
horsemen [a] in Cheapsyde with jauelinges, i c. persons, wherof xl.
gentlemen were apparayled in black velvet and white feathers, and
chaines of gold about their neckes; next them stoode vi^{xx} horsmen
of the Earle of Pembrookes, with blacke jauelinges and hattes with
feathers; next them stoode i c. of the Lord Treasurers gentlemen
and yeomen with jauelinges allso, which 3 rankes of horsemen com-
passed from the Crosse in Cheape to Birchin Lane ende. And
when the sayd nobles had brought hir to Shordich Church, there
they tooke their leaue, and departed home againe. The Sheriffes of
London had the conduction of her to Waltham townes ende, where
the shires of Middlesex and Essex parteth; and harbingers [were] [b]
sent afore into euery shyre to the borders to Scotland, that every
sheriffe in euery shyre, accompanyed with the gentlemen of the
country, [should] [b] receaue her, and make provision in enery shyre
for hir meates, both for hirselfe, familie, and horses, till she come
to the borders of Scotland, at the charges of the Kinges Maiestie

---

[a] "His horsemen standing."—Stow, Annales, p. 606
[b] Supplied from Stow.

A.D. 1551.

and the shyres^a that she should passe thorough till she be in Scotland, euery shire for theyr owne precinct; this first night she lodged in Waltham towne.

The Earle of Arundell and the Lord Pagett sent to the Tower.

The 24 Nouember, at a Court of Aldermen, the warding^b of the gates of the Citye of London was discharged for the day tyme.

The 30 of November, beinge St. Andrewes day the Apostle, at night my Lord Mayor received a letter from the Kinges Maiesties Counsell, Mr. Recorder then being present with the mayor in his house; wherupon my Lord Mayor sent ymmediately to warne the Aldermen and theyr deputyes to be afore him at the Guylde hall the morowe after, beinge the first daye of December, at vii of the clocke in the morninge; at which court, on theyr appearance, the sayd letter was read, which was that the Mayor and Aldermen should see to the safegard of the city for that day and night for feare of suspected and lewde persons; that done by the assent of the Court, euery alderman in his ward should ymmediately by himselfe or his deputy cause euery constable in his warde to warne enery householder within his precinct to see to his familie and to keepe his house, and to haue in a readines a man in harnes in his owne house, and not goo abroade till they should be called, if need were. And further that that night they should cause a good and substantiall double watche to be kept with householders in enery warde, which ymmedyately was done.

For the safegard of the Citye.

The first daye of December, beinge Tuesday, the Duke of Somersett was had from the Tower of London by water and shott London bridge at v of the clocke in the morninge,^c and so went to Westminster, where was made ready a great scaffold in Westminster hall,^d and there the sayd Duke appeared, afore the Lordes and

^a " At the charges of the shires."—Stow, p. 606.
^b " Warders," in MS..
^c The Chronicle of the Grey Friars here adds, " and 1 or 2 drownyd by the waye in the Tems betweene the tower and Westmester."—p. 72.
^d " Where was made in the middle of the Hall a new scaffold."—Holinshed.

Peeres of the Realme, the Lord William Pawlet, Marques of Winchester, and Lord High Treasurer of England, that daye sittinge under the cloath of estate as High Stuard of England; the indytement of the sayd duke beinge read, he was imedyately arraigned on the same for felony and treason, and after tryed by his peeres the nobles there present,^a which did quitt him of the treason but found him guilty of the felony,^b whereupon after their verdite giuen he had iudgment giuen to be had [thence to]^c the place [he came from]^c and from thence to the place of execution, there to be hanged till he were dead; but the people in the hall, supposinge that he had bene clerely quitt, when they see the axe of the Tower put downe, made such a shryke and castinge up of caps, that it was hard into the Longe Acre beyonde Charinge Crosse,^d and allso made the Lordes astonyed, and word likewise sent to London, which the people reioysed at; and about v of the clocke at night the sayd Duke landed at the Crane in the Vintre, and so [was] had thorough Can[dle]wyke Streete^e to the Tower, the people cryinge God saue him all the way as he went, thinkinge that he had clerely bene quitt, but they were deceyued, but hoopinge he should haue the Kinges pardon.^f

[margin: A.D. 1551. The Duke of Somerset arraigned at Westminster.]

The 7 of December there was a mustre before the Kinges Maiestie in St. James [field]^e beyonde Charinge Crosse,^g the Kinges Maiestie

[margin: A muster before the Kinge.]

---

^a His judges were Northumberland, Northampton, Pembroke, and the other leading members of the government,—the very parties against whom he was said to have conspired,—and the witnesses against him were not produced, but only their written depositions read, as was frequently the custom in those days.

^b For having designed the killing of the Duke of Northumberland and the others, although on consideration he had determined to abandon it; "yet," adds Edward VI. in his Journal, "he seemed to confess he went about their death."

^c Supplied from Stow, "from" in MS.

^d "The people, knowing not the matter, shouted half a dozen of times so loud that from the Hall door it was heard at Charing Cross plainly, and rumours went that he was quit of all."—Edward VI.'s Journal.

^e Candleweeke-Street.—Stow.

^f Holinshed says, as he passed through London, "there were both exclamations; the one [party] cried for joy that he was acquitted, and the other cried out that he was condemned."

^g The Chronicle of the Grey Friars (p. 72) reads, "in Tothill fields by Westminster."

A.D. 1551.

sittinge on horse-backe on a hill by St. James with his Maiesties Privie Counsell with him; first came all the Kinges Maiesties pencioners rydinge all in compleate harnes, 4 trumpetters rydinge afore them and then the Kinges standerd borne amonge them, and euery pencioner had two men followinge after them with theire speares; then followed i c of my Lord Treasurers men with a trumpett and a standerd afore them; next them i c of the Duke of Northumberlandes men with a trumpet and a standerd afore them, xl of them with veluet coates on their harnes; next them the Lord Privie Seales men, i c with a trumpet and a standerd; next after them Lord Marques of Northamptons men, i c with a trumpett and a standerd before them; then the Earle of Rutlandes men, l with a trumpet and a standerd afore them, xx of them in blewe veluet cassockes ouer theyr harnes; then l of the Earle of Huntingtons men with a trompet and a standerd; next them i c of the Earle of Pembrokes men with a trumpet and a standerd afore them; next them l of the Lord Darsies, Lord Chamberlaines, men with their trumpet and standerd; next them l of the Lord Cobhams men with theyr trumpet and standerd afore them; last of all i c of the Lord Wardens men of the Cinck Portes with a trumpet and a standerd afore them, which were all goodly horsed. The sayd Lordes seruantes were set in aray in Hide Parke, and in the afternone at 2 of the clock they came thence and so rode about twise afore the Kinge v in a ranke, all in complete harnes and well horsed and euery man his speare in his hand, and then brake of euery lordes company to theyr places, which was a goodly sight.

Ballard araigned upon a rape.

The 12 of December at the sessions of the gayle delivery holden at Newgate, Nicholas Ballard, gentleman, which in August last past was punished for an adulterer with one Middletons wyfe, and after sent to Newegate for a rape, and after was bayled with sureties from tyme to tyme till nowe, was this day araigned for the sayd rape, which was indyted for the same, and by a jury this day found guilty of the rape, havinge great witnes for the proofe of the same rape; and after verdyte giuen against him he asked the benefyte of his booke,ᵃ and read, and so was burnt this daye in the hand and had to the bishops convicte prison.

A.D. 1551.

The 20 of December, beinge Sonday, in the afternone Doctor Dunstall,ᵇ Bishop of Durham, which had lyen longe at his place by Coldharber, in Thames Streete, was had to the Tower of London.

Bishop of Durham sent to the Tower.

The 21 of December, beinge St. Thomas th' Apostles day, Lord Riche beinge Lord Channcellor of England, the Kinges Maiesties great seale was taken from him by the Duke of Northumberland and the Earl of Pembroke in the afternoone. And the morrowe after Doctor Goodricke, Bishop of Elye, had the keepinge of the great seale, as custos, by the counselles commandement, which bishop was one of the Privie Counsell to the Kinges Maiestie.

Lord Chauncellor put downe.

This year before Christmas, the Lord Clinton, Lord High Admirall of England, went into Fraunce to be the Kinges Maiesties deputye to christen the French Kingesᶜ sonne, which bare the Kinges name, where he was highly received and feasted of the French Kinge, and had great gyftes giuen him, and was proclaymed by the French harrouldes after the christninge, *Edwardus Alexander Dux Anguiloniæ.*ᵈ

The French Kinges chylde.

Fryday, the 22 of January, 1551-[2], Edward Seimer, Duke of Somersett, was beheaded at the Tower Hill, afore ix of the clocke in the forenoone, which tooke his death very paciently, but there was such a feare and disturbance amonge the people sodainely before he suffred, that some tombled downe the ditch, and some ranne toward the houses thereby and fell, that it was marveile to see and hear;ᵉ but howe the cause was, God knoweth.ᶠ

[A.D. 1552.]

Death of the Duke of Somersett.

Saterday, the 23 of January, beinge the first day of Hilary

A lord Chauncellor.

ᵃ Benefit of clergy.

ᵇ Cuthbert Tunstall, made Dean of Salisbury 1516, Master of the Rolls and Vice-Chancellor 1516-22, Bishop of London 1521-30, Lord Privy Seal 1523-30, Bishop of Durham 1530, deprived 1552, restored in 1553, deprived again 1559, and died the same year.

ᶜ Henry II. ᵈ Angolismæ, of Angoulème.

ᵉ Stow gives some particulars of the cause of this panic, p. 607.

ᶠ Edward VI. appears to have been perfectly convinced of his uncle's guilt, and in that conviction to have given himself no further concern about the duke, only noting in his diary that "the Duke of Somerset had his head cut off upon Tower hill,

CAMD. SOC.   K

A.D. 1552.

Tearme, and allso the first day of the Session of the Parliament[a] at Westminster, Doctor Goodricke, Bishopp of Ely and custos of the Kinges great seale of England, was sworne in the Chauncery Lord Chauncellor of England, the Lord Treasurer of England giuinge him his oath.

Sir Raphe Vane.

The 27 of January Sir Raphe Vane, knight, was arraigned at Westminster, and condempned for felony, and had judgment to be hanged.

Sir Thomas Arundell.

The 28 of January Sir Thomas Arundell, knight, was arraigned at Westminster, and condempned for fellonie, and had judgment to be hanged.

Sir Myles Patriche.

The 5 of February, Sir Myles Patriche,[b] knight, was arraigned at Westminster and condempned for fellonie, and had judgment to be hanged.

Sir Michaell Stanope.

The 9 of February Sir Michaell Stanope, knight, was arraigned at Westminster and condempned for felonie, and had judgment to be hanged.

The 17 of February, the daye of receivinge the books of the releife of all the wardes of London [towardes the new hospitals][c] by the Kinges Maiesties Commissioners, the Counsell dyned at Mr. Coopers, sheriffe, and after dinner Mr. Thomas Curteis, alderman, came thither to speak to my Lord Chauncellor for a matter he had dependinge before him in the Chauncery, but for his misdeamour in wordes and signes to the Lord Chauncellor at that tyme the sayd Mr. Curteis was committed to warde in the Flete by the Kinges Counselles commaundement.

This yere all manner of victualles was exceedinge dere and at excessiue prices, both of fleshe and fishe, that the lyke hath not bene hard of, for white herringe was sold for xxx s. and xxxii s. the barrell of the best, and redd herring at xiiii and xv s. the cade; sprots at ii s. iiii d. the cade, and meale of the best at xxx s. the quarter.

between eight and nine o'clock in the morning." Grafton indeed says that "the King seemed to take the trouble of his uncle somewhat heavily;" but the King's public demeanour and the Christmas rejoicings at Court certainly do not seem to countenance this assertion.   [a] This session lasted till the 15th of April following.

[b] Sir Miles Partridge.   [c] Supplied from Stow.

A.D. 1552.

The 19 of February was sene in the element ouer the City of Antwarpe, in the Dukedome of Brabant, iiii sonnes with ii rainebowes, backe to backe in the forme as is here set downe, which was sene in the afternone the same daye betwixt iii and iiii of the clocke.

This moneth, on St. Mathies day, the 25 of February, in Barwicke Parke, in Essex, was a shepe that had a lambe with ii netherbodies, with iiii hinder feet and ii tayles, and betwene both the netherbodye the vth legge with ii feete together, and had but one fore part with ii feete and i head, which lambe was brought to Quenhith and shewed to my Lord Mayor after yt was dead, and commaunded to cut it in peeces and bury yt in the feild.

Fryday, the 26 of February, at ix of the clocke in the forenone, Sir Raphe Vane and Sir Miles Partridge[a] were hanged at the Tower hill, and Sir Michaell Stanope and Sir Thomas Arundell were beheaded on the Tower hill; all which iiii persons tooke on theyr death that they neuer offended against the Kinges Maiestie nor against any of his Counsell.[b]

Death of foure knights at the Tower Hill.

Memorandum: the 18 day of March, 1551, beinge Fryday, was sene in the element at a towne called Brykerbery,[c] by Newbery, in Barkshire, iiii sonnes after this manner under written, presented to the Kinges Maiestie by Mr. Weldon,[d] one of the Masters of his Houshould, Mr. Winstome, of Newebery, Mr. Randall, of the Temple,

[a] The Chronicle of the Grey Friars adds: "the wych playd wyth Kynge Henry VIIIte at dysse for the grett belfery that stode in Powlles church-yerde."
[b] They were apprehended and executed as the accomplices of the Duke of Somerset.   [c] Bucklebury.
[d] Master of Queen Catherine Howard's household in 1541

68   WRIOTHESLEY'S CHRONICLE.

A.D. 1552. and Hinde, the Kinges plomer, which persons did see the sayd token betwene ix and x of the clocke in the forenone of the same daye.

The 18 day of March a wyfe of Hamersmith brought two pigges to London to a carpenter dwellinge in Smythfeild, which was taken contrary to a proclamation for eatinge of fleshe in Lent, and by iudgment of my Lord Mayor and Aldermen they did ryde on 2 horses with panelles of strawe about the markettes of the Citie, havinge eche of them a garland on theyr heades of the pyges pettie toes, and a pygge hanginge on ech of their brestes afore them, and lay 2 dayes in the Counter allso, and so discharged after their penance done.

The 19 of March a clothiers sonne of Devonshire brought a duck to the Rose taverne by Flete-bridge in Flete-strete to be rosted, and was taken withall, which boy and one of the boyes of the taverne rode on horsebacke, havinge the ducke on the spitt rosted, caryinge yt betwene them thorough all the marketts of the Citye, which was their penance iudged by my Lord Mayor and Aldermen, and laye in prison one daye and night, and so discharged.

The 15 of Aprill, 1552, the Session of this Parliament brake up and was clerely dissolued at iiii of the clocke in the afternone, which day was Good Frydaye.

The 16 of Aprill, being Easter even, one good wyfe Ryse, an Irishe woman, which was a seller of aqua composita,[a] and dwelled by St. Buttolphes Church without Aldersgate, for a devillishe correction which she had promised a mayde childe of xiiii yeres of age, which she had strypped naked the Wednesday before about iii of the clocke in the morninge and carded all hir body both before and behinde with a payre of wollen cardes,[b] which was too pitifull a sight to be sene, for which she was iudged by my Lord Mayor and Aldermen to ryde in a carre with a picture of a childe and a woman cardinge yt, after the manner that she had punished her, and havinge the cardes hanginge about her necke, which she did this daye, and a proclamation made in diuers places of the Citye of

[a] "a woman that dwelte in Aldersgate strete, that made aqwavyte" [aqua vitæ]. —Grey Friars' Chronicle, p. 74.
[b] "with a payer of carddes, soche as doth carde wolle with-alle."—Ibidem.

hir evill demeanor, which sayd woman was counted in substance i c l. and better, which she had goeinge by usurye, and allso havinge an evill name of hir livinge, which sayd punishment the people thought was too litle for her offence.[a]

_{A.D. 1552.}

Allso this yeare at Easter were but two sermons kept at the Spittle, that is to say, Monday and Tuesday, for the Wednesday should noe more be kept holyday, as by Acte of this Parliament should after appere, and the guestes of the Aldermen that should haue dyned at my Lord Mayors and the Sheriffes that day was put of till Lowe Sonday after Easter daye.

_{Two sermons at Easter at the Spittle and noe more.}

Memorandum: That in Aprill afore St. Georges day, Garter the Kinge of Armes was sent by the Kinges Maiestie to the Lord Pagett, prisoner in the Tower of London, to fetch and take from the sayd Lord Pagett the Garter and George of the noble order of the garter which he was knight of, which Garter and George the sayd Kinge of Armes tooke from him there, being prisoner, in such degree as he was made knight of the same order,[b] which the sayd Lord Pagett was content with seinge yt was the Kinges Maiesties pleasure, and the Kinge sent yt to the Earl of Warwick, sonne and heire of the Duke of Northumberland, who was made knight of the sayd order in his rome.

_{Lord Paget deprived of the order of the Garter in the Tower of London.}

Saterday, the 30 of Aprill, 1552, a gunpowder house in Hogg-lane, beyonde the Tower-hill, toward Stepney, about the houre of vi of the clock in the afternone, by mischaunce of the beatinge of gunpowder, ix persons[c] were cast away and burnt, whereof vi of them dyed out of hand, and three other sore burnt and in daunger of death.

_{A misfortune by gunpowder.}

Memorandum: The 8 of May my Lord Mayor was presented to the Kinges Maiestie at Grenewich, and there made knight of the Kinges Maiestie.

_{Lord Mayor made knight.}

---

[a] Other accounts of this outrage will be found in Machyn, p. 17, and Grey Friars' Chronicle, p. 74.

[b] "upon this pretence, that he was said to be no gentleman, either by father or mother."—Baker's Chronicle, p. 330.   [c] "15 in number."—Stow, p. 607.

A.D. 1552.

Saterday, the 21 of May, Sir Roger Cholmeley, knight, Lord Cheife Baron of the Exchequer, was sworne Lord Cheife Justice of England in the Kinges Bench, and Mr. Bradshawe, the Kinges Atturney, was sworne Lord Cheife Baron of the Kinges Exchequer; the ould Cheife Justice gaue it ouer because of his greate age.

A great hayle in Holland.

Memorandum: The 17 of May, 1552, beinge Tuesday, betwixt iiii and v of the clocke afternone, fell a terrible and dreadfull hayle in Holland in the towne of Dordrike, so that the inhabitors of the sayd towne for great feare shutt their houses, for by the space of halfe an houre there fell so terrible a hayle that the garden hearbes and fruites of the trees were therewith destroyed, and the sayd haylestones were great, some did way halfe a pounde, some 3 quarters or xii ounces, some stones hauinge the naturall shape of the sonne, and some resembled lyke crownes of thornes, and the water that did melt of the sayd hayle and did runne in great aboundaunce through the canelles in the streates did cast forth a smoke as yf it had bene seethinge water; and after this hayle did ryse a myst or smoke so troublous and filthy and with so great a stenche that yt was maruell.

Wednesday, the 8th day of June, and in the Whitson week, the Lordes of the Kinges Maiesties Counsell sat in the Guildhall, afore whom were present the Lord Mayor and Aldermen with the wardens of all the Companies of the Citye of London; to whom was declared by the mouth of the Lord Chauncellor that the Kinges Maiestie had sent them thither to declare that his Maiestie marvayled greately why euery thinge, both of wares and marchandises, and specially victualles, were so dere, and at so excessiue prises with in the Citye, seinge that thoroughout all England it was falne halfe in halfe, and in the Citye noethinge falne; wherefore he layd great fault in my Lord Mayor and the Aldermen for lacke of executinge justice on the offendors, shewinge them that they had diuers tymes warninges both private and allso by letters from the Kinges Counsell, for to see a redresse for the same, and not amended; wherefore he declared to them, and allso other of the Lordes of the Counsell, there present, that if they see not a speedy redresse and reformation shortly, that they should put all their liberties in daunger, to the great undoeinge of the Citie of London.

A.D. 1552.

The Lordes names there present:

The Lord Chauncellor.	The Earle of Pembroke.
The Lord Treasurer.	Lord Chamberlaine.
The Duke of Northumber-	Lord Warden of Sinck
lande.	Portes.
The Duke of Suffolke.	Sir Edward North.
The Lord Privie Seale.	Sir Phillip Hobbie.
The Lord Marques North-	Mr. Mason, Secretarie.
ampton.	Sir Robert Bowes.
The Earle of Huntington.	Sir Richard Cotton.

Saterday, the 11 of June, at a Court of Aldermen kept in the Guildehall, one Thomas Chapell, merchant, occupyinge uphoulstry dwellinge in Cornehill, was iudged by the sayd Court for that he had a yarde of false measure which lacked a good ynche of the length, and presented to my Lord Mayor by one Mr. Holmes, secretary to the Duke of Northumberland; which sayd Chappell was had from the Guyldhall to Leadenhall, and there sett in the stockes, and the yardes hanged ouer his head, with a paper written for false measure, and so satt from a quarter of an hour before xii of the clocke till ii of the clocke in the sayd stockes, and then discharged and sent home to his house. For false measure.

Monday, the 27 of June, 1552, one Thomas Harvie, a baker in Southwarke, was set on the pillory in Southwarke for lackinge six ounces waight in a penny loafe, and judged by a whole Court of Aldermen, the 21 of this moneth, and lay euer since in the Counter, trustinge that he should haue scaped from that punishment, but yt prevayled not. Pillorye.

Monday the 1 of August, beinge the day of the election of the Sheriues of London, Mr. John Grymes, clothworker, was by the Commons elected Sheriff for the year followinge, which sayd Grymes Election of the sheriffes. Jonn Grymes clothworker.

A.D. 1552.

was lame and chosen more for displeasure then for loue, because he intended to goe out of the City into the country, and allso for because he would giue nothinge to the settinge up of the godly acte and provision [which] was beginninge for releife of the poore of the sayd City; wheruppon a court of aldermen was kept in the guyldhall the Fryday followinge, beinge the v of August; the sayd Grymes after longe examination and sute, declaringe his unhability and impotencye, was set to his fyne of ii c t. accordinge to an acte of commen counsell provyded in that behalfe; and was bound to the Chamberlayne with Southwoode, goldsmyth, and Rikethorne, haberdasher, his sonne-in-lawe, to pay i c on Michaelmas even next comminge, which should be payd to him that should succede [in] his rome of the shryvealty, and L t at Christmas next comminge, and the other L t at the Annuntiation of Our Lady next ensueinge, which two payments of c t is due by Act of Commen Counsell to the Chamber of London to the use of the Citie; whereupon the morrowe after, beinge the vi of August, the Commons were newe assembled in theyr liueries againe for a newe election of another sheriffe in his rome; fyrst a Common Counsell called up before my Lord Mayor and th' Aldermen the same daye was declared to them by Mr. Recorder of his dispensation for a fyne of ii c t accordinge to the acte, but then elegible againe; whereupon the sayd Grymes request was to be clerely discharged of that office, and all other for euer, which at length was granted him, but the c t. which the Chamber of London should haue was by this Common Counsell given from the use of the Chamber to the use of the poore newe elected, as a benevolence from the Chamber. Allso that day by this Common Counsell newe enacted, that yf any more hereafter should be set to their fyne after another election that the fyne of 2 c t. should halfe go to the use of the poore and the other halfe to the use of the Chamber. This done my Lord Mayor and Aldermen departed downe into the great hall to a newe election of a sheriffe in his rome; which sayd newe election fell to Thomas Clayton, baker, dwellinge on St. Mary Hill by Bellinesgate, which

2nd election.
Thomas Clayton baker.

that daye was chosen for one of the sheriffes for the City of London and Middlesex for the yere ensuynge. After this the sayd Clayton repayred to my Lord Mayor divers tymes, declaringe his impossibility and great age, whereby he was not able to perfourme the sayd office; whereupon after diuers consultations my Lord Mayor caused a court of Aldermen with a newe assembly of the Commons to be called the xv of August. First the sayd Mr. Clayton called afore the Court of Aldermen declared his great age and impossibility of goodes, beinge willinge to take the office if his substance and power were accordinglye, whereupon they agreed to sett him to his fyne of ii c ł accordinge to the lawe, which at length he agreed unto, which should be to pay i c ł in hand within 3 dayes, which should goe to the poore, and l ł at Christmas next comminge, and l ł at the Annuntiation of Our Lady next ensuynge to the behoofe of the Chamber, upon which he ymedyately should bringe suretyes to be bound with him for the perfourmaunce of the same to the Chamberlaine of London, which he did, and Messrs. Collins, Jackson, Alleine, and Davie, wardens of the bakers, were bound to the Chamberlaine with him for the perfourmaunce of the sayd fyne, which done my Lord Mayor caused a Commen Counsell to be called up, declaringe to them that they had done. And the said Mr. Clayton declaringe his minde afore the sayd Comen Counsell as afore to my Lord Mayor and aldermen, desyred their favour and good willes allso therein, to be clerely discharged of all manner of offices for the sayd fyne for euer, he being put apart; at length it was graunted him. This done, my Lord Mayor and aldermen departed downe to the great hall for a newe election, Mr. Recorder first declaringe to the Commons of the impossibility and age of the sayd Clayton, and allso of his fyne; they then nominatinge vii persons in the election, whereof they draue yt to two, which were Mr. Harper, merchant taylor, and Mr. John Browne, mercier; the sayd Mr. Harper beinge then present in the hall came up into the Hastinges Court ymediately and desired the Commons to be good to him, sayinge that his substance and goodes

3d election, John Browne, mercer.

A.D. 1552. were out of his handes, desiringe them to favour him for that tyme, and hereafter he would be glad to take the office if it shall so chaunce on him, which they agreed unto, and so tryed againe with handes betweene him and Mr. Browne. The election fell whole to Mr. Browne, and so the sheriffes with the heades and wardens of the Company presented the election to my Lord Mayor according to the custome, which done the Commons departed. After yt was declared to my Lord Mayor that the said Mr. Browne should be in towne or ells newly gone forth, whereupon my Lord Mayor sent the common sergeant at armes to his house ymediately to bid him to dine with my Lord Mayor, who had answere that he was rydden into Darbishire with the gentlewoman his wyfe, and had taken theyr horses at x of the clocke, supposinge they would lye that night at St. Albones or at Dunstable at the farthest. Upon this aunswer my Lord Mayor caused the common hunt to ryde that afternone after him; he meetinge with him early on the morrowe, being the xvi day, havinge a letter with him from my Lord Mayor. And so he returned backe to London againe and came to supper to my Lord Mayors. After diuers communications had with him by the sayd Lord Mayor, a court of aldermen was warned againe the morrowe, beinge the xvii of August, before whom the sayd Mr. Browne was called, he declaringe before them that he was not a man of substance nor able to perfourme the rome, but declaringe his obedience, and that he neuer had occupyed no trade of merchaundise, but livinge as a gentleman on his landes and his office as the Kinges seruant, as paymaster in one of the Kinges mintes of the Tower. This done the sayd court desyred him to take respite till the xixth day, and then to make his answere; in the meane tyme the aldermen of the mercers with the wardens of the Company caused the liuery of the Mercers to be assembled at their hall, havinge the sayd Mr. Browne afore them, declaringe to him what worshipp yt should be to him to take the sayd office on him yf he knewe himselfe able for yt, he beinge a citizen borne, his grandfather and father allso both bearinge the offices of the Lord Mayor and sheriffes

of London, and further offringe him diuers thinges to ayde and
help him with; but all would not prevayle; wherupon aunswere was
sent from him to my Lord Mayor. A newe assemblye of the
aldermen and commens was warned to be at the Guildhall the sayd
xixth of August, the which day my Lord Mayor and aldermen
called the sayd Mr. Browne before them to knowe his minde, which
soberly and discretely he declared to them, not beinge of substance
for the sayd rome; wheruppon they desyred him to depart out
of the counsell chamber for a while; they, after debatinge of
the matter accordinge to the lawes of the citye, what might be
done therein; after callinge him afore them againe, shewed him
that they could not dispence with him, but to paye his fyne,
wherupon a Common Counsell was called upp, and there Mr.
Brown declared his minde afore them so soberly and discreetly,
shewinge his unhability and lack of substance, that they had great
marvaile to hear his wisdome. They most hartely desyringe him
to take the rome on him. After my Lord Mayor and aldermen
departed to the counsell chamber againe, shewinge him that eyther
he must take the office on him, or elles he must pay ii c℔ accordinge
to the lawe or euer they could goe to a newe election, who at
length graunted to their requestes; then they further declared to
him that he must fynde suerties with him for the payment of the
sayd fyne afore they must proceede to the election; then he desyringe
their favour for dayes of payment, and on his owne bonde allso, at
last his request was graunted, he to be bound to the Chamberlaine
by recognisance to pay i c℔. at the feast of All Sainctes next comminge, l. ℔ at the feast of the Purification of Our Lady next ensuinge,
and l. ℔ at the feast of Pentecost then next followinge, which bond
he acknowledged, and so they declared yt to the Common Counsell.
And then my Lord Mayor and Aldermen went downe to the great
hall to proceede to a newe election. Mr. Recorder first shewinge
to the Commons howe they should put all malice and partiallity
aparte, and frely accordinge to theyr charter to elect such a sad and
substantiall person to the sayd rome that they noe more proceede

A.D. 1552.

4th election,
John Maynard,
mercer.

A.D. 1552.

to any more election; shewinge them further, that he neuer hard or knewe of so many elections as they lately had made, which might be taken for great slander of the citizens, and allso against theire charter.

This done, my Lord Mayor and Aldermen departed accordinge to ould custome; then the Commons nominatinge John Maynarde, mercer, William Chester, draper, Robert Mellis, merchaunt taylor, and John Richmond, armorer, to be for the election; they tryinge yt by handes, the election fell to Mr. Maynard, mercer, and so presented to my Lord Mayor; and so the Commons departed. This sayd Mr. Maynard nowe elected had bene at Venice this yere, and came from thence to his house at Popler from thence about the 23 of July last past, whereby as the report goeth he should gayne great substance upon bargaines that he had made afore tyme, to be payd when he had bene at Venice, and returned thence againe. Likewise he hath made diuers bargaines aforetyme to be payd when he should be sheriffe of London, so that men thinke this election was procured, which should be for his great advantage and profitt.

Memorandum: The 20 of July the house of the Grey Fryers beganne to be builded [a] for the fatherles children. Allso the latter end of that moneth the church of St. Thomas hospitall in Southwarke was begunne to be built for poore and impotent persons, lame and sicke.

Allso about the 7 or 12 of August, diners strange fishes, as dolphins, were taken in the Thames at diuers tymes betwene Wollwiche and Grenewiche.

The 28 of September, Mr. John Maynard, mercer, was sworne sheriffe with Mr. William Garret,[b] alderman, elected by my Lord Mayor, and received i c t by the handes of Mr. Chamberlaine for John Grymes, clothworker, which refused the sayd office the first of August, beinge the day of the election of the sheriffe.

[a] "The 26 of July, began the preparing of the Gray Friers house in London."—Stow, p. 608.

[b] Variously spelled Gerard, Garrard, or Garrett.

The 29 of September, beinge Michaelmas day and the day of the A.D. 1552.
election of the Lord Mayor, there was a sermon made in the Guildhall Chappell by Mr. Sampson, parson of All Hallowes in Bread
Strete, in the stead of the Communion of late yeares accustomed,
and after that they proceeded to the election of the Lord Mayor, and
then was chosen Mr. George Barnes, alderman and haberdasher,
Lord Mayor for the yeare ensueinge.

About the 7 and 8 of October, two great fishes called whirle-
pooles [a] were taken and slayne about Wollwich, which were chased
2 dayes and 2 nightes ere they were slaine, and they were drawne
at 2 barges through London bridge the ix of October, and so
brought to the Kinges bridge at his place of Whitehall to shewe
the Kinge, who came thither after his progresse the 10 October at
night.

Memorandum: That in this moneth of October, at the shippinge A prest to the Kinge
to Bawmes [b] marte for the Merchaunt Adventurers, the Kinge and by the merchaunt
his Counsell demaunded of the sayd merchauntes by way of prest, adventurers.
of euery brode cloth shipped to the sayd marte xx s. sterling, to be
payd at Antwarpe for [a] certaine debt of the Kinges, and they to
have the Kinges bonde for the repayment of yt againe, which did
amount to xlviii M ł and above.

The 17 of October, beinge the even of St. Luke, the Sergeantes
feast was kept at Grayes Iune, in Holborne, Mr. Robert Brooke,
Recorder of London, beinge the principall of the newe sergeantes
and six more besyde him; my Lord Mayor with the aldermen The Sergeantes feast
bidden to the sayd feast; the aldermen assemblinge at my Lord at Greys Inne.
Mayor's house, and soe rode from thence up Fryday Streat, through
Cheapsyde and out at Newegate, all in their skarlett gownes, to the
sayd Greyes Inne; where sat at the high bord in the hall my Lord
Chauncellor, with other Lordes. At the seconde borde my Lord

---

[a] This word is used in Stow.

[b] Boom, a town in the province of Antwerp, Belgium, at the junction of the
Brussels Canal with the Rupel, 12 miles south of Antwerp city. Boom, being ad-
mirably situated for trade, is a busy inland port.

78 WRIOTHESLEY'S CHRONICLE.

A.D. 1552.

Mayor and the Aldermen and Sheriffes, which were xx in nomber; at the 3rd borde, beinge in the middest of the hall, the judges with the ould sergeauntes at the lawe; at the 4th borde, which was next the cupbord, the newe sergeantes all on one syde, two of them to a measse; and there was another table next to the judges which was voyde; this feast was but one dinner, x dishes to the first course and viii to the last course, and after wafers and ipocras.

EDWARDI VI. Anno 6°.

Newe service in churches.

The first day of November, beinge All Hallowes daye, the newe seruice of the booke called the Common Prayer[a] beganne in Pawles, the Bishop of London executinge himselfe.[b] And in the afternoone the sayd Bishop preached at Pawles Crosse,[c] my Lord Mayor and the Aldermen beinge present at the sermon.

Copes and vestments put downe.

This day all copes and vestments were put downe through all England, and the prebendaries of Pawles left of their hoodes, and the Bishops their crosses,[d] so that all prestes and clarkes should use none other vestmentes, at service nor communion, but surplisses

[a] The new Common Prayer Book, according to the alterations agreed upon in the former year, with the form of making bishops, priests, and deacons, was appointed to be received everywhere after the feast of All Saints. It was, by the King's order, translated into French by Francis Philip, for the use of Guernsey, Jersey, and Calais, which translation was printed in the following year, 1553.—See Collier's Ecclesiastical History, ii. p. 321, and Strype, p. 377.

[b] "The bishop of London, Dr. Ridley, executing the service in Paules Church in the forenoone in his rochet onely, without coape or vestment, preached in the quier." —Stow, p. 608.

[c] The Grey Friars' Chronicle (p. 76) adds, "and stode there tyll it was nere honde v a cloke, and the Mayer nor aldermen came not within Powlles church, nor the craftes, as they were wonte to doo, for be-cause they were so wary of hys longe stondynge."

[d] Several Acts were passed by the Parliament this year, advancing the Reformation in a Protestant sense. Among other things, the marriage of the clergy was declared good and valid, which had been for some time considered by the people as only tolerated.

onely: as by an Act of Parliament in the booke of Common Prayer more at large is sett out.[a]

A.D. 1552.

After the feast of All Saintes, the upper quire in St. Pawles Church, in London, where the high aulter stoode, was broken downe[b] and all the quire thereabout, and the table of the communion was set in the lower quire where the preistes singe.[c]

Memorandum: The 23 of November, the poore children of the City of London were taken into Christes Hospitall, late the house of the Grey Fryers in London: And allso that daye they tooke other sicke and poore people into the hospitall[d] in Southwarke:. In which two places the children and poore people should haue meate, drinke, lodginge, and cloths, of the almes of the citye.

The entringe of the poore children into Christes hospitall.

The 3 of December, 1552, the Earle of Arundell was discharged out of the Tower of London, and went from thence to his place by Strand.

The 9 of December, there was one Anthony Fowlkes, a gentleman, set on the pillory in Cheape, and had his eare hard nayled to the pillory, for deceivinge certeine citizens for mercery wares, hosen, and other, in offringe them a bagge with newe counters sealed for a pawne, sayinge yt was gould, till he would bringe mony, with which he was taken well, and for his deceipt was judged by my Lord Mayor and Aldermen at a court in the guyld hall, the viiith

One sett on the pillory.

---

[a] This relates to the preface prefixed to the First Service Book of Edward VI. concerning ceremonies, the same that is still before the Common Prayer Book, and the Act of Parliament passed in 1549 for its authorisation.

[b] "Item, the xxv day of October was the pluckynge downe of alle the alteres and chappelles in alle Powlles churche, with alle the toumes, at the commandment of the byshoppe, then beynge Nicolas Rydley, and alle the goodly stoneworke that stode behynde the hye alter, and the place for the prest, dekyne, and subdekyne, and wolde a pullyd downe John a Gauntes tome, but there was a commandment [to] the contrary from the counsell, and soo yt was made alle playne, as it aperes."—Grey Friars' Chronicle, p. 75.

[c] About this time David's Psalms began to be turned into English rhyme by Thomas Sternhold, one of the grooms of the King's Privy Chamber; he versified thirty-seven, and the remainder were completed by John Hopkins and others.—See Heylin, p. 127.

[d] "Of Saint Thomas in Southwarke."—Stow.

A.D. 1552.

of December, to haue this penaunce. And when he had stand on the pillory till the clocke was past xii. he would not rent his eare, but one of the bedles slitted yt upwards with a penkniffe to loose yt, and so he was had to prison againe for 2 dayes after.

Memorandum: On Christmas day in the afternone, when my Lord Mayor and Aldermen rode to Pawles, all the children of Christes Hospitall stoode in aray, from St. Lawrence Lane, in Cheape, toward Pawles, all in one liuery of gownes of russet cotton and red caps, both men children and the maydens, [the latter with] kircheifes on theyr heades,[a] all the masters of the hospitall beginninge first, next them the phisicion and iiii surgeons, with bandes about theyr neckes of white and grene satten, and betwene enery xx children, one woman keeper, which children were in number xvii^{xx}.

[A.D. 1553].

This yeare [b] was Mr. George Ferrers [c] Lord of merry disportes at the Court at Grenewich;[d] Mr. Maynard, shiriue of London, had allso a lord of misrule,[e] which received the kinges lord into the City.

A good mayor.

This mayor [f] after Christmas punished diuers colyers by settinge them on the pillory and rydinge about the city for yll fillinge of their sackes, and caused quarters and demi-quarters to be had in diuers places of the city to measure coles, and had halfe a quarter

---

[a] This passage is more clearly expressed in Stow (p. 608): "all in one livory of russet cotton, the men children with red caps, the women children [with] kerchiffes on their heads."

[b] "the 4th day of January."—Grey Friars' Chronicle, p. 76.

[c] George Ferrars.—See Machyn's Diary, p 28.

[d] "After the Duke [of Somerset's] condemnation, it was thought fit to have something done for averting the Kings minde from taking thought; and, to that end, one George Ferrers, a gentleman of Lincoln's Inne, was appointed in the Christmas time to be Lord of Misrule; who so carried himself that he gave great delight to many, and some to the King, but not in proportion to his heavinesse."—Baker's Chronicle, p. 330.

[e] Sergeant Vawce, in Stow, p. 608, where a full account of George Ferrars' visit to the City will be found.

[f] Sir George Barne.

measure caryed after him diners dayes as he rode to way bread, and sold enery halfe quarter of coles for vi d. charginge the constables to see the people serued after that rate; allso, he punished bawdes and whores by rydinge in cartes, and whipped vagabondes out of the city; so that all malefactours feared him for his good executinge of justice.

This yere, after Candlemas, the prises of corne begann to fall, so that wheat was sould for xii s. a quarter, and my Lord Mayor set downe the syse of bread, which syse in the beginninge of his tyme was but xx ounces the peny wheaten loafe, and nowe he raysed yt to xxxiv. ounces, and lyke to be lower.

Memorandum: The first day of March, 1552, beganne the first Session of the seconde Parliament of our Souereigne Lord Kinge Edward the VIth, all the Lordes spirituall and temporall assemblinge that daye in the Kinges Maiesties Court of Whitehall, at Westminster, in their robes; first a sermon made by Doctor Ridley, Bishop of London, in the Kinges chappell, and after the communion was kept; the Kinges Maiestie with diners other lordes received the communion that daye. Then the Kinges Maiestie, with all the Lords in their degrees, went in order into the Kinges great chamber, on the Kinges syde, which that daye was prepared for the Lords House. The Kinges Maiestie sitting there under his cloth of estate, and all the Lordes after their degrees. Then the Bishop of Ely, Doctor Goodrick, Lord Chauncellor of England, made a proposition for the Kinge, for the assemblinge of the sayd Parliament. The knightes and burgesses in London, in scarlet, with diners other knightes and burgesses of other shyres, beinge there present at the sayd proposition, which ended, the Kinge and the Lordes departed. The cause of the assembly in the court this daye was because the Kinges Maiestie was a litle diseased by could takinge;[a] therefore,

A.D. 1553.

The first beginninge of the second parliament of Kinge Edwarde the 6, Anno reg. 7°

---

[a] The young King had been seized ever since January with a distemper, which at length brought him to his grave. In fact, ever since April 2, 1552, when he fell sick of the small pox and measles, his lungs had been slightly affected, "which probably might turn to a consumption."—See Edward's Journal p. 49.

A.D. 1553.

yt was not meete for his Grace to ryde to Westminstr in the ayre; the morrowe after, all the burgesses sat in the Common House at Westminster, and there chose for their Speaker Mr. Dyer, of the Temple, which was one of the newe sergeantes at the lawe that was last made, and so went from thence to the court and presented him to the Counsell.

The 2 day of March all the Bishops and Deanes of the Spiritualty assembled at Pawles for their convocation in their robes, the Bishop of Rochester, Mr. Scorye, makinge the sermon before them in Latten, in Our Lady Chappell behinde the quire.

The parliament ended. The 31 of March, beinge Goodfryday, the Parliament brake up and was clerely dissolued [a] at the Kinges place at Whitehall at vii of the clock at night; the Kinges Maiestie sitting in his robes in the great chamber on the Kynges syde, where the first Session beganne with all the Lordes spirituall and temporall, in their robes likewise.

The children of Christs hospitall. Memorandum: The 3d of Aprill, beinge the Monday after Easter day, the children of Christes Hospitall in London came from thence thorough the City to the sermon kept at St. Maries Spittle, all clothed in plunket coates, with redd cappes, and certeine of the mayden children likewise in the same liuery, with kerchers on their heades, all the aldermen and masters of the house goeing after them with grene staues in their handes, the surgeons and officers with the bedles goeinge before them, and the matron and other women tendinge on them, where was made a great skaffolde with viii seates,[b] one aboue another, and the skaffold couered with canvas and rayled before yt, where all the children sat, all the masters commoners, with the matron sittinge highest, and the children in rowe under them, and all the surgeons and officers before the children, next the rayles, which was a godly sight to behold.

[a] The Parliament sat but one month, the Court having no further need of its assistance after the Duke of Northumberland had procured a subsidy for the King and had succeeded in tarnishing the memory of the late Duke of Somerset.

[b] Stages or forms.

The 10 of Aprill, beinge the Monday after Lowe Sonday, my Lord Mayor was sent for to the Court to the Kinges Counsell, and there the Kinges Maiestie gaue to them for the workehouse for the poore and ydle persons of the City of London his place of Brydewell in Flete Streat, and vii C marks landes of the Savoy rentes, with all the beddes and bedding of the Savoy,[a] towardes the maintenaunce of the sayd workehouse.

<small>A.D. 1553.
Brydewell giuen to the Citie.</small>

Tuesday, the 11 of Aprill, my Lord Mayor was presented to the Kinges Maiestie at his pallace of Whitehall in Westminster, and was made knight of his Maiestie, which day the Kinge removed in the afternoone to Grenewich.

<small>Lord Mayor made knight.</small>

Memorandum: In the monethes of Aprill and May this yeare Commissions were directed through England for all the Church goodes remaininge in Cathedrall and parishe Churches,[b] that is to say, iuelles, plate, ready mony, copes, vestmentes, with other mettalles of brasse and copper, the Churchwardens to make a true inventory of all such goodes, and to bringe [it] to the Commissioners;[c] and, after the inventories were brought in, all such goodes were taken away to the Kinges use, that is to say, all the iewelles of gould and siluer, as crosses, candlestickes, censers, chalyces, and all other iewelles of gold and siluer, and ready mony, which should be delivered to the master of the Kinges iuelles in the Tower of London, and all copes and vestmentes of cloth of gould, cloth of tyssue, and cloth of siluer, to be deliuered to the master of the

<small>The iewells and plate of Churches suppressed.</small>

---

[a] "of the hospitall of the Savoy."—Stow.

[b] Heylin and other favourers of ecclesiasticism urge from hence that the King must have been ill-principled as to the interests of the Church, because he was now in the sixteenth year of his age, and yet made no scruple to sign an order for visiting the churches and taking thence all the plate and ornaments under the flimsy pretext of their being superfluous. All this was done, say they, under colour of selling the superfluities and giving the money to the poor, who had, however, the least share. Burnet, on the other hand, observes, that, when all is done, it was only calling in the superfluous plate that lay in churches, more for pomp than use.

[c] The Commissioners or Visitors had instructions to compare the churchwardens' returns with the inventories made in former visitations, and to see what was embezzled, and how.

A.D. 1553.

Kinges wardrobe in London, and all other vestmentes and copes to be sould, and the mony to be deliuered to the Kinges treasurer Sir Edmunde Peckham, knight. Reserued to euery cathedrall and parishe church a chales or cup, or more, with tableclothes for the communion borde, at the discretion of the Commissioners.[a] Pawles Church suppressed the latter ende of Maye;[b] my Lord Mayor, the Bishop of London, and my Lord Cheife Justice, with other, beinge Commissioners for all the churches of London; all the belles remayninge still in euery parishe church by inventorye, with such other chalisses or communion cups at the Kinges pleasure.

This yeare in Whitson hollidayes were noe sermons kept by my Lord Mayor but one sermon on Whit Sonday at Pawles, made by the Bishop of London, beinge the 21 of May, 1553.

Attaint passed in the Guildehall.

The 3 of June, beinge Fryday, Lord Montague, Cheife Justice of the Commen Place, with Justice Browne, Justice Hale, and Justice Brooke, all Justices of the Commen Place, sat on attaint in the Guildhall in the afternone, in my Lord Mayor's Court, which was shewed by Sir John Ayliffe, Alderman of London, and Holte keeper of Ludgate, against a jury that passed at the suyte of Througher, xxiii substantiall Commoners of the Citye, charged upon the ishewe of the pety jury; Mr. Browne, which was elder sheriffe last yere, beinge foreman of the xxiii. Mr. Pary and Grafton allso of the sayd jurye, which sayd persons remayned all that night till Saterday in the morninge at viii of the clocke in the Counsell chamber without meat or drinke, and then gaue theyr verdyte, Justice Hales and Justice Browne takinge their verdyte,

[a] They were to leave in every church one or two chalices of silver, with linen for the communion table and for surplices; and to bring in all other things of value to the Treasurer of the King's Household, and to sell the rest of the linen, copes, altar-cloths, &c. for the benefit of the poor.

[b] "The 25 day of May satte in Powlles the comyssioners with the lord cheffe justes, with the lorde mayer, and soo had away alle the platte, coppys, vestmenttes, wyche drewe unto a gret gooddes for the behoffe of the Kynges grace."—Grey Friars' Chronicle, p. 77.

and gaue their verdite against the petty jury, sayinge they gaue an untrue and false verdyte, which was the first attainte that had passed in many years in London.

A.D. 1553.

Saterday, beinge the 8 of July, 1553, my Lord Mayor was sent for to the Court at Grenewich by a letter, and to bringe with him 6 or 8 Aldermen, 6 Merchaunt Staplers, and 6 Merchant Adventurers; which he did the same day in the afternone; and when they were before the Counsell, there was declared secretly the death of the Kinges Maiestie, which dyed the 6 day of July, beinge Thursday; and allso howe he had by his letters patents ordayned for the succession of the imperiall crowne of England and Ireland; which, opened unto them by the mouth of the Counsell, they were sworne to yt and to keepe yt secret. The sayd Kinge Edward had rayned 6 yeares full the 28 of January last past,[a] and so much more, since which was in the 7th year of his raigne.

Death of Kinge Edward the 6.

Monday the 10 of July, at 3 of the clock in the afternone, Lady Jane, wyfe to the Lord Gilford Dudley, one of the sonnes[b] of the Duke of Northumberland, was brought by water from Grenewich to the Tower of London and there received as Quene of England, appointed by the Kinges letters patentes under the great seale of England,[c] which sayd Quene was eldest daughter to the Lady Frances, wyfe to the Duke of Suffolke, and the daughter of the late Lady Mary, the French Quene, [one] of the daughters of Kinge Henry the VIIth and sister of Kinge Henry the VIIIth.

The cominge of the newe Quene to the Tower.

Sequitur initium Regni Reginæ Jahannæ:

[a] The sixth year of King Edward VI.'s reign terminated on the 27th January, 1553.

[b] The fourth son.

[c] Her pretensions to the throne, and the history of the succession to the Crown under the Acts and will of Henry VIII. and the letters patent of Edward VI. are fully stated by Sir Harris Nicolas in his notes to the "Literary Remains of Lady Jane Grey," 8vo. 1825.

JAHANNÆ REGINÆ. Anno 1°.

Queen Jane.

The 10 of July at v of the clock [a] in the afternone was proclamation made,[b] with a trompetter, and 2 of the harouldes Kinges at Armes, and Mr. Garret, the sheriffe, rydinge with them, of the death of our late souereigne Kinge Edward the VIth, and howe he had ordeyned by his letters patents, bearinge date the 21 of June last, the sayd Quene Jane to be heyre to the crowne of England and the heyres males of hir body [c] lawfully begotten; which proclamation was made in 4 partes of the City of London, under the great seale of England, bearinge date the 10 daye of July, in the Tower of London, and the first yeare of the raigne of Queue Jane, Quene of England, Fraunce, and Ireland, Defender of the Fayth, and of the Church of England and Ireland the supreme head.

Execution.

Tuesday the 11 day of July was one Gilbert Pott, drawer to Ninion Saunders, vintner, dwellinge at the St. John's Head within Ludgate, set on the pillory in Cheapsyde, and had both his eares nayled to the pillory and cleane cut of for seditious and trayterous wordes [d] speakinge at the tyme of the proclamation of the Quene [e] yesternight, a trumpetter blowinge, and a harould with his coate readinge his offence at the cuttinge of his eares, and Mr. Garrett,[f] the sheriffe, seinge the execution; and after he was had to warde againe to the Counter in the Poultry, where he had lyne all night, which punishment was done by the Counselles commaundement.

Misfortune.

And about v of the clock at night the same afternone the master of the sayd Gilbert Pott, which was Ninion Saunders, vintner, and

---

[a] "after 7 a clocke at nyght."—Grey Friars' Chronicle, p. 78.

[b] This proclamation is printed by Grafton, and has been reprinted by most of the biographers of Lady Jane Grey.

[c] Stow, after quoting the first part of this paragraph, ends here abruptly with "&c."

[d] Full particulars of the story of Gilbert Potter or Pott will be found in the Chronicle of Queen Jane and Queen Mary, pp. 115-121.

[e] Lady Jane.   [f] William Garrard or Garrett.

one John Owen, a gunner, [happening] by misfortune ^a to shote through London Bridge toward the Blacke Fryers, were drowned about St. Mary locke at London Bridge; the wherry men were saved by their oares.

A.D. 1553.

Memorandum: This Tuesday, beinge the 11 of July, at v of the clocke at night, Sir Raphe Warreine, knight, alderman, departed out of this lyfe at Bednalne Grene at his house, which sayd Warreine had borne the office of the mayraulty two tymes [b] in the City of London, and was the auntient alderman of the Bench, and euer a trewe and good citizene and a specyall benefactor to the same, and that night, about x of the clocke, his bodye was brought in a horse litter to his house in London, and when he was rypped there were three great stones in his bladder, and another litle one in one of his kidneis.

Death of Mr. Warreine Alderman.

This 11 day [c] allso tydinges came to the Counsell that the Lady Mary had proclaymed herselfe as Quene and heyre to the Crowne of England in Norfolk and in a part of Suffolke, and had certeine noblemen, knightes, and gentlemen come to her to mainetaine her tytle, and allso with inumerable companies of the comon people.

Lady Mary.

Thursday the 13 of Julye the Duke of Northumberland with other lordes and knightes with a great power of horsmen with artillery and munitions of warre departed from London toward Norfolke to suppresse the rebelles, as he tooke them which had taken the Lady Maries parte.

Saturday the 15 of July the gates of the City beganne to be warded with the citizens by day, and at night 2 aldermen or their deputies with 8 of the Common Counsell to ryde about the Citye

Wardinge gates in London.

---

^a Some words have evidently been omitted here by the transcriber. Stow reads: "Gilbert Pot and John Owen, a gunmaker, both gunners of the Tower, comming from the Tower of London in a whirry, and shooting London bridge towards the Black Friers, were drowned at St. Mary lock, and the whirry men saned by their ores."

^b Viz. in 1536 and 1543.   ^c Stow apparently refers this to the 12th.

A.D. 1553.

A sermon at Pawles Crosse.

both within and without to peruse and see the constables watches that were substantially kept from 8 of the clock at night till 5 of the clocke in the morninge.

Sonday the 16 of July Doctor Rydley, Bishop of London, preached at Pawles Crosse, where he declared in his sermon of the death of Kinge Edward. And also declared further, the Lady Mary and the Lady Elizabeth, sisters to the Kinges Maiestie departed, to be illegitimate and not lawfully begotten in the estate of true matrimony accordinge to Gods lawe. And so found both by the clargie and actes of Parliament made in this realme in Kinge Henry the VIII^{ts} dayes their father, which the people murmured sore at.

Wednesday the 19 of July my Lord Mayor, rydinge in the afternone about the wood wharfe westward, as he came at Pawles Wharfe mett with the Earle of Shrewesbery and Sir John Mason, clarke of the Counsell, which spake to the Lord Mayor secretly, that he with both the sheriffes should mete with him and the Counsell at the Earle of Pembrokes place at Baynardes Castle within lesse then an houre and such other of the aldermen as he should thinke best; the Lord Mayor departinge incontinently home, sent for certeine aldermen with the Recorder to meet him incontinent at Paules Church, which they did, and so went to Baynardes Castle to the Counsell, and there spake with them.

Joyfull newes.

Then they declaringe to the Lord Mayor and his brethren that he must ryde with them into Cheape to proclaime a new Quene, which was the Lady Maries Grace, daughter to Kinge Henry the 8, which was so ioyfull newes that for ioy all the people present that hard yt wept, and ere the Counsell had rydden up the hill to Pawles Churchyard the people were so great assembled runninge into Cheap that the Lordes could scarse passe by; the Lord Mayor and the counsell comminge to the Crosse in Cheap, where the proclamation should be made, Mr. Garter, the Kinge of Armes, in his riche coate of armes, with a trumpetter being ready, and, [when] the trumpett blewe, there was such shoute of the people with castinge up of cappes and cryinge, God saue Quene Mary, that the style of the proclamation could not be hard, the people were so ioyfull, both man, woman, and childe. The proclamation there ended, the Lord Mayor and all the Counsell rode strayght to Pawles Church and went up into the quire, where the Canticle of Te Deum laudamus was solemply songe with the organs goinge, and that done the Counsell departed and commaunded Mr. Garret the sheriffe with the Kinge of Armes and trumpetter to see the proclamation made immedyately in other accustomed places within the City. All the people and citizens of the City of London for so joyfull newes made great and many fires through all the streates and lanes within the sayd City, with setting tables in the streates and banketting allso, with all the belles ringinge in enery parishe church in London till x of the clock at night,[a] that the inestimable joyes and reioysinge of the people cannot be reported.

A.D. 1553.

Queue Mary.

 Lords present at the proclamation:

The Lord Mayor of London.	Lord Darcy.
The Earle of Bedforde.	Lord Chamberlaine.
The Earle of Arundell.	Lord Cobham.
The Earle of Shrewesbery.	Lord Warden.
The Earle of Pembroke.	Sir Richard Cotton, comptroler.
Lord Pagett.	John Baker.
Lord of Worcester.	Sir John Masson.

This night, about ix of the clock, the Earle of Arundell and the Lord Paget rode in post to the Quene with xxx horse with them, and cheeringe the people that sat banketting about the bonfyres, askinge them yf they reioysed not at their good newes, which all thanked God, and sayd God saue Quene Mary.

Thursday the 20th of July all the Lordes of the Counsell dyned at my Lord Mayors, and the Duke of Suffolke and the Bishopp of Canterberry, and the Bishop of Ely, Lord Chauncellor, with them,

---

[a] "and for the most parte alle nyght tyll the nexte daye to none."—Grey Friars' Chronicle, p. 80.

and satt there in counsell after dinner till yt was past iiii of the clocke, and so departed. And this day was Te Deum songe in all the parishe churches in London, and all the belles ringinge all the day longe.

Fryday the 21 of July tydinges came to London that the [day]^a past about v of the clocke at night the proclamation came to Cambridge, where the Duke of Northumberland lay with his army, and that he hearinge of yt, callinge for foure trumpetters and a harrould, which could not be founde, rode into the market place with the Mayor and the Marques of Northampton, and there made proclamation himselfe, and castinge up his capp after as if he had bene ioyfull of yt; but the Quene caused him and his sonnes to be arested that night as traytours in the Kinges Colledge, and to see them safely kept; and this daye the campe scattered away and departed from him euery one towarde his countrye, but all his goodes there and all the ordinaunce and horses were stayed for the Quene.

Saterday the 22 of July the gates of London were warded with citizens in harness at enery gate, and to stay all suspected persons that came from the campe.

Sonday the 23 of July my Lord Mayor chose in his house at dinner Mr. Thomas Offley, alderman, sheriffe of London for the yeare ensueinge.

Monday the 24 of July the Duke of Northumberlande with his sonnes and other were caryed by the Earle of Arundell and the Lord Pagett from Cambridge towarde London, and lay at Ware this night.

The Duke and other prisoners had to the Tower.

Tuesday the 25 of July, beinge St. James day, at iii of the clocke in the afternone, the Duke of Northumberland came to the Towre of London by the conduction of the Earle of Arundell, with a great number of light horsemen, bowes, and spearmen, and came in at Bishopsgate, all the streates as he passed by standinge with men in harnes afore enery mans dore till he came to Tower Wharfe,

^a Omitted in MS.

all the streetes full of people, which cursed him and callinge him traytor without measure. A.D. 1553.

The prisoners names that came with him.

The Duke of Northumberlande.	The Earle of Huntington.
	Lord Hastinges.
The Earle of Warwicke.	Sir John Gates.
Lord Ambrose Dudley.	[Sir][a] Henry Gates, his brother.
Lord Henry Dudley.	Sir [Thomas][b] Palmer.
Sir Andrewe Dudley.	Doctor Sanders.[c]

But when they came within the Tower the Earle of Arundell discharged the Lord Hastinges, and had him out of the Tower with him.

The 26 of July the Lord Marques of Northampton, the Bishop of London,[d] Lord Robert Dudley,[e] and Robert Corbet, were brought from the Quenes campe to the Tower. *More prisoners.*

The 27 of July Sir Roger Chomley, Lord Cheife Justice of the Kinges Benche, Sir Edmunde Montague, Lord Cheife Justice of the Common Place, were sent to the Tower, [where were also confined][f] the Lord Gilford, Lady Janes husband, and Lady Jane late pro claymed Quene, and Rowland Dee, mercer.

The 28 of July the Duke of Suffolke and Sir John Cheeke were had to the Tower.

The 29 of July Sir Martin Bowes, Sir Henry Hobathorne, Mr. Recorder, Mr. Whight, and Mr. Garret, sheriffe, rode to the Quene *A benevolence sent to the Quene.*

---

[a] Omitted in MS.   [b] John, MS.

[c] Dr. Edwin Sandys, Vice-Chancellor of the University of Cambridge, who had impugned Queen Mary's rights from the pulpit.

[d] Nicholas Ridley, "the byshoppe of London, that was goynge unto the queene to begge his pardon, but he was tane at Ipsege, and there was put in warde."—Grey Friars' Chronicle, p. 81.

[e] The Duke's second son, afterwards Earl of Leicester.

[f] The words in brackets would appear to have been omitted in MS. or else the passage is misplaced; for the Lady Jane was already within the dismal walls of the Tower when Queen Mary was proclaimed. Stow omits the latter portion of this paragraph altogether.

to Newehall, in Essex, and there presented to hir Highnes in a purse of crimson velvet v cł in halfe souereignes of gould in the name of my Lord Mayor, Aldermen, and the Commons of the City of London, giuen to hir Highnes of a benevolence, which gift she highly and thankfully accepted, and caused the presenters to haue great chere in hir house.

This mony was levyed amonge the Commons of the City of London, euery Company after their degrees, to be payd to the Chamberlaine by the first day of August next comminge, but enery alderman lent xx ł in gould the 28 of July aforehand, to haue yt speedily sent to hir Highnes.

Allso Mr. Richard Grymes, clothworker, did this moneth make great suyte by himselfe and his frindes to my Lord Mayor and Aldermen to be dispensed from the office of sheriffe and alderman, and after longe suyte, because of his lamnes in his lims, by the assent of a Court of Aldermen, he was judged to pay out of hand to the Chamber of the City of London, to the use of the City, 2 c markes, and so he was discharged for euer.

The 30 of July Lady Elizabethes grace, sister to the Quenes Highnes, rode from hir place at Strand, where she had lyen the night afore, through the Citie of London at xii of the clocke in the forenone, beinge Sonday, and rode out at Algate toward the Quenes Highnes, accompanyed with a M horses of gentlemen, knightes, ladyes, and their seruanntes.

The 31 of July the Duke of Suffolke was discharged out of the Tower by the Earle of Arundell and had the Quenes pardon.

And the same day was Sir John Yorke had from his house to the Tower by Sir Richard Cotton, Comptroller of the Kinges house, and all his goodes seased to the Quenes use; howbeyt he was kept in his house viii dayes before by my Lord Mayors officers, and Mr. Garret, sheriffe, and had all the cheife places in his house sealed and sequestred with my Lord Mayors seale, Mr. Recorder and Mr. Garret, sheriff, with an inventory made by them.

The 1 of August, which is the day of the election of the sheriffe, was chosen by the Commons in the Guildhall Mr. Thomas Offley, alderman, chosen before by my Lord Mayor, and nowe to associate [with] him the Commons chose Mr. Thomas Lodge, grocer, which was then in Flaunders.

The 3 of August 1553 the Quenes Majestie came from Wanstead, and about vi of the clocke at night she lighted at Mr. Bramstons house at Whight Chappell, and there chaunged her apparell, and then, accompanyed with gentlemen, squires, knights, and lords, with a great number of straungers all in velvet coates rydinge before her, which were aboue v C. horse, [a] with all the Kinges trumpetters, harrouldes, and sergeantes at armes, she proceeded to passe thorough the citye, and, when she came to the barres without Aldgate, there were rayles made where my Lord Mayor[b] and his brethren the aldermen stoode, and at her highnes comminge, which was in rich apparell, her gowne of purple velvet French fashion, with slenes of the same, hir kirtle purple satten all thicke sett with gouldsmithes worke and great pearle, with her foresleues of the same set with rich stones, with a rich bowdricke of gould, pearle, and stones about her necke, and a riche billement of stones and great pearle on her hoode, her pallfray that she rode on richly trapped with gould embrodred to the horse feete, and another rich trapped pallfray led after her highnes by Sir [Edward] Hastinges, master of the horse, my Lord Mayor and Mr. Recorder, kneelinge afore her highnes at the entringe of the barres, saluted her highnes with a proposition after this manner, Mr. Recorder sayinge, "Pleaseth your highnes, my Lord Mayor, here present, in the name of his brethren and all the commons of this your highness city and chamber of London, most humbly beseecheth your highnes to be good and gracious Sovereign to theise commens of this your city lyke as your highnes noble progenitors aforetyme haue bene, and, according to theyr bounden duety at your highnes cominge, my Lord Mayor presenteth here your high-

---

[a] "the number of velvet coates that did ride before her, as well strangers as others, were 740, and the number of ladies and gentlewomen that followed was 180."—Stow, p. 613.   [b] Sir George Barnes.

nes with the scepter perteyninge to the office, in token of loyalty and homage, most humbly wellcome your highnes to this your highnes city and chamber of London." Then my Lord Mayor kissinge the scepter deliuered it to her highnes, she holdinge yt, answering, " My Lord Mayor, I hartely thanke you and all your brethren the aldermen of your gentlenes shewed unto me, which shall not be forgotten, for I haue knowne you euer to haue bene good toward me." And then she deliuered the scepter to my Lord Mayor againe, which words were so gently spoken and with so smylinge a countenance that the hearers wept for joye. Sir Anthouy Browne leaninge on her horse, haveinge the trayne of hir highnes gowne hanginge over his shoulder, and all her footemen goeinge afore her and the guarde on enery syde; next her highnes followed the Lady Elizabethes Grace, hir sister, then the Duches of Norfolke, the Lady Marques of Exeter, and so great number of ladyes after them, enery one in their degrees. And when her highnes came against St. Buttolphes church, there was a great stage couered with canvas where all the children of Christes Hospitall sat, with all the gouernours and officers belonginge to the same: one of the children, salutinge her highnes kneelinge on his knees, made an oration to her highnes, in Latin. After she eutred in at Algate, which was richly hanged with arras and set with streamers, the wayghtes of the city playinge in the battlements of the gate, her highnes then passinge to Leadenhall downe Gracechurch Streat, up Fanchurch Streat, downe Marke Lane, and so to the Tower; where, at hir Graces entringe at the stone, my Lord Mayor tooke his leave of her highnes, who rode allwayes before her highnes bearinge the scepter before the sworde with Garter Kinge of Armes rydinge with him; the Earle of Arundell bearinge the sworde before her highnes. And at the gate entringe into the Tower, Sir John Gage, Constable of the Tower, and Sir John Bruges,[a] Leiftenant of the Tower, and Mr. Thomas Bruges, his brother, with him receaved her highnes, and so passed into the

[a] Sir John Bryggys.

Tower. The Duke of Norfolk, Doctor Gardner, late bishop of
Winchester, and Mr. Henry [Edward] Courtney, prisoners in the
Tower, kneeld on the hill within the Tower askinge pardon, whom
she gently saluted, biddinge them ryse up,[a] and so she lighted and
passed to her highnes chamber. All the streates in London, from
Algate up to Leadenhall and so to the Tower, were richly hanged
with clothes of arras and silke, the streates gravelled all the way, and
the citizens standinge at rayles with theyr streamers and banners of
enery Company or occupation standinge at theyr rayles, enery
Company in their best liueryes with theyr hoodes. Allso there
were iiii great stages betwene Algate and the Tower where clarkes
and musicians stoode playinge and singinge goodly ballets, which
reioysed the Quenes highnes greatly. Allso there was such a
terrible and great shott of guns shot within the Tower and all about
the Tower wharfe that the lyke hath not bene hard, for they neuer
ceased shootinge from the tyme her highnes eutred in at Algate till
she came to Marke Lane ende, which was like great thunder, so
that yt had bene lyke to an earthquake. And all the streets by the
way as her highnes rode standing so full of people shoutinge and
cryinge Jesus saue her Grace, with weepinge teares for ioy, that the
lyke was neuer seene before. After her highnes ladyes and gentlewomen came rydinge, which mett her Grace at Wansted Heath,
aboue v^m horse of noble mens seruantes, knightes, and gentlemen,
enery one in his masters liuery, with speares and jauelinges, which
rode three in a ranke, which was a goodly sight to behoulde. But
when they came at Algate the Earle of Worcester, Lord Fitzwater,
Sir William Croft, knight marshall, with typstaves, stayed them,
and would not suffer neuer a Company to enter into the citye, but
turned them back to other gates of the city to returne such as lay
within the city to their lodginges, and the rest to such places without the city wher they laye, and thus this night fynished, which
was on a Thursday.

[a] " and she came to them and kissed them, and said, these be my prisoners."
Stow, p. 613.

96   WRIOTHESLEY'S CHRONICLE.

A.D. 1553.
Mr. Henry Courtney and Dr. Gardiner.

The 4 of August the Duke of Norfolke, Mr. Henry [Edward] Courtney,[a] and Doctor Gardener, late Bishop of Winchester, prisoners in the Tower, had the Quenes pardon; and that night the Duke of Norfolke and Doctor Gardner were sworne of the Counsell.

Dr. Boner and Dr. Dunstall pardoned.

The 5 of August, beinge Saterday, Doctor Bonner, the ould Bishop of London, prisoner in the Marshalsea, and Doctor Dunstall,[b] the ould Bishop of Durham, prisoner in the Kinges Bench, had their pardon sent them by the Quene, under the great seale of England, and were discharged out of prison; the Bishop of London went to his house at Pawles ymmediately.

Dr. Cox brought to prison.

And at his departinge out of the Marshallsea Doctor Cockes, the Kinges almoner and Deane of Westminster, was brought thither to prison.

Warders at the gates discharged.

Sonday the 6 of August the warders at the gates in London were discharged.

And this day the Duke of Northumberland was twise examined by the Quenes Counsell in the Tower, with other prisoners.

The 7 of August the Duke of Northumberland was examined againe, with other prisoners.

An obsequy kept by the Queue.

The 9 of August, in the afternone, the Quene helde an obsequy for the Kinge[c] within the church in the Tower, her Grace beinge present, and had a solemne dirige songe in Latine.

The morrowe, beinge Thursday the 10 of August, the Quenes highnes had a solemne masse of *Requiem* songe within the chappell in the Tower for the Kinge; hir Highnes offringe at the masse with all her ladyes and gentlewomen.

The buriall of Kinge Edwarde the Sixt.

Allso this day the corps of the Kinges Maiestie was solemnely caryed from Whitehall, at Westminster, to the minster of St. Peters Church,[d] where was a rich hearse made like an imperiall crowne without lightes afore the steps where the high aulter stoode;

---

[a] Stow (p. 613) reads: "Edward Courtney, sonne and heire to Henry, Marquesse of Excester."   [b] Cuthbert Tunstall.
[c] The late King Edward VI.   [d] Westminster Abbey.

where his Highnes body remayned, till the Communion sernice and a sermon made by Doctor Day, Bishop of Chichester, was done; and then the corps was honourably conveyed from thence up into the chappell, where Kinge Henry the VIIth lyeth, where the Kinges Majesties body was buryed. The solemnity of the offringe by the estates, mourners, and other was lyke the enterment of Kinge Henry the VIII. his father, savinge the seruice of the Communion and buryall, which was all in Englishe, without any copes or vestmentes, but onely surples, accordinge to the Booke of Common Prayer last sett forth by Act of Parliament.

A.D. 1553.

And this day was a great dole of mony geven within euery warde within the City of London, euery poore house-hould havinge viii d. the peece.

A dole for the kinge.

The Duke of Norfolke and my Lord Courtney were deliuered out of the Tower this 10th of August

The 11 of August, Doctor Gardner, Bishop of Winchester, was deliuered out of the Tower, and went to his place at St. Mary Oueries, which the Marques of Northampton had.

Allso this daye the Duchesse of Somersett was deliuered out of the Tower.

Saterday the 12 of August the Quenes Highnes removed from the Tower of London, and went by water to Richmond.

Sonday the 13 of August Doctor Borne,[e] one of the Prebendaries of Pawles, preached at Pawles Crosse by the Quenes appointment. And in the sermon tyme, because he prayed for the soules departed, and allso in declaringe the wrongfull imprisonment of Doctor Bonner, late Bishop of London, certeine leude and ill disposed persons made a hallowinge and suche a cryinge thou lyest, that the audyence was so disturbed, that the preacher was so affrayd by the commotion of the people, that one Bradford, a preacher, pulled him backe, and spake to the people, desyring them in Christes name and for the bloude of Christ to pacifie themselues, which people were so rude that they would not, but one lewde person

[a] Gilbert Bourne.

A.D. 1553.

drewe a dagger and cast yt at the preacher, which, has God would, hett against one of the postes of the pulpit. My Lord Mayor then and Aldermen rysinge from their places, went about the churchyard to cause the people to departe away, which were so rude that in a great space they would not departe, but cryed kill him; and so, with great payne and feare the sayd Borne was conveyed from the pulpit to the scholehouse in Pawles Churchyard. The Lord Courtney and the Lady Marques of Execeter stoode aboue my Lord Mayor, with Doctor Bonner, Bishop of London, which were sore astonyed to se the rumour[a] of the people, and had as much adoe by their meanes to see the sayd Bishop conveyed in safetye through the church, the people were so rude.

The liberties of the city like to have bene lost.

This busines was so heynously declared to the Quene and her Counsell, that my Lord Mayor and Aldermen were sent for to the Quenes Counsell to the Tower the 14 and 15 of August, and yt was sore layd to theyr charge, that the liberties of the city had lyke to [haue] bene taken away from them, and to depose the Lord Mayor, straightly charginge the Mayor and Aldermen to make a direct answere to them on Wednesday the 16 of August whether they would rule the city in peace and good order, or ells they would sett other rulers ouer them, whereupon my Lord Mayor caused all the Commons of the liuerye to be warned to appeare at the Guildhall on Tuesdaye the 15 of August. And, they beinge assembled, Mr. Recorder declared to the Commons the sore wordes and threatninges of the Queues Counsell, prayinge them to shewe theyr myndes whether they would sticke to my Lord Mayor and his brethren, to se such malefactors and rude people refourmed, or elles theyr libertyes should be taken away from them; the Commons answeringe, that by the good healp and meanes of my Lord Mayor and his brethren they would be so aydinge and assistinge to them, that they trusted the Quenes Highnes nor the Counsell should haue noe more such cause against the citye, but that such malefactours and offenders should be punished ; which aunswere was made by

---

[a] Probably a clerical error for "humour."

my Lord Mayor and Aldermen to the Quenes Counsell, at the Tower, on Wednesday the 16 of August, and was well accepted and taken.

A.D. 1553.

Allso, my Lord Mayor caused a proclamation to be made in the city, that if any person could bringe knowledge who threwe the dagger at the preacher on Sonday, at Pawles Crosse, should haue v t̃ for his labour.[a]

Fryday the 18 of August 1553 Sir John Dudley, Duke of Northumberland, and his eldest sonne [John] Earle of Warwick, [with] Sir William Parre, Marques of Northampton, were arraigned at Westminster hall, which after there enditements read confessed their endytements of treason,[c] without passinge of any jurye of their Peeres, and so had iudgment to be drawne, hanged, and quartered: The Lord Thomas Haward, Duke of Norfolke, sitting under the cloth of estate, and gaue judgment.

The arraingnement of the Duke of Northumberland [b] with other.

The 19 of August Sir Andrewe Dudley, Sir John Gates, Henry Gates, his brother, and Sir Thomas Palmer, knights, were arraigned at Westminster, and confessed their treasons without passinge of any jurye on them, and had judgment to be drawne, hanged, and quartered, Sir William Pawlet, Marques of Winchester, and High Treasurer of England, sitting that daye as chiefe, without any cloth of estate, and gaue judgment.

More traytors arraigned.

Sonday the 20 of August Mr. Watson, a Bachelor of Divinitye and Chaplaine to the Bishop of Winchester, preached at Pawles Crosse by the Quenes appointment, and, because of the sedicion that was on the Sonday before at the sermon tyme, the Quenes Highnes had appointed certeine Lordes of the Counsell to be at the sermon, and to see the order of hir people: First, satt next my Lord Mayor the Lord Treasurer, Marques of Winchester, then Lord Privie Seale, Earle of Bedford, the Earle of Pembroke, the Lord Wentworth,[d] the Lord Rich, and Sir John Jarningham,[e] captaino of the guard, who had 2 c. of the guard with him, which stoode about the

A sermon at Pawles Crosse.

---

[a] neighbour in MS.   [b] Norfolk in MS.
[c] Stow's account is fuller, and gives a more correct notion of this trial (p. 614).
[d] Wenford in MS.   [e] Sir Henry Gerningham.—Stow.

A.D. 1553.

pulpit, with their halberdes, Allso my Lord Mayor and Aldermen had warned all the Companies of the city to be there present at the sermon, which stoode in their liueries and hoodes all the sermon tyme, to herken yf any leude or sedicious persons made any rumors or misorder, which was well accepted of the Quenes Counsell. The preacher preachinge Godes worde on the Epistle of that present day, and declaringe the obedience of subiectes, and what erronious sectes are raigninge in this realme, by false preachers and teachers; to the godly edyfyinge of the audience there present at the sayd sermon, and so was quietly ended without any tumult.

At a masse in the Tower which the Bishop of Worcester sayd.

The 21 of August 50 persons of the head Commoners and Commen Counsell of the Citye of London were apointed by a letter sent to my Lord Mayor from the Quene to be that daye in the Tower, to hear the confession of the Duke of Northumberland and other, at the receivinge of the Holy Communion there, in the chappell of the Tower, at a masse there sayd before them; which sayd duke with other there acknowledged afore the audience that they had erred from the true Catholicke fayth xv yeares and had bene a great setter forth of the yll doctrine nowe raigneinge, which he sore lamented, and there desyringe the people to beware of such yll doctrine; and so he with other received the sacrament after masse, after the ould use afore tyme used.

A preist set on the pillory.

Allso this 21 of August John Daye, parson of St. Alborow [a] within Bishopsgate, was set on the pillory in Cheape, and had one of his eares nayled, for seditious wordes speakinge of the Quenes Highnes. And allso a surgeon by Pawles was likewise set on the pillory with him, and had one of his eares nayled allso for seditious wordes speakinge of the preacher at the sermon at Pawles Crosse on Sonday the 13 of August. And when they had stoode on the pillory 3 houres the nayles were pulled out with a payre of pinsers, and they were had to prison againe.

The Duke and other beheaded.

Tuesday the 22 of August the Duke of Northumberland and Sir John Gates, late Captaine of the Guarde, and Sir Thomas

[a] St. Ethelberga, Bishopsgate Street within.

Palmer, knights, were all three beheaded on the Tower hill, betwene 8 and 9 of the clocke in the forenone, and after their bodies and heades wear caryed into the Tower againe.

A.D. 1553.

Allso this daye was a vagabond set on the pillory in Cheap for sedicious wordes speakinge of the Lord Gray, deputy of Guynes,[a] howe that he should haue betrayed the towne; and after he had stoode an houre on the pillory he was well whipped at the post of the sayd pillory, and after had to warde againe, and was whipped againe at a cart the 25 of August, and so banished.

One whipped on the pillorye.

The 23 of August John Day, parson of St. Alborowes[b] within Bishopsgate, was set on the pillory againe, and had his other eare nayled, and after xii of the clock at none it was pulled out with a payre of pinsers, and then he went to ward againe; but that night he was discharged of his imprisonment upon suretes to abyde further order at the Quenes pleasure

A preist set on the pillory againe.

Allso this daye, beinge the even of St. Bartholomewe, the Quenes Highnes deliuered the great Seale of England to Doctor Stephen Gardner, Bishop of Winchester, and made him Lord Chauncellor of England, and Mr. Sargeaunt Brambe[c] was made Lord Cheife Justice of the Kinges Bench, and Sargeaunt Morgan[c] was made Lord Cheife Justice of the Common Place, and Mr. Brooke,[d] Sargeant, was made Lord Cheife Baron of the Exchequer, and Sir Nicholas Hare made Master of the Rolles.[e]

A newe Lord Chancellor and other officers.

Thursdaye, the 24 of August and St. Bartholomews daye, the olde service in the Lattin tongue with the masse was begun and sunge in Powles in the Shrowdes, now St. Faythes parishe. And lykewise it was begun in 4 or 5 other parishes within the Cittie of London, not by commaundement but of the peoples devotion.

The olde service in Latin with the masse begun.

Allso this day was no wrestlinge nor shootinge. Noyther was

[a] Guisnes, a town of Picardy.
[b] St. Ethelburga, Bishopsgate Street within.
[c] Sir Thomas Bromley, Chief Justice of the King's Bench, and Sir Richard Morgan, Chief Justice of the Common Pleas. [d] Sir David Brooke, knt.
[e] From this point the MS. is continued in a different handwriting.

A.D. 1553.	any kept at all this yeare, because of the troblesome tyme in this realme.
Olde service.	Sonday the 27 of August the service begone in the Cathedrall Churche of St. Paule in London, in the Latin after the use of Sarum. And the worke that was broken downe of stone, where the highe altare stoode, was begun to be made up agayne with breke.
A prest to the Queene.	The first day of September the Queene demaunded a presse of the Cittie of London of xx^{tie} thowsand powndes and to be payed agayne within 14 dayes after the feast of St. Michaell next comminge. To the levyinge of the which summe the aldermen and vi^{xx} of the heade Commoners of the Cittie made the performance of the sayde somme. So that he that lent least lent one hundreth powndes, which must be payde to Mr. Weldon, the Queenes coferer, and Sir Martin Bowes, alderman, on this syde the viii day of September, which the moste parte of the Commons were verie glad to accomplishe and to make shift, that had not readye money, allthoughe it were to their losses.
	Sonday the 3 of September Mr. Edward Corteney was created Earle of Devonshire at Richmonde.
Newe coynes of golde and sylver.	Mundaye the 4th of September the Queene by a proclamation set owt certeyn newe coynes of golde and sylver: viz. a sovereigne of fyne golde of xxx s.; the halfe sovereigne of fyne golde called a ryall of fyne golde, xv s.; an angell of fyne gold x s.; the halfe angell v s.; a peece of fyne sylver called a grote of iiii d.; another peece of sylver ii d.; and another peece of sylver of a i d.: and all other base coynes of this realme to be currant and goe as they be at this daye.
A subsidye pardoned.	The same day another proclamation made by the Queene for pardon of the last subsidie of iiii s. the pound [lands],[a] and of ii s. viii d. the pound moveable goods by Act of Parlement in the last Session of King Edward the Sixt.

[a] Supplied from Stow.

The 6 of Septembre Lorde Ferys, and Sir Roger Cholmeley, and Montague were discharged out of the Tower of London and sett to paye great fynes.[a]   A.D. 1553. Prisoners discharged.

The 14 and 15 of September Mr. Latimer and Dr. Cranmer, Archbishop of Canterburie, were sent to the Tower of London.   Bishops sent to the Tower.

The 27 of September the Queene removed from St. James and tooke her barge at Whitehall in the afternoone aboute iii of the clock, so to passe to the Tower of London,[b] shooting the bridge at a full sea.   The Queen removinge to the Tower.

The xxx[th] of September in the forenoone there was made in the Tower of London 15 knightes of the Bathe by the Queene. And the same daye Sir William Pawlett, Marques of Winchester, was sworne Lord Treasurer of Englande, and Mr. Brooke, sergeant at the lawe, was sworne Lord Cheife Baron of the Exchequer.   Knightes of the Bathe.

Allso the 30 of September, in the afternoone, at two of the clocke, the Queene rode from the Tower of London throughe the Cittie to her coronation in a riche charlott of clothe of golde. The Ladie Elizabeth and the Ladye Anne of Cleve ridinge after her in another riche chariott covered with cloth of sylver, and iii other riche chariotts followinge with ladies. All the streetes from the Tower to Temple barre were richelye hanged with divers costlye pageantes, &c.   The Queen rydinge through London to her coronation.

Sundaye the 1 of October the Queene was crowned at St. Peters Churche in Westminster by the Bishop of Winchestre.   The coronation of Queene Marye.

Thursdaye the 5 of October the parlement began at Westminster, the Queene ridinge from White Hall in her parlement robes with all the lordes spirituall and temporall in their parlement robes; and had a solemne masse of the Holie Ghoste sunge in Westminster Churche, with a sermon made by Dr. Heath, Bishop of Chichester.   A Parlement.

---

[a] Stow (p. 616) reads: "The Lord Ferrers of Chartley, the Lord Chiefe Justice, Sir Roger Cholmley, the Lord Montague, Sir John Cheeke, and other, were delivered out of the Tower."

[b] Stow adds, "accompanied with the Lady Elizabeth her sister and other ladies."

A.D. 1553.

MARIÆ ANNO PRIMO.

Sacrament at Paules.

Againste the feaste of All Sayntes the sacrament of the bodie and blond of Christe was hanged up agayne in Paules Churche over the highe alter under a riche canopie of cloth of golde, after the olde custome of the Churche.

The weather-cock of Paules new mendid and set up.

The 3 of November 1553, at x of the clock in the forenoone, the weather cock of Paules steeple, which was taken downe and new mended, was sett up agayne by Peter, a Dutchman, that stoode on it when the Queene rode to her coronation. The cocke with the winges wayed 40 lb., his length from the bill to his tayle was 4 foote, and his bredth over the wings 3 foote and an halfe, and was gilded under the wings with the bodye, which weather cock is of copper, and the bolle under the crosse also.

Arraynment of Archbishop Cranmer and others at the Guylde-Hall.

The 13 of November Thomas Cranmer, Archbishop of Canterburie, Gilford Dudley, esquier, and Ladie Jane his wife, Ambrose Dudley and Henry Dudley, esquiers, were arrayned at the Guilde Hall in London of highe treason againste the Queene, and were there condemned and had iudgment to dye.

A priest punished.

Fridaye the 24 of November one Sir Tho. Sothwood, priest, alias parson Chekin, parson of St. Nicholas olde abbaye in Old Fishe Street, rode aboute the Cittie in a carte with a ray hood for sellinge his wife, which he said he had maried.

The light in Paules steeple on St. Katherin's night.

Saterdaye the 25 of November, and St. Katherins daye, the light in Paules steeple went about the steeple that night; and the singinge men of Paules Queer with the children singinge anthemes, as of old had bene accustomed.

General processions.

The xxx[th] of November, beinge Thursdaye and St. Andrewes eeve, a generall procession in Paules, with a sermon made by Mr. Borne,[a] one of the Residentiaries of Paules, the Litaine sunge in Latin, the bishopp and the priests of everie parishe followinge after the

---

[a] Gilbert Bourne, prebendary of London.

crosse round about the churche. The Lord Maior and Aldermen A.D. 1553.
followinge after the Queere.

The first of December was lykewise another generall procession, with a sermon made by Harpesfylde.

The vi of December the Parliament brake up, and was clean dissolved in the afternoone. Parliament dissolved.

Sunday the xth of December the Lord Maior, Mr. Thomas White, was presented to the Queene at Whitehall, and there made knight by the Earle of Arundell, the Queenes deputie. Lord Maior made knight.

Thursdaye 14 of December, in the afternoone, the Lord Maior and the sheriffes went to these three common bowlinge allies, that is to say, Northumberland alley by Algate, St. Nicolas shambles alley, and an alley in the Old Baylie; and with mattockes did breake and digge up all the said alleys. Bowlinge allyes digged up.

The xxith of December, beinge St. Thomas day afore Christenmas, all the service began agayne in Latin in all the churches throughe the Queenes dominions by Act of Parlement, as it remayned the last yeare of King Henry 8. The service of the Church in Latin.

This yeare, about Christenmas and after, wodd and coles was at excessive and highe prices in London by scarcitie thereof. For billetts at xx s. a .^{a} and above. And coles of the cart were sold at x d. the sack, and horse coles at xiiii and xv d. a sacke. The faggotts at v s. and vi s. the c and above. Wherefore the Lord Maior caused lighters of sea coles to be sold at Billingsgate and Quenehith for iiii d. the busshell, which greatlie helped tyll better provision might be fownde. Derth of wood and coles.

The 2 of January there came certayne ambassadours from the Emperoure out of Dutchland,^{b} and had great presentes given them of victualls by the Maior and Cittie of the cost of the chamber. The principall ambassadour lodged at Durham Place, and he was called Countie de Augmonte.^{c} Another lodged at Suffolke Place by Charinge Crosse, called Countie de Shulinge. Two other lodged at Salisburie [A.D. 1554]. Ambassadours from the Emperoure.

---

^{a} Blank in MS. ^{b} Charles V. of Germany.
^{c} This was the brave Count Egmont.

A.D. 1554.

Place by Bridewell, called Monsieur Corier and Monsieur Chauncellour Negri; which saide embassadors had great feastinge of the Queene and Lordes. They came to intreat of a marriage from the Emperour for the Queene and the Prince of Spayne.

One drawne for treason.

The xiiith of Januarie, one called Harvy was drawne from the Tower of London to Tyburne, and there hanged and quartered for counterfeytinge the Q[ueen's] hande in a patent, and allso brake out of prison in the Tower afore Christmas, and was taken in a shipp and arreigned at Westminster on Twelft Eeven of the same treason.

Lord Maior goinge in Procession in Paules on Sundayes.

Sundaye the 14 of January Procession began in Paules Churche after the olde fashion before highe masse : The Lord Maior and Aldermen goeinge in Procession in their violett gownes and clokes furred, as they used everie Sundaye in King Henry the VIII. tyme, afore the sermon began.

A monition to the Maior from the Queene.

Munday the 15 of January the Lord Maior and Alldermen were sent for to come to the Cowrt and to bringe with them xl. persons of the heade commoners of the Cittie. And when they came afore the Councell the Lord Chauncellour declared to them the Queenes pleasure, which was that she intended to marrie with the King of Spayne, which should be for the great preferment of this realme. And that they like obedient subiects to accept her Graces pleasure, and to be content and quiett themselves: And, further, that Godes religion, which she used and had sett forthe new of late might be so observed and kept within the cittie that they might be a spectacle to all the realme, which they had yett verie slacklye sett forthe, or els, if they will not be diligent to doe and observe her lawes and commaundements, that they should run in her highe indignation and displeasure, and to be further punished accordinge to their deserts.

Sir Robert Dudley arreigned.

Munday the 22 of January Sir Robart Dudley, knight, one of the Duke of Northumberlands sonnes, was arreigned at the Guyld hall of treason, the Lord Maior sittinge as highe commissioner, the Earle of Darbye, the Earle of Devonshire, the Earle of Sussex, with other lykewise commissioners, and after his arreignment he

confessed his treason, and had iudgment given by the Earle of Sus-   A.D. 1554.
sex, to be drawne, hanged, and quartered.

The 25 of Januarie tidinges were brought to the Lord Maior, by A risinge in Kent by Wyatt.
Sir John Gage, Lorde Chamberleyn to the Queene, that [Sir Thomas
Wyat, with][a] certayne rebells, were up in Kent, about Maydstone.
Whereupon a courte of Alldermen was called immediatlie in the
afternoone; and that night the Lord Maior rode to peruse the watch
of the citie, and so everie night after two aldermen to ride to peruse
the sayd watches.

Allso, that night, by the Councells commaundment, the Lord Lorde Marquesse sent
Maior secretlie with the sheriffes apprehended the Lord Marques of to the Tower.
Northampton, lying in Mr. Warners howse, by Carter Lane, and
brought him to his owne howse, where he lay that night; and
Mr. Warner[b] lay with Mr. Huett, sheriffe.

The 26 of January the Lord Marques was sent from the Lord
Maiors howse to the Tower of London by the Sword-bearer, and
Mr. Warner was sent thither lykewise by Mr. Huetts officers, by
the councells commaundment.

Allso, this day the gates of the cittie began to be warded by the The gates warded.
citizens.

The 27 of January the Lord Treasurer came to the Guildhall 500 men sent out of
from the Councell to declare that the cittie should make owt v C. Rebells.
footemen, well harnised, to goe against the rebells, whereupon a
Common Councell was called in the afternoone to haue their assents
thereunto, which they grawnted, and had them readie that night
among the Companies of the cittie; which was putt of till the morrowe. And the 28 of January, beinge Sundaye, the saide v C. men
were assembled at Leadenhall, and there delivered to the Capteyns,
and sent by water to Gravesend. The Lo. Vrmon,[c] beinge Capteyne
of one hundreth, with other capteynes for everie C. men, appoynted
by the Councell.

The 29 of January the Duke of Norfolke, with the Capteyne of The Londoners flyinge
to the Rebells.

[a] Supplied from Stow.   [b] Sir Edward Warner.—Stow, p. 618.
[c] Sic.

108   WRIOTHESLEY'S CHRONICLE.

A.D. 1554.

the guard[a] that were sent from the Queene, with certeyn other souldiers and yeomen of the guard, with the capteyns and souldiers that went out of the cittie, offred to assault Rochester Castle, where the traytor Wyatt and his rebells laye, and the capteyns of the cittie with their souldiers fledd to the rebells over Rochester Bridge and drue up the bridge, so that the Duke was fayne to flie, and then the rebells tooke the Queenes ordinance and treasure.[b]

The 30th of January Wyatt removed with his rebells from Rochester and came to Blackheath, and there camped with the Queenes ordinance and lay in the towne of Greenwich and there about.

This day allso ordinance was layde at everie gate of the cittie.

The 31 of January Wyett removed to Greenwich and Detforde with his campe.

The first day of February a proclamation was made in the cittie of London with an harrold, a trumpett, and the Comon Crier, the knight Marshall ridinge with them; which was that the traytor the Duke of Suffolke, which was fled westward, was discomfited, and his horsemen and bagage taken, and he and his two bretheren fledd in servinge mens cotes. And allso that Peter Carowe and his uncle Gawyn Carowe and Gibbes were fledd into France, and that certeyn of their adherents were taken and kept in Exeter. And, further, that whosoever should take the traytor Wyatt should haue a c l̄ landes to him and his heires for ever.

The flyinge of the Duke of Suffolke.

The same day in the afternoone, beinge Candlemas Even, all the Commons of the Cittie were assembled in their liveries at the Guildhall. The Queens Majestie, with her Lords and Ladies ridinge from Westminster to the sayde Guildhall, came thither by iii of the clocke the same afternoone. First she went up to the Councell Chambre, where the Alldermen use to sytt, and there pawsyd a litle, the Lord Maior and Alldermen receavinge her Majestie at the stepps, goeinge up to the Mayres Cowrt. Then her Majestie came downe into the great hall up into the place of the hustinges, where

The Queenes cominge to the Guildehall in London.

[a] Sir Henry Jerningham.
[b] This is given at much fuller length in Stow, p. 618.

was hanged a riche cloth of estate, she, standinge under it, with her owne mowth declared to the audience there assembled the wicked pretence of the traytor Wyett, which was utterlie to deprive her of her crowne, and to spoyle the Cittie; which was so noblie and with so good spiritt declared, and with so lowde a voyce, that all the people might heare her Maiestie, and comfortinge their hartes with so sweet wordes [a] that made them weepe for joye to heare her Majesty speake. This done she came downe and went up agayne into the Councell Chamber and dranck, and then departed and rode through Bucklersburie to the Crane in the Vintree, and there tooke her barge, and so to Westminster by water.

A.D. 1554.

The 2 of February, beinge Candlemas day, the citizens made preparation for a M. men of the howsholders of the said Cittie, well har[n]ised, to defend the Cittie, the Lord Mayre and Alldermen everie one in his warde takinge the mustre of them. Wherefore, this daye the goeinge to Paules in the afternoone was left; and allso that day the Lord Mayres officers served him at dynner in harnis.

The 3 of February, beinge Saterday, in the afternoone, the traytor Wyatt with his rebells came into Southwarke, and there trenched at the bridge foote, and sett 2 peeces of ordinance againste the gate at London Bridge.[b] And then came the Lord William Howard, Lord Admirall, to the Lord Mayre, with a commission from the Queene, and made a proclamation against the said Wyatt, and that the Queen had sent him to be Capteyne Generall, with the Lord Mayre, for the defence of the Cittie, declaringe to the citizens that he would die in the defence of it. And that night the said Lord Admirall watched the bridge with iii C. men, and brake the drawebridge, and sett rampeers with great ordinance there.

Lord Wm. Howarde Lieutenant of the cittie.

Sundaye the 4 of February the Lord Admirall made stronge defence on the bridge and warded with iii C. of the citizens with him

[a] The Queen's harangue may be read in Foxe.

[b] Wyatt placed two pieces of artillery in battery at the Southwark end of the bridge, and caused a deep trench to be dug between the bridge and the place where he was encamped.

A.D. 1554.

all the daye till viii of the clock at night; and then releeved them with other iii C. fresh men to warde all the night, and by 5 in the morninge other iii C. freshe men came to releeve them, and everie morninge and eveninge fresh releefe was sett.

Wyatt removed out of Sowthwerke and marched towards Kingston.

The 6 of February, beinge Srove-Twesdaye, afore six of the clock in the morninge, Wyatt with his rebells went out of Southwarke, and went to Kingeston, over the bridge, and came towarde Braynforde; and that afternoone were 2 men hanged on a gibbett, in Paules Churche yearde, by marshall lawe, one beinge the Duke of Suffolkes servante, a richeman and under-sheriffe of Lecester, and the other a baker, one of the rebells.

Allso, the same day tydinges came that the Duke of Suffolke and his brother were taken by the Earle of Huntingdon. And that day allso the Lord Cobham [a] and Harper [b] were committed to the Tower.

The viith of February, beinge Ash-Weddensday, earlye in the morninge, the Earle of Pembroke, Lieuetenant of the Queens armie, with the horssemen and footemen of the noblemen, gathered their armies together with the Queens ordinance, and pitched their field by St. James beyond Charinge Crosse,[c] to abide the said traytor Wyatt and his rebells. The Lord Mayre and the Lord Admirall sett the citizens in good arraye at Ludgate, Newgate, and from Creeplegate to Bushopsgate, lest the rebells would drawe to Finnesburie field, they to defend that syde. Then Wyatt with his rebells came to the park pale by St. James about 2 of the clocke in the

The victorye of the Queen and takinge of Wyatt.

afternoone, and Knevett, one of his capteynes, with his rebells went by Towtehill, through Westminster, and shott at the Cowrt gates. Butt Wyatt, perceavinge the great armie of the Queens campe, and

[a] Upon suspicion of favouring Wyatt's rebellion.—Chronicle of Queens Jane and Mary, p. 36.

[b] Sir George Harper, who had been excepted in the Queen's proclamation of pardon to the Kentish men.

[c] "By ten of the clocke the Earle of Pembroke had set his troupe of horsemen on the hill in the high way aboue the new bridge, ouer against St. James: his footmen were set in two battels, somewhat lower, and neerer Charing-Crosse, at the lane turning downe by the bricke wall from Islington ward, where hee had set also certaine other horsemen, and he had planted his ordinance upon the hill side."—Stow, p. 620.

ordinance bent againste him, sodenlie returned by the wall of the parke at St. James, toward Charinge Crosse, with the lightiest of his souldiers, where the Earle of Pembrokes men cutt of his trayne and slue divers of the rebells; but Wyatt himselfe with divers other came in at Temple barre, and so thorowe Fleet street to the Bell Savage, cryinge " a Wyatt! a Wyatt! God saue Queen Marie!"[a] Butt when he sawe that Ludgate was shutt against him, and the ordinance bent, he fledd back agayne sayinge, " I haue kept touche;" and by Temple barre was taken,[b] with the Lord Cobhams sonne, and other of his capteyns and rebells, and brought to the cowrte gate, and from thence sent by water to the Tower of London. And then all the Queens hoste came throughe London in goodlye araye, and Te Deum was sunge in the Queens Chappell for ioye of the sayde victorie, and so fewe slayne.

The xth of February the Lord Mayre with other justices satt on the rebells by commission of Oyer and determiner at the justice hall in the olde Baylie, where that day were condemned of treason iiii[xx] ii persons of Kent and other places; and xxxii were condemned at Westminster, and had iudgment to be drawne, hanged, and quartered.

Allso the same daye in the afternoone the Duke of Suffolke, which was taken in Lecestreshire, was brought thorowe the Cittie of London by the Earle of Huntington, and one of his bretheren with ii c. light horsemen, and so had to the Tower. *The Duke of Suffolke sent to the Tower.*

The 12 of Februarie Guilforde Dudley was beheaded at the Tower hill. And Ladie Jane his wife was immediatlie after his death beheaded within the Tower upon the greene. *Guilforde Dudley and Lady Jane beheaded.*

The 14 of February divers of the rebells were putt to death, that is to saye, Bothe, one of the Queenes footemen, one Vicars, a Yeoman of the Garde, great John Norton, and one Kinge, were hanged at Charinge Crosse. And three of the rebells, one called *Rebells hanged and quartered.*

---

[a] Or, according to other authorities, " Queen Mary! God save Queen Mary, who has granted our petition, and will have no Spanish husband."

[b] After a brave resistance Wyatt threw away his broken sword, and quietly surrendered to Sir Maurice Berkley, who, mounting him behind him, carried him off instantly to the Court.

112   WRIOTHESLEY'S CHRONICLE.

A.D. 1554. Pollarde, were hanged at the parke pale by Hide Parke; three allso in Fleet street, one at Ludgate, one at Bishopsgate, one at Newgate, one at Aldgate, three at the Crosse in Cheape, three at Soper Lane ende in Chepe, and three in Smythfield, which persons hanged still all that daye and night tyll the next morninge, and then cutt downe.[a] And the bodies of them that were hanged at the gates were quartered at Newgate, and the heades and bodies hanged over the gates where they suffred.

Rebells hanged. The 15 of February were hanged of the rebells iii against St. Magnus Churche, iii at Billingsgate, iii at Ledenhall, one at Moregate, one at Creplegate, one at Aldrigegate, two at Paules, iii in Holborne, iii at Tower hill, ii at Tyburne, and at 4 places in Sowthwerke 14. And divers others were executed at Kingston and other places.

Signes in the firmament. Allso this daye about ix of the clock in the foorenoone was seene in London in the middest of the Element a raynebowe lyke fyre, the endes upward, and two sunnes, by the space of an hower and an halfe.

Duke of Suffolk arrayned. The 17 of February the Duke of Suffolke was arreigned at Westminster and there condemned of Treason.

Proclamation. The same day a proclamation was made in London for strangers, not being denizens and merchants knowne, using the trade of merchandize, should departe and avoyde the realme within xxiiii dayes after this proclamation, upon payne to forfeyt all their goods movable, and allso upon payne of imprisonment.

Rebells executed in Kent. The 18 of February Bright,[b] one of the capteyns of the Londoners that fledd to Wyatt, and xxii persons more of the Kentish men, were delivered to the sheriffe of Kent, to be executed in divers places in Kent appoynted by the Queens Councell.

Rebells pardoned. The 22 of February certeyne of the rebells which lay in Newgate, both the Counters, the Kings Benche, the Marshallsie, and Westminster, to the number of iiii C. and more, were ledd to West-

---

[a] The Grey Friars' Chronicle (p. 88) adds: "the whych ware of London that fled from the Duke of Norfoke."

[b] In most chronicles spelt Brett, but in the Diary of a Resident in London Bart.

minster to the Cowrte, coupled together with collers and halters abowte their neckes, and there in the Tylt-yeard kneeled afore the Queen lookinge owt at the gallerie by the gate, and cried for mercye, who most gratiouslye gave to them their pardon.

A.D. 1554.

Fryday the 23 of February Lorde Gray, Duke of Suffolke, was beheaded at the Towerhill.

Duke of Suffolk beheaded.

The first daye of Marche, the parsons and curates of the Cittie of London that were wedded were cited to appeare in the Consistorie in Paules afore the Bishop of Londons Commissioners, and there deprived from their benefices. And those that were and had bene religiouse men were deprived both from their wives and benefices allso.

Wedded priests put from theyr wives and benefices.

The 9 of Marche one Fermer a woodmonger was sett on the pillorie in Chepe with 4 billetts hanginge at his shoulders, 2 before him and 2 behinde him, for buyinge wodd at viii s. iiii d. the M¹ and sellinge it agayne for xviii s. the M¹, which pennance was enioyned him by a Cowrt of Alldermen the 8 of Marche.

A woddmonger sett on the pillorie.

The xv of Marche Wyatt, capteyn of the rebells, was arregned at Westminster and there condemned of highe treason.

Wyett arraygned.

And the same daye the Earle of Devonshire was committed agayne to the Tower.

Earle of Devon sent to the Tower.

The xviii of Marche, beinge Palme Sunday, the Ladie Elizabeth was had to the Tower from Westminster by water privelie, after the Queene had gone a procession, which was about x of the clock in the forenoone.

Ladie Elizabeth sent to the Tower.

The same Palme Sunday the old service after the usé of Sarum in Latyn was begone agayne and kept in Paules and other parishes within the Cittie of London, with allso bearinge of Palmes, and creepinge to the Crosse on Good Fridaye, with the Sepulcher lights and the Resurrection on Easter daye.

Creepinge to the Crosse with sepulcher lights.

Allso the Scriptures written on Rood-lofts and about the churches in London, with the armes of England, was washed out againste the feast of Easter in moste parte of all the parishe churches of the

Scriptures in churches washed owt.

CAMD. SOC.   Q

A.D. 1554.

diocesse of London. And Dr. Feknam[a] was made Deane of Paules, and Dr. May putt owt, and the sacrament of the aulter hanged or sett on the aulter in everie parishe churche.

New Bishopps.

The first day of Aprill was consecrated at St. Marye Overies churche in Southwerke vi new Bishopps after the olde sorte, the Lord Chauncellor and Bishop of Winchester singinge the masse, the Bishop of London and the Bishop of Durham assistinge him.

A Parlement.

Munday the 2 of Aprill, 1554, the Parlement began at Westminster, which should haue bene kept at Oxforde, the Queens Majestie ridinge in her Parlement robes from her pallace of Whitehall to St. Peters churche with all her Lordes spirituall and temporall in their robes, and there heard masse of the Holie Ghoste and a sermon. And that afternoone the Common Howse did chuse Mr. Robert Brooke, esquier, and sergiant at lawe and Recorder of London, for their speaker in this Parlement.

A catt hanged in Cheape.

Sunday the 8 of Aprill was a villanouse fact done in Cheape[b] earlie or daye. A dead catt havinge a clothe lyke a vestment of the priest at masse with a crosse on it afore, and another behinde put on it; the crowne of the catt shorne, a peece of paper lyke a singinge cake putt betwene the forefeete of the said catt bownd together, which catt was hanged on the post of the gallowes in Cheape beyond the Crosse in the parishe of St. Mathewe, and a bottle hanged by it; which catt was taken downe at vi of the clock in the morninge and caried to the Bishop of London, and he caussed it to be shewed openlye in the sermon tyme at Paules Crosse in the sight of all the audience there present.

A proclamation for the catt.

The Lord Mayre, with his bretheren the alldermen of the Cittie of London, caused a proclamation to be made that afternoone that whosoever could utter or shewe the auctor of the sayde fact should haue vi l. xiii s. iv d. for his paynes, and a better rewarde, with hartie thancks. But at that tyme, after much enquirie and

[a] John Feckenham.
[b] This is mentioned by Stow and several other chroniclers.

searche made, it could not be knowne, but diverse persons were had to prison for suspicions of it. _{A.D. 1554.}

The xi of Aprill Sir Tho. Wyatt, cheefe capteyne of the late rebellion in Kent, was beheaded at Towrehill, at ix of the clock in the foorenoone, and his bodie after quartered on the scaffolde. His head was sett on the gallowes at the parke pale beyond St. James,[a] where Pollard and two other were hanged in chaynes. And his 4 quarters were hanged on gibbetts in chaynes at 4 severall places without the Liberties of the Cittie. _{Wyatt putt to death.}

The xvii of Aprill Sir Nicolas Trockmorton was arreigned at the Guildhall of treason, and was quitt by a jurie of the citizens of London, which jurie after their verditt given were bownd in vc l. a peece, to appeare in the Starre Chamber afore the Queens Councell at all tymes when they shal be commanded. _{Sir Nic. Throckmorton arraygned.}

The 25 of Aprill the jurie that quitt Sir Nicholas Throckmorton appeared before the Lord Chauncellor and the Queens Councell in the Starre Chamber at Westminster and were committed to warde. Thomas Whetstone, haberdasher, which was the foreman of the jurie, and Emanuell Lucare, marchant taylor, were sent to the Tower of London, and all the rest of the jurie were sent to the Fleete. _{The jurie of London sent to warde.}

Frydaye the 27 of Aprill Lord Thomas Grey, brother to the Duke of Suffolke, was beheaded at the Tower hill. _{Duke of Suffolkes brother beheaded.}

The 29 of Aprill Sir James Croft, knight, was arrayned in the Guildhall of treason, and there by a jurie of the citizens of London condemned and had iudgment of death. _{Sir James Croft arrayned.}

Saterdaye 5 Maii the Parliment brake up and was quite dissolved.

Monday 7 Maii the parishe clerkes of London kept the procession agayne after the olde use, goeinge from the Guyldhall chappell in riche copes of clothe of goulde with longe streamers and banners and three riche crosses borne afore them, and the sacrament of the aulter borne under a riche canopie after them. _{Clerks procession.}

---

[a] The Grey Friars' Chronicle (p. 89) adds: "and the hed with the qwarter was stolne awaye."

116   WRIOTHESLEY'S CHRONICLE.

A.D. 1554.

William Thomas arraygned.

The ixth of May William Thomas, esquier,^a was arreigned at the Guyldehall of highe treason for cons[p]iracie of the Queenes death, and there by a iurie of the citizens of London condemned and had his iudgment to dye.

King Henrye the VIIth aniversarie.

The xith of May King Henry the VIIth anniversarie was kept at Westminster agayne, accordinge to his last will and testament. The Lord Mayre and the sheriffs with the Lordes of the Councell beinge then present at the masse and offered, which anniversarie had bene putt downe longe, and now renned by the Queene.

William Thomas executed.

Fridaye the xviiith of May William Thomas was drawne from the Tower of London to Tiburne, and there hanged, headed, and quartered, and after his head sett on London Bridge, and his quarters sett in 4 severall places, one myle out of the Cittie of London.

Ladye Elizabeth sent to Woodstocke.

The xixth of May, beinge Saterday and the eeven of the feast of the Holie Trinitie, Ladye Elizabeth was had out of the Tower and went thorowe London Bridge in her barge at 3 of the clock in the afternoone, lyeinge at Richmond that night; and from thence conveyed to Woodstock, Mr. Benyfield,^b Lorde Williams of Tame, and Sir Leonard Chamberlayne, waytinge on her, with ii c horsemen, there to remayne at the Queenes pleasure.

Earle of Devonshire sent to Fodringay.

Frydaye 25 Maii Sir Edward Courtney, Earle of Devonshire, was had out of the Tower at 3 of the clock in the morninge, Mr. Chamberlayne of Suffolke and Sir Tho. Tresham, knights, ridinge with him, with certeyne of the Queens garde and others, to Fodringay^c Castle in Northamptonshire, and he there to remayne under theyr custodie at the Queens pleasure.

---

^a "late Clerk of the Council."—Machyn, p. 63. His works, consisting of a very curious and circumstantial account of the reign of Henry VIII. and the origin of the Reformation, together with six essays on questions of state, written at the command and for the information of Edward VI. have been edited by D'Aubant from the Cotton. MS.

^b Sir Henry Bedingfield, the recently appointed Constable of the Tower.

^c Fotheringay.

This moneth allso divers persons both men and weomen were sett on the pillorie in Cheape for slaunderouse and seditiouse wordes speakinge against the Queene and her Councell, and had their eares nayled to the pillorie.

<small>A.D. 1554. Divers sett on the pillorye.</small>

The xth of June, beinge Sundaye, an handgun was shott of neare to Paules Churchyeard in the sermon tyme, the pellett hitting the churche wall next where the Lord Mayre satt, and after fell on a mans shoulder, and taken up and delyvered to the Lord Mayre; and after the sermon was done,[a] searche was made all about the precinct of Paules in everie howse, but no knowledge could be fownd but that a gonne was shott in Foster Lane neare St. Fausters Churche. But the partie that shott it (by reporte) fleed, and within vi dayes after was taken and examined afore the Lord Mayre and sent to prison, and divers witnesse allso examined for the same, which agreed not one with another, and the partie allso himselfe denieinge that he shott anye, nor no gun could be founde in the howsse that the reporte was spoken where it should be shott. So that after x or xii dayes imprisonment he was bayled upon suerties, and bound to be forthcomminge at all tymes when he should be sent for; and so was discharged out of warde.

<small>A gun shott in the sermon tyme at Paules.</small>

The xith of June Lord John [Thomas] Grey,[b] one of the bretheren of the Duke of Suffolke late putt to death, was arreigned at Westminster in the Kings Benche of treason, and there condemned to dye.

<small>Duke of Suffolkes brother arrayned.</small>

The 15 of Julie, beinge Sundaye, one Elizabeth Crofte, a yonge mayden, stood at Paules Crosse on a litle scaffolde neare the preacher, which was taken in Aldersgate Streete in Aprill last past, called the whyte byrde, or the byrde that spake in the wall.[c] Her confession was readd by the precher openlye, which declared that one Drakes, a servant of Sir Anthony Nevills,[d] which gaue her a whistle, and

<small>The birde in the wall.</small>

---

[a] The sermon was preached by Dr. Pendleton.—Strype.

[b] Lord Thomas Grey.—See Chronicle of Queen Jane and Queen Mary, p. 75.

[c] "called the Spirit in the Wall."—Stow.

[d] "John Drake, Sir Antony Knevett's servant."—Diary of a Resident in London, p. 66; but Stow agrees with the text.

118   WRIOTHESLEY'S CHRONICLE.

A.D. 1554.

by theyr develish pretence feyned[a] her to speake divers thinges of the Queen and Prince of Spayne, of the masse and confession; as that one Myles, clerk of St. Butolphes in Aldersgate Street, and a player, and one Hyll, a weaver[b] in Reddcrosse Streete, declared to the people,[c] which caused great assemblie of people to drawe thither, which there openlye lamented in the presence of all the people. After her confession read she kneeled downe, and asked God forgivenes, and the Queens Maiestie, desyringe the people to praye for her, and to beware of heresies. The sermon done she went to prison agayne in Bred Street, where she had bene a litle tyme, but afore that she was in Newgate. And after Dr. Scorye resorted to her divers tymes to examin her; and after this she was released.

Landinge of the prince of Spayne.

Fryday the xxth of Julie tydinges came to the Lord Mayre that the Prince of Spayne was come into Englande, and landed at Southampton this daye, and came with viii^{xx} sayle of Spanish shippes well appoynted, beside the navie of Flaunders and the Queens navie, which were to the number of lx shippes and more, Lord Wm. Howarde, Lord Admirall of England, conductinge them, after they came into the costes of Englande.

Proclamation for the marriage with bone-fyers.

The xxith of Julie proclamation was made in London that all noblemen, gentlemen, ladies, and other should repayre to the Cittie of Winchester, there to doe their attendance at her graces marriage accordinge as they are appoynted. And that night were bone-fyers made in everie parishe within the Cittie of London, with all the bells ringinge in everye parishe churche for the ioyfull tydinges of the Princes landinge in safetie.

King Phillip receaved into Winchester.

The 23 of Julie the Prince of Spayne came to Winchester[d] about vi

[a] feigned.

[b] Stow reads: "a player, a weaver, Hill, clerk of St. Leonard's in Foster Lane, and others confederate with her."

[c] These confederates, putting themselves among the press, took upon them to interpret what the spirit [in the wall] said [when she whistled], expressing certain seditious words against the Queen, &c.—See Stow.

[d] Philip lingered a few days at Southampton, where he disembarked, as if in order to ascertain the humour of the nation, as one of his ambassadors, the Count of

of the clock at night, accompanied with noblemen as well of England as of his owne countrie,ª with trumpetts blowinge and bells ringinge, and came to the Cathedrall churche, where he alighted. And there the Bishop of Winchester, Lord Chauncellor, with 4 bishops more, with the priests, singinge-men, and children, receaved him with procession in riche copes and with iii crosses up into the quiere, where was a riche traves richlye hanged for him; and there he kneeled downe before the sacrament; and then the Lord Chauncellor began Te Deum, the organs playinge and the quier singinge the rest. This done he was brought out with torche light to his lodginge throughe the cloyster to the Deanes howsse, all the Queens garde standinge in their riche cotes all the waye. He was apparelled in a riche cote richlie imbroydered with goulde, and an hatt much like the same with a feather in it. The same night after he had supped, which was about x of the clock, certeyne of the Councell brought him to the Queen by a secrett waye, where she receaved him right lovinglye and kissed him, and after halfe an howre they tooke their leave, eche kissinge the other, and so departed that night to his lodginge. A.D. 1554.
His first meetinge with the Queene.

The 24 of Julie, aboute 3 of the clock in the afternoone, he came from his lodginge on foote, the Lord Steward, the Earle of Darbie, the Earle of Pembrooke, and divers other lordes and gentlemen, both Englishe and Spanishe, goeinge afore him to the Courte, where everie bodye might see him, and so was brought up into the hall where the Queene was standinge upon a skaffold richelye hanged, she meetinge him halfe waye, receivinge him, and kissinge him in the presence of all the people.ᵇ And then she tooke him by the hand, she goeinge on his right hand out of the hall in her great The meetinge of the Prince and the Queen openlye.

Egmont, had been recently violently assaulted by the populace, who mistook him for his master.

ª He came well attended with a bodyguard and troops.

ᵇ Mary took no pains to conceal her impatience, being enabled in her conscience to plead her anxiety for a legitimate Roman Catholic succession, as the only means of securing the faith in England.

A.D. 1554.

chamber of presence. And there in the presence of all the lordes and ladies they stoode a quarter of an hower under the clothe of estate talkinge together; and then after a while he toke his leave of her Grace and came forthe into the open cowrte, where all the pentioners stood in araye and the garde all alonge on both sides the waye in theyr riche cotes to the Court gates; and from thence the lords brought him to the Cathedrall churche to evensonge, and after to his loginge agayne.

The prince made Kinge before the marriage.

The same night, about 12 of the clock, the Emperor sent a message to the Queen, declaringe to her that his sonne which should marrie with her was not then a Prince onelye but a Kinge; and that he was Kinge of Naples and Jerusalem before the marriage, and so did send his writings of the same under his great seale.

The marriage of King Phillippe and Queen Marye.

The 25 of Julie, beinge Weddensdaye and St. James daye,* about xi of the clocke the Kinge and Queene came from their lodgings towards the churche all the way on foote, verie richelye apparelled in gownes of cloth of golde sett with riche stones, he with his gentlemen and garde and she with hers, eche of them havinge a sworde borne before them, the Earle of Darbye bearinge the sworde before her Maiestie, and the Earle of Pembroke before the Kinge; and when they were come into the churche he went into one traveys and the Queen to another richlye hunge, where they were shriven. This done they came forth of their traveys to the place appoynted for the marriage, where the Lord Chauncellor, beinge before with 5 other bishops assistinge him, used all thinges, both in the banes-byddinge and otherwise, as hath bene in all marriages of olde tyme, and spake it both in Latin and in Englishe, her Grace on the right syde standinge and the King on the left syde. Her marriage ringe was a rownd hoope of gould without anye stone, which was her desire, for she sayde she would be married as maydens were in the olde tyme, and so she was.

* The feast of St. James, the titular saint of Spain.

After the marriage knott thus knitt the King and Queen came hand in hand under a riche canopie, beinge borne over them with 6 knightes and 2 swordes before them, all the lordes both Englishe and strangers richelye apparelled goeinge afore them, the trumpetts then blowinge tyll they came into the quier, where all the priestes and singinge men all in riche copes began to singe a psalme used in marriages, the King and Queen kneelinge awhile before the aulter, eche of them havinge a taper afore them; then after her Majestie went into her traveys on the right syde, and the King into another on the left syde; after the gospell they came owt and kneeled before the alter openlye all the masse tyme, and the carecloth was holden ouer them; and he kissed the bishopp at the Agnus and then her Majestie. The masse done the Kinge of Herroldes openlye in the churche, and in presence of the King, the Queen, the lordes and ladies, and all the people, solemnlye proclaymed their Maiesties Kinge and Queene, with their title and style, in manner as followeth:

A.D. 1554.

Philippe and Marie, by the grace of God Kinge and Queene of Englande, France, Naples, Jerusalem, and Irelande, Defenders of the Faythe, Princes of Spayne and Sicilie, Archdukes of Anstriche, Dukes of Mylane, Burgundye, and Brabant, Countes of Aspurge,[a] Flaunders, and Tyrrole. Which proclamation ended, the trumpetts blue and other noyses playde. And then the Kinge and Queene came furthe hand in hand, with their lordes, ladies, and gentlemen waytinge on them, and 2 swordes borne afore them in manner afore sayde; and so went on foote to the courte, and there dined openlye in the hall, both together at one table.

The Kinge and Queenes style.

Sundaye 5 August the King was stalled in Windsore of the noble order of the Garter, and there kept St. George's feast in his royall estate himselfe; where was kept a great feast. And the Earle of Sussex was made knight of the Garter at that tyme allso.

The King stalled in Wyndsore.

The 7 of August was a general huntinge at Wyndsore forest, where was made a great toyle of 4 or 5 myles longe.

A generall huntinge.

[a] Haspurgi, Hapsburg.

122   WRIOTHESLEY'S CHRONICLE.

A.D. 1554.   The 11 of August the King and Queen removed to Richmond.

The 17 of August[a] the King and Queen came by water from Richmond in the after-noone, and landed at my Lord Chancellors stayers in St. Marye Overies, and there had a banquett in the Lord Chauncellors howsse, and then passed throughe the parke to the howse at St. Georges, of which Sir John Gage, Lord Chamberlayne to the Queene, had the keepinge, and there lay that night and dyned there the next daye.

The comminge of the Kinge and Queen through London.

Saterdaye the 18 of August, in the after-noone, the King and Queenes Majesties rode throughe Sowthwerke, over the bridge, and so throughe London; where they were with great provision receaved of the citizens, pageants in places accustomed, the crosse in Cheape new gilte, &c.

Duke of Norfolk deceased.

Memorandum: In the moneth of September the Duke of Norfolke died at Framlingham in Norfolke, and there was honorablye buried amongst his auncestors.

Allso this moneth the Bishop of London visited all his dioces, and had sermons in everie parishe and place where he satt, and sett owt divers goodlye articles in print for the true religion.

Churche holydayes.

Allso he commaunded that the feast of everie saynte that was patrone of the churche, called *Festum loci*, in everie parishe, should be kept holiedaye in everie parishe throughe his diocesse as a principall feast used in olde tyme, after the custome of the churche.

Lord Chauncellor preached.

Sunday the xxx[th] of Septembre 1554 Dr. Steven Gardiner, Bishop of Winton and Lord Chauncellor of England, preached at Paules Crosse, divers Lordes of the Queens Councell beinge present

---

[a] The authorities differ widely as to this date. The Grey Friars' Chronicle (p. 91) says: "They came not unto London tyll it was the 18th day of August, and then came bothe unto the place in Sothwarke, and lay there that nyght, and the 19th day came into London." And Stow (p. 625): "The 11 of August, the King and Queene remooued to Richmond, from thence by water to Southwarke, &c. And the next day, being the 12 of August, they rode through Southwarke ouer the bridge, and so through London, &c." While Baker's Chronicle reads: "The eleventh of August they remoued to Richmond, the seven-and-twentieth to Suffolk Place in Southwark, and the next day to London," &c. (p. 342).

at his sermon, and goeinge afterward to dynner to the Lord Mayres howsse.

The first Sundaye after Michaellmas daye was kept the dedication of the churche throughe all England, accordinge to the olde costome.

The 18 of Octobre, beinge the day of St. Luke, the Kinge rode from his pallace of Whitehall to Paules Church in the forenoone, and there heard masse, which was sunge by the Spaniards of his owne quier.

Frydaye the 26 of October there was a Spaniarde hanged at Charinge Crosse, which had shamefullie slayne an Englishe man, servant to Sir George Gifforde. There would have bene given v c. crownes of the straungers to have saved his life.

PHILIPPI ET MARIÆ. Annis 1º et 2º.

Sundaye the 4 of November 5 persons did open pennance in Paules, whereof 3 were priestes that were wedded; and the other 2 were seculare men, that had 2 wives apeece lyvinge.

Munday the 12 of Novembre the Parliament began at Westminster.[a]

Saterdaye the 24 of November Doctor Reynold Poole,[b] Cardinall, came to the Cowrte to Westminster, and was receaved of the King and Queens Majesties, which had longe bene a banished man out of this realme, and now restored to his bloud agayne by Acte of Parlement.

Weddensdaye the 28 of November the Lord Mayre and Alldermen assembled in Paules in their scarlett gownes and clokes, with all the Commons in their liveries, at ix of the clock in the foor-

marginalia: A.D. 1554. Dedication of the church. The Kinge cominge to Paules to masse. A Spaniard hanged. Open pennance. A Parlement. Cardinall sent from the Pope.

---

[a] In the new parliament the Commons consisted wholly of Roman Catholics or of men indifferent to the great question of religion, and the Lords were as subservient to the Crown as ever.

[b] Cardinal Reginald Pole was son of Sir Richard Pole by Margaret, Countess of Salisbury, the daughter of George, Duke of Clarence, brother of Edward IV.

noone. The highe masse done, Dr. Chadsey, one of the Prebendaries in Paules, went into the pullpitt in the quiere, the Bishop of London present in his stall, and ix other bishopps sittinge on the north syde of the highe alter, against the Lord Mayre and the Aldermen. First the preacher redd a letter sent to the Bishop of London from the Queens Councell; the tenure whereof was, that the Bishop of London shoulde causse *Te Deum* to be sunge in all the parishe churches of his dioces, with continuall prayers[a] of the priestes in their masses, for the Queens Majestie, who was conceyved and quick with childe.[b] The letter redd, he began a collation with this antheme: *Ne timeas, Maria; invenisti enim gratiam apud Deum.*[c] His sermon ended, *Te Deum* was sunge, and solemne procession was made of *Salve, festa dies*, goeinge the circuite of the churche.[d]

Saterdaye the first of December the Lord Mayre and Aldermen went to Lambeth by water in the afternoone, to salute the Lord Cardinall Poole and Legatt de Latere, which he thankfullie tooke.

Sunday the 2 of December Cardinall Poole came from Lambeth by water, and landed at Paules wharfe, and went from thence to Paules Churche, with a crosse, 2 pillers, and 2 polleaxes of sylver borne before him. He was there receaved by the Lord Chauncellor with procession; where he taried tyll the King came from Westminstre by land, at xi of the clock. And then the Lord Chauncellor entred Paules crosse and preached a sermon, takinge for his theame these wordes: Fratres, scientes quia hora est jam nos de somno surgere, &c., which was a parte of the Epistle for this Sundaye. In which sermon he declared that the King and Queen had restored

---

[a] Several of the prayers used on this occasion have been preserved. They were composed by different priests, but nearly all contain a clause praying that the child might be a male, "well favoured and witty," with strength to repress his enemies.

[b] In her exceeding anxiety for issue, Mary mistook the commencement of a dropsy for the sure sign of pregnancy, and, when Cardinal Pole was first introduced to her on his return to England, she fancied that the child was quickened, even as John the Baptist leaped in his mother's womb at the salutation of the Virgin.

[c] Luke i. v. 30.   [d] In thanksgiving for the Queen's quickening.

the Pope to his supremacie; and that the 3 estates assembled in the A.D. 1554.
Parliment (representinge the whole bodie of the realme) had submitted themselves to the same. The sermon beinge ended, the King departed towardes Westminster, and with him the Lord Cardinall. But the Lorde Chauncellor went with the Lord Mayre to dynner.

This moneth allso, in Christenmas weeke, the daye of St. Thomas of Canterburie was kept holydaye, by the Bishop of Londons com maundement.

Allso in the Christenmas holydayes came over the seas to see the Prince of Piamont.
King and Queens Majestie a nobleman of the Emperors linage called Prince of Piament, or Duke of Savoy;[a] and was lodged at Somersett Place by the Strande without Temple barre, and had great chear in the cowrt.[b]

The xi of Januarie was a Spaniarde hanged at Charinge Crosse, [A.D. 1555.]
for slayinge an Englishe man at the cowrt gate at Westminster in A Spaniarde hanged.
Christenmas holydayes, cowardlie runninge him thorowe with a rapere whilst 2 Spaniardes held him by the armes; who allso were arrayned and cast, but after pardoned by the Queene.

The 16 of January the Parlement brake up, and was elene dissolved.[c]

The 18 of January all suche persons as remayned in prison Prisoners discharged.
within the Tower of London condemned of treason were delyvered out of prison by the Queens Councell, which satt there at their delyverie, and had the Queens pardon.[d]

[a] Emanuel Philibert, Prince of Piedmont and Duke of Savoy, was cousin-german to King Philip by their mothers.

[b] The Queen caused him to be elected into the order of the Garter, and shewed him much hospitality, expecting that he should marry the Princess Elizabeth.—See Tytler's Edward VI. and Mary, ii p. 418.

[c] Mary dissolved the parliament in ill humour.

[d] Philip recommended the instant release of some of the most distinguished prisoners in the Tower; and it is generally stated to have been at his instigation that Mary consented to release Elizabeth and the Earl of Devon from the Tower, and to restore to their entire liberty the Lord Henry Dudley, Sir George Harper, Sir Nicholas Throgmorton, Sir William Sentlow or St. Low, and four others.

126 WRIOTHESLEY'S CHRONICLE.

A.D. 1555.
A generall procession.

Frydaye the 25 of January, beinge the Conversion of St. Paule, there was kept a solemne generall procession in London. To the which about xi of the clocke the Kinge and the Lord Cardinall Poole came ridinge from Whitehall to Paules Churche. This night allso were great bonefires made in everie parishe within London. The which sayd procession and fyers were done to give God laude and prayse for the conversion of this realme to the catholique faythe and churche, &c.

Heretykes condemned.

The 28, 29, 30 of January, the Lord Chaunccellor, with other bishopps, satt in the churche of St. Marye Overies in Sowthwerke for heresies,[a] where was condemned for heresie Mr. Hooper, quondam Bishop of Glocester and Worcester; and Rogers, quondam vicar of St. Sepulchers in London, and one of the Prebendaries of Paules; and Cardemaker,[b] quondam Deane of Wells, reconciled him[self] to the order of the churche; Bradforde, Dr. Taylor of Hadley, and one Saunders, quondam parson of Allhallowes in Bred Street, were lykewise condemned of heresie, and committed to the sheriffs of London, who sent Rogers[c] and Hooper to Newgate; Bradford,[d] Taylor,[e] and Saunders[f] to the two Counters, in the Poultrie and Bred Street.

[a] Without the least hesitation the late parliament revived the old barbarous laws against heretics, enacted statutes against seditious words, and made it treason to imagine or attempt the death of Philip during his marriage with the Queen.

[b] John Cardmaker, *alias* Taylor, late Vicar of St. Bride's, was Chancellor of the Cathedral of Wells.—See Foxe, and Le Neve's Fasti.

[c] John Rogers was instituted to the prebend of St. Pancras, in St. Paul's Cathedral, 24th August, 1551, and was also reader of the lecture in St. Paul's. He is fully commemorated by Foxe as the proto-martyr of the Marian persecution. He was burned at Smithfield for "being a Lutheran," writes Noailles, the French ambassador, and "he met his death, persisting in his opinion, so bravely that the greater part of the people here took such pleasure that they did not fear to give him many acclamations to comfort his courage."

[d] John Bradford.

[e] Dr. Rowland Taylor had lived for some time in the family of Archbishop Cranmer, who preferred him to the rectory of Hadleigh, in Suffolk, to which town he was sent to be burnt. From him was descended the learned and amiable Jeremy Taylor.

[f] Laurence Saunders was sent to Coventry to be burnt.

⁰ The 14 of Marche, about ix of the clock at night, an image of St. Thomas of Canterburie, which was new made in stone (by the commaundement of the King and Queenes Councell) by the wardens of the Mercers, and sett over the Chappell doore of the Mercers hall and Churche in Cheape, was broken and defaced, but the auctor of that fact could not be heard of or fownd out, notwithstandinge a Proclamation made in that behalfe. A.D. 1555.

The 16 of Marche Thomas Tompkins, of Shorditch, weaver, afore viii of the clock in the foorenoone, was brent in Smythfielde. Tomkins burned.

Sundaye the 24 of Marche, before 5 of the clock in the morninge, Sir John Lawrence, priest, Thomas Cawston, Thomas Hikbye,^a Stephen Knight, William Hunt, and William Pigott, were had out of Newgate and delyvered by the sheriffes of London to the sheriffes of Essex to be brent. Parsons brent.

The 4 of Aprill, beinge Easter daye, was a lewde fact done in the parishe Churche of St. Margarett, in Westminster: Sir John Shetheur, priest, ministringe the sacrament to the parishioners, and holdinge the challis in his left hand, one William Branch *alias* called Flower, in a servinge mans cote,^b suddenlye drue a woddknife and strooke the priest on the heade, that the bloud ran downe and fell both on the challes and on the consecrated bread. The sayde person was apprehended and committed to the Gatehowse in Westminster. A lewd parte.

The 17 of Aprill, beinge Weddensday in Easter weeke, in the afternoone, was a solemne obsequie and dergie, kept in Paules Churche, and in all the parishe churches in London, for Pope Julius the thirde, who died about the xth day of March ^c last past. Obsequye for the Pope.

---

^a Apparently a clerical error for Thomas Hawkes, an Essex gentleman, who was burned at Coggeshall.

^b He had been a monk of Ely, and is called by other authorities Fowler.—See Machyn's Diary, p. 85.

^c Pope Julius III. was elected, 8th February, 1550, by only two votes over Cardinal Pole. He was crowned on the 22nd of the same month, and died 5th March, 1555.

A.D. 1555. Lord Courtney and Ladye Elyzabeth.	Allso, againste this tyme of Easter, Lord Courtney, Earle of Devonshire, came to the cowrte agayne: And allso, a x dayes after, the Lady Elizabeth came lykewise to the Queene, both at Hampton Cowrte, where the Queen had taken her chamber to be delyvered of childe.[a]
Fryers observants.	The 7 of Aprill, beinge Palme Sunday, the Queene set up the Howsse of Friers Observants in Greenewich, which friers, both Englishe and strangers, [were dressed] [b] in gray habittes barefooted.
William Flower condemned and disgraded in Paules.	The xxth of Aprill in the foorenoone, in the consistory of Paules, was arreyned the sayde William Branch *alias* Flower, who struke the priest on Easter-day in the parishe churche of St. Margaretts, in Westminster. And, beinge condemned of heresie, he was delyvered to the sheriffes of London and Middlesex. This Flower was once a muneke in Ely Abbey, professed at his age of xvii yeares, and after made priest, and then married and had 3 or 4 children; and then ran about the countrie usinge the arte of surgerye.
William Flower burnt at Westminster.	The 24 of Aprill the sayde William Flower for his sayde fact had his right hand smitten of, and for opinions in matters of religion was burned in the sanctuarye nigh to St. Margaretts churchyarde.
iii persons hanged, buryed, and burnt at Charinge Crosse.	The vii[th] of May was the bodie of one John Towley, a poulter, taken up by the gallowes at Charinge Crosse, where he and 2 persons moe were hanged the 26 of Aprill last past. These three dyd a great robberye in Westminster of a Spaniarde to a great summe of golde and jewells afore Shrovetyde last past.
Two weomen at Paules Crosse.	Sunday the 19 of May two weomen did recant, at Paules Crosse, certeyne slaunderouse wordes by them spoken, that a childe should speake when it was new borne, saying "fast and praye," upon which sayinge the sayd woman was examined by the Bishop of London, and after afore the Queens Councell in the Starre Cham-

[a] It appears from Mary's will, which was dated the 30th April 1558, or about seven months before her death, that down to that time she was confident of being *enceinte,* for she made a provision for settling the crown on her issue.—See Sir F. Madden's Privy Purse Expenses of the Princess Mary; with Introductory Memoir and copy of Will in Appendix.

[b] Omitted in MS.

ber, and there confessed the truthe: That the childe never spake, but groned and rattled in the throate after it was borne, and died. For which fact they were enioyned to recant at Paules Crosse.

A.D. 1555.

Weddensdaye, the 22 of May and Assencion Eeven, was one ^a that named himself King Edward had from the Marshallsie in South werke, rydinge in a carre in a fooles cote with papers written on his head and brest, rydinge throughe London into Westminster Hall, and carried rownd aboute the sayde hall, first to the Kings Benche, then to the Chauncerie and the Common Place, and then to the Hall doore, and then st[r]ipped naked, and bownd to the cart, and whipped rownd about the pallace there: And after was had throughe Westminster and [so] into London, whipping him still, till he came to the middest of Smythfield, and there putt on his clothes, and banished into the north countrie, where he was borne. He was a lackey upon viii yeres past to Sir Peter Mewtas.

One whipped, sayinge he was King Edwarde

Saterdaye the 25 of May, in the afternoone, the Lord Maior satt in Paules Churche, in the consistorie, with the Bishop of London, where afore them divers were condemned for heresie against the Sacrament of the Aulter.

Thursday the xxxth of May John Taylor alias Cardemaker, priest, and John Warne,^b were burnt in Smithfield for heresie against the Sacrament of the Aulter.

John Taylor, priest, brent.

Munday the 17 of June 1555 was a solemne obsequie in Paules^c for the Kinges grandmother, Ladye Jane, Queen of Spayne, Ar[a]gon, &c.^d

Obsequie for the Queen of Spayne.

Mundaye the first of Julie John Bradford and a boye were brent in Smythfielde for heresie.

Bradforde brent.

This yeare, on St. Bartlemew Eeven, after the Lord Mayre and

The disputation of schollers in the hospitall of Christes Churche.

---

^a William Featherstone was the real name of this youth, who was the son of an honest miller; he was seized at Eltham, in Kent, but not till the month of May.

^b An upholsterer of London — See a full relation of his execution in Foxe.

^c A full account of the hearse and ceremonial will be found in Machyn's Diary, pp. 90, 341.

^d Jane, Queen of Spain, here mentioned, was heiress of Castile and Aragon; besides being King Philip's grandmother she was Queen Mary's maternal aunt.

A.D. 1555.

Alldermen had ridden aboute the fayre, they came to Christes Churche by Newgate Markett, where disputation of the children of Paules Schole, St. Anthonies, and the children of the Hospitall was heard, and three severall games made for them.

The King and Queen ridinge throughe London.

The 26 of August 1555, beinge Mundaye, the King and Queene came by water from Hampton Cowrte to theyr pallace of Whytehall to dynner; and about 4 of the clock in the afternoone they rode from thence throughe the Cittie of London to Tower wharfe, where they tooke bote to Grenewich.[a]

The Queen gave all spirituall promotions that were in her possession to the clergie agayne, and allso pardoned them of the First Fruites and Tenths from thenceforward.[b]

Kinge passinge over the seas into Flanders.

The 4 of September the Kinge tooke shippinge at Dover and so passed over to Calys, and about xi of the clocke that daye was highlye receaved of the Lord Deputie, and the Mayre of the Staple of Calies. He was there presented with a purse and a thowsand markes of golde in it. On the morrowe he departed from Callies towards Brussells, in Brabant, to visitt the Emperoure his father. At his departinge he gave amonge the souldiers of Calies for a reward a thowsand crownes.

The Popes bulls of plenarie remission.

The 15 of September was declared at Paules Crosse the Popes Bull of plenarie remission, named Paulus Quartus,[c] to all people beinge penitent, full remission of all their synns, &c.

A great fludd.

The last daye of September by occasion of great wynde and rayne that had fallen were suche great fluddes that that morninge the Kings pallace in Westminster and Westminster Hall was overflowen with water up to the stayrefoote goinge to the Chauncerie and Kings Bench. And by reporte there that morninge a whirie-

---

[a] The Grey Friars' Chronicle adds: "towarde hys jurné unto hys fader the Emperar, and there toke hys leffe," p. 96.

[b] It was with much difficulty Parliament was brought to legalise these restorations.

[c] Giampietro Caraffa, Archbishop of Chieti and a Cardinal, was elected by the title of Paul IV. 23rd May, and crowned 26th of the same month, 1555.

man rowed with his boate over Westminster Bridge ª into the pallace cowrt there, and so thorowe the gate into the Kings Street.

A.D. 1555.

This yeare on Michaelmas even the prisoners that laye in the Counter in Bread Street were removed to a new Counter made in Wood Street of the Citties purchace and buyldinge.

A new counter in Wood street.

‹ The 16 of October Dr. Ridley, quondam Bishop of London, and Hugh Latimer, quondam Bishop of Rochester,ᵇ were brent at Oxforde.

Ridley and Latimer brent.

Munday the 21 of October 1555 the Parliament began at Westminster, the Queen ridinge from her pallace at St. James, throughe the parke, to the Tilt yeard gate by Whitehall, and so to St. Peters Churche in Westminster.ᶜ

A parliament.

Allso this moneth Dr. Storye and other were appoynted by the Cardinall ᵈ to visitt everye parishe churche in London and Middlesex, to see their roode-loftes repayred, and the images of the Crucifixe with Marye and John thereon to be fixed.

For settinge up roode loftes.

Allso about the 5 of November the Lord Cardinall begane a synode ᵉ in the Queens pallace of Whitehall in Westminster, where

A synode.

ª This was not a bridge across the Thames, but one of those landing stages or staiths which ran out into the stream on the Westminster side, near Whitehall.

ᵇ We should here read "Worcester." The confusion has evidently arisen from Ridley, who was just before mentioned, having held the see of Rochester before he was translated to London, whereas Latimer never held any other see than Worcester, of which he was consecrated bishop in September, 1535, and resigned 1 July, 1539. These two prelates were burnt at the same stake, the Vice-Chancellor of Oxford University, with the other commissioners appointed by the Court, and a multitude of Oxford scholars and gentlemen, standing by.

ᶜ After a short session, the Queen dissolved this parliament on the 9th of December.—See Journals.

ᵈ Cardinal Pole, now Archbishop of Canterbury. This enlightened Roman Catholic prelate was averse to these frantic attempts to maintain one standard of faith by means of fire and sword, and endeavoured, though in vain, to prove to Mary and her government that the practice of persecution was not only dangerous to themselves, but the scandal of all religion.

ᵉ "The 11th day after the meeting of parlament began the Cardinalles senod at Lambyth, and contynewyd tylle the 12th day of February after."—Grey Friars' Chronicle, p. 96.

A.D. 1555.   all the Bishopps with the rest of the clergie.satt twice everie weeke for a reformation of the clergie according to the olde antiquitie of the Churche, which latelye had bene putt downe.

Philippi et Mariæ, Annis 2° et 3°.

Dr. Gardiner deceased.   The 12 of November Steven Gardiner, Bishop of Winchester and Lord Chauncellor of England, died at Yorke Place in Westminster, and his bodie after was caried by water to his place at St. Marie Overies, where it was closed in leade, and x dayes after layde in a vaute of brick made for it, tyll the springe of the yeare.   For his will was to be buried in Winchester. But because of the great waters that haue fallen this winter it could not convenientlie be carried. Some suppose that he had beene poysoned [a] when he went over the seas to intreat a peace betwene the Emperor and the French Kinge.

Philpott brent.   The 16 of Decembre the Lord Mayre satt in Paules with the Bishop of London in the afternoone, afore whom one Phillpott, late Deane of Winchestre,[b] a gent and learned in the lawe, was condemned.   And the 18 of December he was brent in Smythfeild.

[A.D. 1556.]
A new Lord Chancellor.   This yeare on newe yeares daye the Queen gave the Great Seale of Englande to Dr. Heath, Archbishop of Yorke, and made him Lord Chauncellor of Englande,[c] and gave the Privie Seale to the Lord Pagett, and made him Lord Privie Seale. These were both Londoners borne.

Persons brent.   The 27 of Januarie vii persons were brent in Smythfielde for denieinge the presence of Christe in the Sacrament, &c.

[a] He attended at the opening of the Parliament, and displayed his usual ability and energy; but on the third day his bodily sufferings obliged him to quit his post, and he expired of a painful disease on the 12th of November.

[b] John Philpot, Archdeacon of Winchester.

[c] The new Chancellor, though keen in the persecution of Protestants, had not the talent and address of the old one.

This yeare letters came from beyond the seas that in Netherlande (with tempest of weather and fire that fell out of the element) were burned 20 churches, a myll, and a bridge, and much grownde where flaxe grewe.

A.D. 1556.

The 14 of February Thomas Cranmer, late Archbishop of Canterburie, was disgraded of all his orders and dignities of bishopp and priesthoode at Oxforde,[a] by Dr. Bonner, Bishop of London, the Bishop of Ely, and others, being with him in commission sent from the Pope, and after was committed to the laitie as a layeman to suffer at the King and Queenes pleasure.

Dr. Cranmer disgraded at Oxford.

The 24 of February the corps of Dr. Gardiner, Bishop of Winton, were translated and caried from the parishe churche of St. Marye Overye throughe Southwerke toward Winchester, there to be buried. His corps were sett in a chariott covered with blacke, and a picture made lyke unto him lyeing on his coffin, with a miter on the heade, and a cope of golde on the bodye of the picture, with gloves and ringes on his fingers, &c. The Lord Vicount Montacute, the Bishop of Ely, and other his executors, ridinge to the buriall, and above 200 horse of gentlemen and yeomen all in black.[b]

The cariage of the Bishop of Winchesters corps.

The 26 of February, one William Constable, alias Federstone, was arreigned at the Guildehall of London, who had caused letters to be cast abrode that King Edwarde VI. was alyve. And to some he shewed himselfe to be King Edward, so that manye persons, both men and weomen, were troubled by him. For the which sedition the said William had bene once whipped and delyvered. But now he was condemned and iudged to be drawen, hanged, and quartered.

A traytor naminge himselfe King Edward.

---

[a] In the Magliabechiana, which is on the same staircase as the Florentine archives, a document of some interest to students of English History has recently been turned up. Its date is March 8, 1554, and it is an application to Pope Julius III. for the deprivation of Thomas Cranmer from the see of Canterbury on account of his evil life. It is signed Roger Ascham, and is apparently written by him; and is countersigned by Mary and her husband Philip. It is in perfect order and beautifully written. Mary signs "Maria" in a small, round, and clear hand.

[b] A fuller account of the obsequies will be found in Machyn's Diary, p. 100.

A.D. 1556.	This yeare in the beginninge of Lent was sent by commission of
Images sett up agayne.	the Bishopps [order]^a that in euerie parishe churche in London and throughe England an image of the Saynte that everie churche bare the name of should be made and sett on the end of the highe aulter.
A peace.	This yeare in February a peace was concluded betwene the Emperor Charles the V. and Philipp his sonne King of England and Henrie the Second, French King, for 5 yeares to endure.
A traytor executed.	The 4 of Marche William Constable, afore condemned for naminge himself King Edwarde the VI. was drawne from the Tower of London to Tyborne and there hanged, headed, and quartered, and after his head sett on London bridge.
Dr. Cranmer brent.	The 21 of Marche Dr. Cranmer, late Archbishop of Canterbury, afore disgraded, was brent at Oxforde.
Cardinal Poole made priest and Archbishop of Canterbury.	The same daye the Lord Cardinall Poole was made priest at Lambeth, and the morrowe, being Sunday, he was consecrated Archbishop of Canterburie at Grenewich in the Friers churche. And the Weddensdaye after, beinge the feast of the Annunciation, he receaved the pall in his churche of St. Marye the Arches, *alias* Bowe Churche in Cheape.
Newgate on fyer.	Saterday the 28 of Marche, at x of the clock in the forenoone, a parte of Newgate was on fyre called Mannings-hall and was brent to the grownd,^b and no prisoners lost.
Black Fryers.	This yeare at Easter the churche of Great St. Bartlemewes, in Smythfeilde, was sett up with black friers; Fryer Perwyn beinge head thereof.
Persons brent for religion.	Frydaye 24 of Aprill 1556 were six Essex men brent in Smythfeild.

Monday 27 Aprill were vi Essex men sent out of Newgate to be brent in divers places in Essex.

Allso iii weomen brent in Smythfeilde.

^a Omitted in MS.
^b The Grey Friars' Chronicle reads: "but thangkes be to God that there was but lyttyll harme done, for it was sone qwenched." P. 97.

The 28 of Aprill John Throckmorton and Richard Udall[a] were drawen to Tyborne and there hanged and quartered for treason.

A.D. 1556.
Traytors executed.

The 19 of May William Stanton was likewise executed for treason.

The 8 of June, Rossey, Bedyll, and Derike,[b] were lykewise executed at Tiburne for treason.

The 18 of June, Frances Vernam,[c] esq., and Edw. Turner, gent., arreigned at the Guildehall for treason and condemned. Vernam confessed his treason.

Memorandum: the same daye, one Sandes, gent., a yonger sonne of the Lord Sandes, was hanged at St. Thomas Watrings for a great robberie that he and other had committed on Whit Sonday last of iii M t.

Sandes hanged.

Saterday 27 Junii were 13 persons caried from Newgate in three carrs to the end of the towne of Stratford the Bowe, and there brent.

Persons brent at Stratforde.

Tewsday the xxx[th] of June Wm. West, esquier, callinge himselfe De la Ware, was arreigned at the Guylde Hall in London for treason. But in the beginninge of his arreignment he would not aunswere to his name of Wm. West, esquier, but as Lord De la Ware, and to be tried by his pieres, which the judges there with the heraldes proved he was no lorde, because he was never created nor made a lorde by anye writt to the Parlement, nor had anye patent to shewe for his creation; wherefore that plee would not serve, and so had like to haue had judgment without triall; but at last he aunswered to the name of Wm. West, esq., and so was tried by 12 men, and condemned of treason, as consentinge to Henry Dudley and his adherents; and so had iudgment as a traytor.

William West, esquier, naminge himselfe Lord De la Ware, condemned of treason.

[a] "Mr. Waddall, captayn of the yle of Wyth."—Machyn's Diary, p. 104; but Stow agrees with the text.

[b] These names are spelled Rosey, Bedyll, and Dethick in Machyn's Diary, and Rosselle, Bedelle, and Darrelle in the Grey Friars' Chronicle, while Stow names them William Rossey, John Bedell, and John Dedike.

[c] Frances Varney.—Machyn's Diary, p. 108.

136   WRIOTHESLEY'S CHRONICLE.

A.D. 1556. The 8 of Julie Henry Peckham [a] and John Daniell were hanged
Peckam and Daniell executed. and beheaded at the Tower hill; and theyr bodyes buried in Barking Churche.[b]

A new order for a weekelye procession. This moneth the Bishop of London and other the Queenes Commissioners caused a new order to be made for processions, viz.: That everie Munday, Weddnesday, and Fridaye, weekelye, the children schollers in everie parishe should goe in procession afore the crosse, with the schole-master followinge them; and mens apprentices followinge the crosse, then the priests and clerks, and after the parishioners. And that everie of the sayde dayes one of everie howse at the least to goe in procession upon payne of xii d.

PHILIPPI ET MARIÆ.   Annis 3° et 4°.

An abbott in Westminstre. Saterdaye the 21 of November Mr. Dr. Feknam, late Deane of Paules in London, was made Abbott of Westminster, and stalled, and tooke possession of the same; and 14 muncks moe receaved the habitt the same daye with him of the order of St. Bennett. And the Queen gave to the sayde abbott all suche landes as remayned that day in her handes suppressed and taken by King Henry the 8 for ever.

One brent on the cheekes. The same day was one brought from Westminster Hall ridinge with his face to the horse tayle with a paper on his heade to the Standerd in Cheape, and there sett on the pillorie, and then burned with an hotte iron on both his cheekes with two letters, F and A, for false accusinge one of the Cowrt of the Common Place of treason.

A wicked faete done, and a sharpe punishment for it. The 16 of December 1556, at a sessions kept in the justice hall of the Olde Baylie without Newgate, one Gregorie Carpenter, blacksmith, beinge there prisoner, suddenlye with a knife stroke one William Whitrents his fellowe prisoner into the right side of his

---

[a] Henry Peckham, son to Sir Edmond Peckham.—Stow, p. 628.
[b] All Hallowes church, Barking.

shoulder that he fell downe as dead; for which fact he was im-   A.D. 1556.
mediatlye taken from the barr into the street before the justice
hall, where, his hand beinge first taken of, he was hanged on a
gibbett sett up for that purpose; his hand was nayled on the topp
of the gibbett, his bodie hanginge iii dayes after on the sayde jebbett
or he was cutt downe.

Fridaye the 26 of February the Lord Sturton was arreigned   [A.D. 1557.]
at Westminster for a felonie and murder done by him and his   Lord Sturton arreigned and hanged.
servantes in murderinge one Mr. Argile and his sonne, and con-
demned to death for the same; and after conveyed from the Tower
of London throughe the Cittie and so to Salisburie, and there hanged
with four of his men servantes the 6 of Marche. He caused the
sayde Argile and his sonne first to [be] stricken downe with clubbes,
then their throtes to be cutt, and after to be buried in his howse 15
foote deepe.

The 27 of February the Lord Mayre and Aldermen receaved a   Ambassadour from Russia.
Greate Duke which came from the Emperor of Russia, and by
casualtie of sea was lyke to be drowned on the coste of Scotland, &c.ᵃ

Thursdaye the 18 of Marche 1556 the Kinge landed at Dover   King Phillips retorne into Englande.
about x of the clock in the night. And the 23 of Marche passed
throughe London with the Queen and nobles of the realme to the
pallace of Whitehall by Westminster.

Saterdaye the 3 of Aprill 1557 diverse persons were condemned   Heretikes brent.
in Paules for heresie, and were brent in Smythfield 12 Aprilis.

Saterdaye 1° Maii ᵇ Mr. Thomas Percy, Esquier, was made knight   Percye, Earle of Northumberland.
and after lorde. And the morrowe after he was created Earle of
Northumberland, and had given him all the landes which had been
his auncestors remayninge in the Queens handes that daye.

     ᵃ After "&c." the transcriber has added the following note: "The rest is at large
sett downe in Mr. Stowes Annales of England, pa. 1067."—This reference refers to
the edition of 1592, a copy of which is in Lambeth Library.

     ᵇ "The last of April," according to Stow, who is supported by Sir Harris Nicolas.
The date in our text must therefore be taken as that on which Percy was created
Earl of Northumberland, although that event is here stated to have taken place on
the morrow after.

A.D. 1557. Stafforde rebelles tooke Scarborough Castle.	This yeare, about the latter end of Aprill, one Thomas Stafforde, second sonne to the Lord Stafforde, with certeyn other traytors, tooke Scarboroughe Castle in the countie of Yorke; which came out of France and made proclamation there, naminge himselfe to be Protector of this realme, and the Queen to be unrightfull Queene. But by the good pollicie of the Earle of Westmorland and others the saide Stafforde was apprehended with the other his complices without effusion of bloude, and brought up to London and sent to the Tower.
Stafford and others executed.	The 28 of May, beinge Fridaye, Thomas Stafforde was beheaded on the Tower Hill. And on the morrowe iii of his companie; viz. Stetchley,[a] Bradforde, and Proctor were drawne to Tiburne and there hanged and quartered.
Proclamation against the French Kinge.	Mundaye the 7 of June was a proclamation made in the Cittie of London againste the Frenche Kinge to be taken as the Queenes ennemie.
An armye sent over to the Kinge.	The 6 of Julie the King passed over the seas to Caleis,[b] and in the same moneth the Queen sent over an armie of men[c] to ayde the King, the Earle of Pembroke beinge Lord Generall and Livetenant of the armie.
Death of the Ladye Anne of Cleve.	This yeare in Julie[d] died the Ladie Ann of Cleve,[e] at Chelsey, and the 5 of August her corps[f] were solemnlye brought from thence to the Abbey of Westminster, and there buried by the highe aulter.

[a] Stretchley.—Stow.

[b] Stow (p. 631) adds: "and so into Flanders, where he made great prouision for warre against the French King."

[c] "viz. a thousand horsemen, foure thousand footemen, and two thousand pyoners." —Stow, p. 631.   [d] July 16.

[e] Sometime wife and queen of King Henry VIII. but, as she was never crowned, she is generally designated the Lady Ann of Cleves.—See Machyn's Diary, p. 144.

[f] The body of the late Queen, which had been sered, *i.e.* inclosed in waxed cloths, the night following her death, was interred with great pomp in Westminster Abbey on the 3rd August.—See Machyn's Diary, p. 145; and was buried, as Stow says, "at the head of King Sebert," where "she lyeth in a tomb not yet finished."—See Vetusta Monumenta, ii. pl. 35.

The 18 of August was a solemne obsequie kept in Paules for John, late King of Portingale,[a] who died in Julye last.

This yeare on Bartlemew-daye was kept a wrestlinge at Clarkin well. And the Sunday after was a shootinge kept in Fynnesberie feild.

This yeare allso in August the King with a great armie royall passed into France, of L^m men or more. And the xth daye of the same moneth was slayne by the Burgonians and Swartrotters[b] the Prince of Piamount, beinge capteyne above iiii^m Frenche men, and divers noblemen taken prisoners. This victorie was within 5 myles of St. Quintyns.

This moneth the King layde siege to the towne of St. Quintins by the water of Some, and on Fridaye the 27 of August[c] the towne was wonne by the King with the helpe of Englishmen.[d]

This sommer reigned in England divers straunge and new sycknesses, takinge men and weomen in theyr heades; as strange agues and fevers, whereof manye died.

A.D. 1557.
Death of the King of Portingale.
A wrestlinge and shootinge.
A victorye in France by the Kings armye.

St. Quintins wonne.

Strange syckness.

PHILIPPI ET MARIÆ ANNIS 4 ET 5.

This yeare the 6 of November, beinge Saterdaye, in the afternoone, certeyne persons were condemned of heresie in Paules Churche, and the 13 of November followinge were burned in Smythfeilde.

The xxxth of November, beinge St. Andrewes daye, in the forenoone, the Queen came from St. James to Whitehall to masse, where the Lord Cardinall Poole did preach before her Maiesty. At the masse there Sir Thomas Tresham, knight, receaved the order of the Crosse, and was made Lord of Saynt Johnes of England.

This yeare on New-yeares daye, beinge Saterday 1557[-8], the

Persons brent.

A new Lorde of St. Johns in England.

Caleis lost.

---

[a] John III. King of Portugal, who succeeded his father Emanuel in 1521, and died in July, 1557, was the husband of Jane, aunt of King Philip, and hence arose the special observance of his obsequies in England.

[b] Switzers.   [c] 18 August.—Stow.

[d] At the siege the Lord Henry Dudley, youngest son of John, late Duke of Northumberland, was slain with a gun.

140   WRIOTHESLEY'S CHRONICLE.

[A.D. 1558.] French King sent a great power and armie to Caleis[a] and tooke Risebancke and Newnam Bridge,[b] and after layde siege to the towne,[c] and won it the Frydaye after, beinge the 7 of Januarie. They found great riches both of ordinance and goodes both in the Staple hall and in the towne. They tooke the cheefest of the marchauntes and inhabitantes of the towne prisoners, and lett the rest of men and weomen goe without any baggage. It is supposed it could not so sone be wonne without treason.[d]

An armye. The 6 of Januarie, beinge Twelft-daye, the cittie of London sent out v C. men toward Caleis, but they came too short.

A parlement. Thursdaye the xx[th] of Januarie began the Parlement at Westminster.

Guisnes lost. This moneth[e] also, the castle and towne of Guisnes was wonn by the Frenchmen; the Lord Gray capteyn thereof defendinge it, tyll they with ordinaunce had beaten downe all the walls.[f]

A meteor in the element. The 29 of January, being Saterday, at 8 of the clock at night, was seene in the element a rownde circle lyke a hoope, coloured much lyke the raynebowe; the mone standinge right in the middle of the compasse, and all the element clere within the said compasse, which was seene tyll after x of the clock that night.

A prest demaunded of the Londoners, &c. This moneth the Queen demaunded a prest of the Cittie of London of C[m] marks. But by great labor of the Lord Mayre and

[a] Under the command of the Duke of Guise.

[b] Nieulay, one of the outworks of Calais, situated within the English pale.

[c] of Calais. Of which the English Council had greatly reduced the garrison, considering it as impregnable and secure from assault during the winter.

[d] In the preceding November two skilled Italian engineers, Strozzi and Delbene, had reconnoitred the town and all the forts adjacent, having gained admittance in disguise.

The Duke of Guise, having so unexpectedly captured Calais, on the 13th of the same month, marched with his army to assault the town and fort of Guisnes, situated five miles distant from thence.—Grafton.

[f] Though miserably fortified, the castle of Guisnes was most gallantly defended by Lord Grey de Wilton, who had obtained some 400 Spanish and Burgundian soldiers from the army of King Philip; but, the Spanish auxiliaries having been killed almost to a man and the walls completely shattered, the garrison forced their officers to capitulate.

Alldermen to the Queenes Councell, declaringe the povertie of the ^{A.D. 1558.}
Cittie, they brought it to xx^m ł which was levied of the Companies
of the Cittie. For which sum to be repayed the Queen bownd
certeyn landes. And allso for interest of the money xii ł of everie
hundreth for a year. Allso she demanded lyke prest in everye
shire and towne throughe all England.

About the 15 of Julie the Frenchmen that afore had gotten Dun- *Dunkirke lost and won*
kirke in Flaunders went to assaulte the towne of Gravelinge. But *agayne.*
the Flemminges prepared an armye towarde them, the counte of
Egmont beinge their head capteyn, and assaulted the Frenchmen
betwene Gravelinge and Dunkirk (certeyne of the Queenes shipps
beinge that tyme in the seas neare to the place where the Frenchmen laye, and shott out of their shipps). There were slayne of the
Frenchmen about 6 or 7 thowsand and the rest fledd, and the
towne of Dunkirke taken agayne by the Fleminges. But the
Frenchemen that were in the towne sett fyre in divers places thereof
at their departinge, and allso brent the shipps that lay in the haven.

This yeare, about September, dyed in Spayne Charles the 5th
late Emperor of Rome, and two of his sisters, wydowes; one [the]
late French Queene to Fraunces late French Kinge, and the other
Queene of Hungarie.

PHILIPPI ET MARIÆ ANNIS 5 ET 6.

Thursdaye the xviith of November, 1558, aboute sixe of the *Death of Queene*
clock in the morninge, Queene Marie died at her manor of St. James *Marie.*
by Charinge Crosse.

And that daye at xi. of the clocke in the forenoone the Ladie *Queene Elizabeth pro-*
Elizabeth, her sister next inheritor to the Crowne, was proclaymed *claymed.*
Queene of Englande, France, and Irelande, Defendor of the Faythe,
&c. in London, with herraldes of armes and trumpetors, &c.

ELIZABETHÆ. Anno 1.

Fridaye the xviiith of November Dr. Reynolde Poole, Cardinall *Death of Cardinall*
Poole.

A.D. 1558.

The Queene cometh from Hatfielde.

The Queene removeth to the Tower.

The Queene removeth to Somersett Place.

Queene Marye buried.

Obsequie for Charles the Emperoure.

[A.D. 1559.]

and Archbishopp of Canterburie, died at Lambeth, in the morninge, and was afterward buried at Canterburie, in Christes Churche.

Weddensdaye the 23 of November Queene Elizabeth came from Hatfielde to the Lord Northes howse, in the late Charter-howse in London, the sheriffes of London meetinge her Grace at the further ende of Barnett towne, within the shire of Middlesex, and so rood afore her tyll she came to Charterhowse gate, where she remayned tyll the Munday after.

Mundaye, the 28 of November, at 2 of the clock in the afternoone, the Queen rode from the Lord Northes howse, alonge the Barbycane, and in at Creple-gate, and alonge London-wall to Bishopsgate, which was richlye hanged, and where the waytes of the Cittie played, &c.

Mundaye the 5 of December the Queene departed from the Tower of London by water to her place by the Strande, called Somersett Place, at x of the clock in the fore-noone, and went throughe London bridge.

Tewsdaye, the xiiith of December, the corps of Queen Marie was honorablie caried from the mannor of St. James in the after-noone to the Abbaye in Westminster. Her picture lyeinge on the coffin apparelled in her royall roabes, and a crowne of gould on the heade. And in the Abbay was a sumptuous and riche hearse made, under which the corps stood all night. And the morrowe beinge Weddensdaye, after the masse of Requiem, the corps were caried from thence to the new chappell, where King Henry VII. lieth, and there in the side chappell, on the left hand, her corps were buried for a tyme.[a]

Saterday 24 Decembris was a solemne obsequie kept in the Abbay of Westminster for Charles the 5, late Emperoure, who died in Spayne in September last.

Sunday the 1 of Januarie the Lord Mayre and Aldermen gave

[a] She was interred on the north side of Henry VII.'s chapel with all the solemn funeral rites used by the Roman Catholic Church, but no monument was raised to her memory. Even at the present day no other memorial remains to point out the spot, except two small black tablets at the west base of the sumptuous tomb erected by order of James I. over the ashes of Elizabeth.

in commaundement to everie warde within the Cittie of London, that the parson or curate in everie parishe churche in London shoulde reade the Epistle and Gospell of the daye in the Englishe tongue in the masse tyme; and the English procession now used in the Queen's Chappell, accordinge to a proclamation sent from her Maiesty and her Privie Councell, proclaymed in the Citte of London xxx Decembris, which commaundement was that day observed in moste parishe churches of the Cittie. *Procession, epistle, and gospell in Englishe.*

Munday the ixth of January, in the morninge, the Image of Thomas Beckett, which stood over the dore of the Mercers Chappell in London toward the street, was fownd broken and cast downe, and a bill sett on the churche dore depravinge the setters up thereof. *Image of Thomas Beckett throwne downe.*

Thursday the 12 of January the Queenes Maiestie removed from her place of Whitehall to the Tower by water. *The Queen removeth by water to the Tower.*

Saterdaye the 14 of January the Queenes Maiestie at 2 of the clock in the after-noone roade from the Tower throughe the Cittie of London to her pallace at Westminster, the Londoners havinge then made sumptuouse provision of pageantes and otherwise, as hath bene accustomed. *The Queen rydeth in her chariott throughe London to her coronation.*

Sunday the 15 of January the Queenes Maiestie was with great solemnitie crowned[a] in Westminster Abbay, and after satt at dynner in Westminster hall, which was richlye hanged. *The Queenes coronation.*

Weddensdaye the 25 of January the Parlement began at Westminster; the Queenes Maiestie ridinge in her parliament robes from Whitehall to the Abbay, &c. *Parliament.*

Frydaye 17 Februarii one of the Honninges servants which was one of the takers of freshe fishe for the Queene was sett on the pillorie in Cheape, in the Fish markett, for buyinge smelts for xii d. the c. and sellinge them agayne for x d. the quarter, which punishment with more was by commaundment of the Queen by her owne mowthe appoynted, as a good example of justice. *One of the Queenes takers sett on the pillorye.*

[a] By Dr. Oglethorpe, Bishop of Carlisle, the ceremony being regulated strictly in the ancient manner, and as in the Roman Catholic times.

144   WRIOTHESLEY'S CHRONICLE.

A.D. 1559.   This yeare, in the Easter holidayes, preached at the Spittell,
Preachers at the   Dr. Byll, the Queenes Almoner, Dr. Cox, and Dr. Horne, which
Spittle and at Paules
Crosse.   two last parsons had bene in Geneva all Queen Maryes tyme.

Sunday the 2nd of Aprill, beinge Lowe-Sunday, Mr. Sampson, one of the new preachers, made the rehersall sermon at Paules Crosse. But when the Lord Mayre and Alldermen came to their places in Paules Church-yarde the pulpitt dore was locked, which was at viii of the clock in the forenoone, and could not gett the key; wherefore the Lord Mayre sent for a smyth to open the pullpett dore, which was verie vile arayde within with ordure and fylth.

Conference appoynted   Mundaye the 3 of April 1559, a daye prefixed by the Queenes
betwixt the olde   Maiesty and her Councell, the Bishopps satt in Westminster Abbaye
bishops and other
preachers.   in the Queere, where the monks satt at a table on the one syde, and the new prechers that came late over at another table againste the Bishopps; and the Queenes Councell that were judges appoynted satt at the head of the Queere at another table. But, when the Bishopps should haue delivered their booke of certeyn questions to the other parte, they were not readie, but made excuse, wherefore the Councell was sore moved, and so arose and departed. And that
Bishops committed to   night [a] Dr. White, Bishop of Winton, and Dr. Watson, Bishop of
the Tower.   Lincoln, were sent to the Tower of London.

Peace proclaymed.   Saterday the 8 of Aprill, at one of the clock in the afternoone, proclamation was made in the Cittie of London for a perpetuall peace betwixt the Queenes Maiestie, the Frenche kinge, and Scotland.

Sundaye, the ixth of Aprill, Mr. Dr. Bill preached at Paules Crosse, and redd a Bill in his sermon tyme concerninge the controversie betwene the Bishopps and the preachers that came late over out of Germanie and Geneva, towchinge their disobedience in matters of religion, as afore is declared.

Lord Wentworth ar-   Saterdaye 22 of Aprill Lord Wentforth,[b] late Deputie of Caleis,
reyned and quitt.   was arreyned in Westminster hall for treason, and was quitt by his

[a] The 5th of April.—Stow.   [b] Thomas Lord Wentworth.

peeres, the Lord Marques of Northampton sittinge under the clothe of estate that daye.

The 8 of Maye the Parliament brake up, where was a subsidie grawnted by the laitie of ii s. viii d. the £ for moveable goods.[a] *Parlement dissolved. A subsedie.*

The 14 of May, beinge Whitsonday, the service began in English in divers parishes in London, after the last booke of service of Common Prayer used in the tyme of King Edward the VI. *English service.*

Sundaye the 2 of Julie the citizens of London had a muster afore the Queens Maiestie at Greenewich, in the Parke, of 1,400 men, whereof 800 were pikemen, all in fyne corseletts; 400 harquebutts, in shirts of mayle, with morins;[b] and 200 halberters in Alman rivetts, which were furnished and sett furth by the Companies of the Cittie of London. *Citizens of London mustered at Greenwich.*

Allso about the beginnmge of this moneth of Julye all the olde Bishopps of England then beinge alive were called and examined afore the Queens Maiesties Councell; as Yorke, Ely, London, with other, to the number of xiii or xiiii. And because they refused to take the oathe towchinge the Queens Supremacie, grawnted by Act of Parlement, and other articles, they were deprived. And lykewise were divers deanes, archdeacons, parsons, and vicars deprived from their benefices, and some committed to prison in the Tower, Flecte, Marshallsie, and Kings Bench. *Bishops deprived.*

Allso this moneth the Queens Maiestie appoynted certen commissioners to ride aboute the realme for th' establishinge of true religion. For London, were appoynted Sir Richard Sakvile, knight, Dr. Horne, a devine, Dr. Huicke, a civilian, and Mr. Salvage, for the temporall lawe: who called before them divers persons of everie parishe of the Cittie, and sware them upon certen Iniunctions newlye sett owt in print. *Commissioners.*

This moneth allso, the howses of Religion erected by Queen Marye, as the moonkes of Westminster, nuns and bretheren of Sion, the *Howses suppressed*

---

[a] Stow adds: "and foure shillings of lands, to bee payd at two severall payments of euery person, spirituall and temporall."

[b] Morions were a kind of open helmet without visor or beaver, copied by the Spaniards from the Moors.

146   WRIOTHESLEY'S CHRONICLE.

A.D. 1559.

Death of the French Kinge.

Aulter and images put downe in Paules.

Churche images burned.

A tempest.

An obsequie for the French Kinge.

Black Friers in Smithfield, and the friers of Greenewich, were all suppressed.

This moneth allso tydinges were brought to the Queen that Henry, the French kinge, was dead of a hurt that he had at a triumphe in justinge at the marriage betwixt his sister, the Ladie Margarett of France, and Phillipp, Duke of Savoy, at Midsomer last in Paris.

Saterdaye the 12 of August the aulter in Paules, with the roode, and Marye and John in the rood-loft, were taken downe, and the Prebendaries and Pettie Canons commaunded to leave of the grey amises of furre, and to use onelye a surplesse in the service tyme, by the commaundement of Dr. Grindall, Bishop of London elect, and Dr. Mey, the new deane of Paules, and other of the commissioners.

This moneth allso, on the Eeven of St. Bartlemewe, the daye and the morrowe after, were burned in Paules Church-yarde, Cheape, and divers other places of London, all the roodes and images that stoode in the parishe churches. In some places the coapes, vestments, aulter clothes, bookes, banners, sepulchers, and other ornaments of the churches were burned; which cost above 2,000*l.* renuinge agayne in Queen Maries tyme.

The 5 of September there fell a 3 howres tempest in London in the forenoone, and ended at one of the clock, at the end whereof was a terrible thonder-clapp with lightninge, which by violence strake All Hallowes steeple, in Bred street, about x foote beneath the topp; out of which fell a stone that slue a dogge, and overthrue a man playinge with the same dogge. But the steeple was so perished, that there was no mendinge of it but to take it downe.

Frydaye the 8 of September was kept in Powles an obsequie for Henry the Second, late French kinge, departed, where was a riche hearse made lyke an imperiall crowne, with 8 pillers covered with black velvett, with a valence fringed with golde, and richlye hanged with scutchions, penons, and banners of the French kinges armes, without any lightes, &c.

INDEX.

Abbeville (Abireld), in Picardy, i. 9
Abley (Abell), Thomas, i. 121
Abram, John, butcher, ii. 8
Alane, John, a priest, i. 77
Aldermary, i. 142
Aldermen, Court of. *See* London
Aldersgate, ii. 6, 20, 68, 117, 118
Aldgate, London, i. 82, 94, 96, 179, 183; ii. 18, 19, 43, 92, 94, 95, 105, 112
Allen or Aleyn, Christopher, Alderman, ii. 43, 73
—— Sir John, mercer, twice Lord Mayor, i. 31, 32, 39, 161
—— John, Archbishop of Dublin, i. 26
—— John, ii. 21
—— Mrs. i. 76
All Hallows, Bread Street, ii. 77, 126, 146
—————— Barking, i. 72; ii. 136
Ambleteuse (Hamylkewe) by Boulogne, ii. 22
Amcottes, Sir Henry, Lord Mayor, ii. 6, 9, 12, 13, 15, 20, 23
Ampthill in Bedfordshire, i. 18, 126
Amsterdam, ii. 6
Anabaptists, persecution of, i. 28, 89, 90
Ancrum Moor, battle of, i. 153
Angoulême (Anguiloniæ), Edward Alexander, Duke of, ii. 65
Angus, Earl of. *See* Douglas
Annebaut (Denybowte), Claude d', Admiral of France, i. 171-173
Antwerp, i. 136; ii. 67, 77
Apprentices of London, insurrection of, i. 11
Arches, Court of, i. 130
Argile, Mr. ii. 137
Arnold, Captain of Bullenberg, near Boulogne, ii. 11
Arras, cloth of, ii. 28

Arthur, Prince, i. 1, 5, 6, 18, 34
Articles, book of, i. 54, 65
Arundel, Earl of. *See* Fitzalan, Henry and William
—————— Humphrey, ii. 30, 32
—————— Sir Thomas, ii. 57, 66, 67
Ashley, William, i. 132
Aske, Robert, i. 57, 58, 63, 65
Askew, Anne, alias Keyme Anne, i. 155, 167, 168, 169
Audley, Mr. John, i. 84
Audley, Sir Thomas, Lord Audley, Lord Chancellor, i. 3, 33, 34, 36, 37, 41, 45, 47, 48, 50, 62-64, 78, 90, 91, 94, 96, 98, 99, 115, 123, 125, 126, 147
Augmentation, Court of, i. 112, 154
Aylesbury, ii. 21
Ayliffe, Sir John, Alderman and Master of Bakewell Hall, ii. 5, 9, 40, 84
Ayton (Hemitton), laird of. *See* Home

Baker, Sir John, Attorney-General, i. 50, 136, 187; ii. 27, 89
—— Mr., Recorder of London, i. 19
—— Roger, ii. 21
Bakewell, or Black-well, Hall, ii. 5, 40
Baldwin, Sir John, Chief Justice of Common Pleas, i. 161, 168
Ballard, Nicholas, ii. 52, 64
Balthasar, a surgeon, ii. 34
Banester, Mr. ii. 58
Bangor, Bishop of. *See* Salcot, John; Bird, John
Barbican, ii. 142
Barford, co. Oxford, ii. 21
Barker, Sir Christopher, Garter, i. 178
—— Nicholas, i. 127

INDEX.

Barking in Essex, i. 72, 132; ii. 136
Barking Abbey, i. 108
Barkley, Dr. i. 82
Barlow, Dr. Bishop of St David's, ii. 1
Barnes, George, Alderman, Sheriff, and Lord Mayor, i. 155; ii. 77, 93
────── Dr. Robert, i. 72, 81, 83, 114, 120, 121
────── his works to be burnt, i. 169
Barnet, Middlesex, ii. 142
Bartholomew Fair, i. 85; ii. 21
Barton, Elizabeth, called the Holy Maid of Kent, i. 23, 24, 85
Basiley, i. 169
Basill, Theodore. *See* Beacon, Thomas
Bath, Bishop of. *See* Clerk, John
Bath, Earl of. *See* Bourchier, John
Battle Abbey in Sussex, i. 82
Battle Bridge, ii. 42, 55
Bayfield, burnt for heresy, i. 17
Baynam, burnt for heresy, i. 17
Baynard Castle, i. 4, 99,151; ii. 88
Baynton, Lady, wife of Sir Edward, i. 131
Beach King, the, i. 44
Beacon, Thomas, *alias* Basill, Theodore, i. 142
Beauchamp's Tower at Windsor Castle, ii. 27
Beauchamp, Viscount. *See* Seymour, Sir Edward
Beaulieu, sanctuary at, i. 3
Becket, Thomas à, image of, ii. 127, 143
Bedingfield (Benyfield), Sir Henry, ii. 116
Bedington, Surrey, ii. 49
Bedyll (John), ii. 135
Bell, Dr. John, Bishop of Worcester, i. 103
Bell, sign of the, in Newgate Market, ii. 6
Belle Savage, ii. 111
Bennet, John, i. 132
────── Margaret, i. 132
Berkwaye. *See* Berkeley
Bermondsey, St. Saviour's Abbey, i. 77
────── monks of, i. 32
Bermondsey (Barnesey) Street, ii. 13
Berwick Park in Essex, ii. 67
Bery, a rebel, ii. 30, 32
Bethlehem (Betchlem Bridge), i. 122
Bethnal Green, ii. 87
Bevis Marks, ii. 16

Bible, the, i. 74; act restricting the reading of, i. 145; in French, i. 184
Biéz, Oudart du (M. le Bees), Governor of Boulogne, i. 152, 165
Bigod, Sir Francis, i. 60, 63, 64
Bill, William, Master of St. John's College and Almoner to Queen Elizabeth, ii. 14, 144
Billingsgate, ii. 37, 47, 72, 105, 110, 112
Bilney or Bylney, Thomas, burnt for heresy, i. 16
Birchin Lane, ii. 61
Bird, John, Bishop of Bangor, i. 106
Bishopsgate, i. 134, 138; ii. 20, 61, 90, 100, 101, 112, 142
Blackfriars, i. 169; ii. 87, 146
Blackheath, i. 12, 111; ii. 108; battle of i. 3
Blackness by Boulogne, ii. 22
Blackwall, i. 172
Blage, George, i. 169, 170
Blake, Thomas, Alderman, i. 134
Blanck Chappeltone. *See* Whitechapel
Bletchingly (Brenchingley), Surrey, ii. 49
Blount, Gertrude, Marchioness of Exeter, i. 88, 102
Blount or Blunt, Eliz. *See* Talboys
Bockinge, Dr. i. 24
Body, William, ii. 4
Boleyn, Anne, Queen of Henry VIII. i. 17-42, 101; created Marchioness of Pembroke, i. 17, 18; proclaimed Queen, *ib.*; her coronation, i. 20-22; brought to bed of a fair daughter, 22; her miscarriage, i. 33; committed to the Tower, i. 36; her household at Greenwich broken up, i. 37; arraigned for treason, i. 37-39; beheaded, i. 41; her dying declaration, i. 41, 42; buried in the chapel in the Tower, i. 42; reported to have poisoned Henry Fitz-Roy, i. 53
────── Sir Thomas, Earl of Wiltshire, i. 20, 49
────── George, Lord Rochford, i. 35, 36, 39, 40, 53; his widow. *See* Rochford, Lady
────── Lady, i. 38
Bonner, Dr. Edmund, Bishop of London, i. 123, 132, 164, 168; ii. 24, 33, 96, 97, 98, 114, 122, 124, 125, 129, 132, 133, 136, 145

INDEX. 149

Bonvise, Anthony, ii. 34
Boom (Bawmes), near Antwerp, ii. 77
Boroughe, Lord. *See* Burgh, Thomas, Lord
Borough, the, added to the City of London, ii. 41
Bothe, footman to Queen Mary, hanged, ii. 111
Boulogne (Bulleine), i. 149, 152, 156, 157, 160, 161, 165, 166, 173, 174; ii. 11, 22, 31, 37, 39; base, i. 156, 157; Old Man at, i. 157; ii. 22
Bourbon, Charles, Duke of, Constable of France, i. 14
Bourchier, Henry, Earl of Essex, i. 21, 68, 113
———— John, Lord Fitz-Warine, created Earl of Bath, i. 51
Bourne, Dr. Gilbert, prebendary of St. Paul's, ii. 97, 98, 104
Bowdley, St. Marie. *See* Beaulieu
Bowell, Sir William, priest, i. 176
Bower, Alderman, i. 127
Bowes, Sir Martin, Lord Mayor, i. 123, 163, 167; ii. 12, 23, 43, 55, 91, 102
———— Sir Robert, ii. 71
Bowling-alleys and playhouses at Paul's Wharf, ii. 43
Bowyer, Sir William, Lord Mayor, i. 146, 147
Boxley, abbey of, i. 74, 75
Brabant, i. 136, 174 ; ii. 67, 130
Bradford, John, a preacher, ii. 97, 126, 129, 138
Bradshaw, Mr. the King's attorney, ii. 70
Bramston, Mr. ii. 93
Branch *alias* Flower, William, ii. 127, 128
Brandon, Charles, Viscount Lisle, 1513, 4th Duke of Suffolk, 1514, married as his third wife, Mary Tudor, sister of Henry VIII. and Dowager of Louis XII. 1515, Great Master of the Household, 1540-45; Lord President, 1540-45; died 22 August, 1545; i. 14, 16, 18, 21, 22, 34, 37, 38, 41, 46, 50, 56, 67, 68, 80, 96, 98, 131-133, 151, 154, 160; ii. 85
———— Charles, brother of Henry, Duke of Suffolk, ii. 50
———— Henry, 5th Duke of Suffolk, ii. 50
Bread Street, i. 128, 135; ii. 4, 8, 42, 43, 77, 118, 126, 131, 146

Breme, Mr. i. 117
Bremen (Bremberland), i. 147, 156; ii 30
Brentford (Braynforde), ii. 110
Brereton, William, i. 36, 39, 40
Brett or Bright, Capt. ii. 112
Bridewell in Fleet Street (royal palace), i. 13; ii. 83, 106
Bridgehouse, the, ii. 12, 18, 40
Bridg Ward in the City, ii. 40
Bridlington, Prior of, i. 63, 64
Brighton (Brighthelmston), i. 157
Bristol (Bristowe), i. 104; ii. 13, 44; haven, i. 7; mint at, ii. 7
Brittany in France, i. 2, 157, 160; ii. 47
Brochty-Crag (Burthecragge), ii. 31
Broken Wharf, ii. 10
Bromley (Brambe), Sir Thomas, Chief Justice of the King's Bench, ii. 101
Brooke, Sir David, Chief Baron of the Exchequer, ii. 101, 103
———— George, Lord Cobham, ii. 64, 89, 110, 111
———— Richard, ii. 84
———— Robert, Recorder of London, and Speaker of the Commons House, i. 162, 168; ii. 77, 114
Browne, Sir Anthony, Viscount Montague, i. 115, 177, 179; ii. 94, 133
———— Sir Humphrey, i. 155 ; ii. 12, 84
———— John, sheriff, ii. 73, 74, 75, 84
———— sergeant at law, i. 116
Bruges, ii. 166
Brussels, ii. 130
Brygges (Bruges), Sir John, Lieutenant of the Tower, ii. 94
———— Thomas, ii. 94
Bryndholme, Edmond, i. 121
Buckden (Bugden), in Hunts, i. 33
Buckingham, Duchess of, i. 84
———— Duke of. *See* Stafford, Edward
Bucklersbury (Brykerbery), ii. 67, 109
Bugden. *See* Buckden
Bulbeck or Bolebec, Lord. *See* Vere, John de, Earl of Oxford
Bullenberg (Bulleine Barke), fortress by Boulogne, ii. 11, 22
Bulmer (Bolner), Sir John, i. 63, 64
———— Ralph, his son, i. 63
———— Lady. *See* Cheney, Margaret
Bures, Mistris, i. 83
Burgart, Francis, Vice-Chancellor of Saxony, i. 81

150 INDEX

Burgh or Borough, Thos. Lord, i. 20
Burgundian (Burgonian) fashion, i. 117
Burgundians (Burgonions), ii. 139
Bury St. Edmund's, Abbey, i. 108
Bush, Richard, goldsmith, i. 176
Butcher (Bocher), *alias* Barne, Joan *alias* Joan of Kent, ii. 37

Calais (Callis), i. 2, 61, 115, 121, 126, 142, 148, 160; ii. 130, 138, 144
—— Staple of, i. 104; ii. 130, 140
—— taken by the French, ii. 140
Calveley, Sir Hugh, i. 169
Cambridge, ii. 14, 50, 90
Campeggio, Cardinal, his reception in London, i. 12
Candlewick Ward, ii. 63
Canterbury, i. 86, 109
—————— Priory of St. Sepulchre at, i. 24
—————— Christ Church, i. 24; ii. 142
—————— St. Austen's Abbey at, i. 86, 109
—————— Archbishop of. *See* Cranmer
Cap of maintenance, presented to Henry VII. i. 2
Capon, a Florentine, i. 122
Cardmaker, John, *alias* Taylor, vicar of St. Bride's and Chancellor of Wells, ii. 3, 126, 129
Carew, Charles, i. 121
—— Gawen, ii. 108
—— Peter, ii. 108
—— Sir George, i. 117, 158
—— Lady, i. 121
—— Sir Nicholas, i. 93
Carlisle, i. 137, 140
Carmarthen (Karmarden), Lord of. *See* Herbert, Sir William
Carmichaell (Carmell), John, Captain of Crawford Castle, i. 139
Carpenter, Gregory, blacksmith, ii. 136
Carter, an Irishman, ii. 11
Carter Lane, ii. 107
Cassilis (Castell and Cassells), Earl of. *See* Kennedy, Gilbert
Castile, King of. *See* Philip, Archduke
—— Queen of. *See* Juana
Casymghurst, John, i. 150

Catharine of Arragon, fourth daughter of Ferdinand II. King of Spain, married first, 1501, to Prince Arthur; and, secondly, 1509, to Henry VIII. i. 4-6, 18, 43, 51, 67; crowned, i. 6; divorced, 17, 18; dies, 33
Catharine Parr, widow of Lord Latimer, and Queen of Henry VIII. i. 143, 173, 174
Catharine, infant daughter of Henry VII. i. 5
Cavendish (Candishe), Sir Edmund, ii. 27
Cawston, Thomas, burnt, ii. 127
Chadsey, Dr. prebendary of St. Paul's, ii. 124
Chaliner, Mr. Clerk of the Council, ii. 26
Chamberlain, Mr. ii. 116
—————— Sir Leonard, Lieutenant of the Tower, ii. 25, 33, 116
—————— Sir Robert, beheaded, i. 2
Champagne, province of France, i. 120
Champnes, an Anabaptist, ii. 10
Chancery, Court of, i. 179, 187; ii. 129, 130
—— Lane, i. 179
Chapel, Thomas, ii. 71
Chapman, a yeoman of the Guard, i. 125
Charing Cross, i. 96, 135; ii. 19, 63, 105, 110, 111, 123, 125, 128, 141
Charles V. Emperor of Germany, i. 14, 60, 97-99, 142, 143, 145; ii. 35, 105, 106, 120, 125, 130, 132, 134, 141, 142
—— visits England, i. 13
—— his ambassadors, i. 44, 98, 99; ii. 36, 105, 184
—— solemn obit at St. Paul's for his wife, i. 97-99
Charter House in London, i. 27, 29, 34, 88, 95, 121, 184, 185; ii. 142
—————— late prior of. *See* Houghton, John
—————— the Mount beside, i. 95
—————— of Sheen. *See* Richmond, Surrey
Cheapside, i. 11, 12, 19, 59, 67, 95, 149, 150, 153, 164, 165, 178; ii. 4, 8, 27, 42, 54, 61, 77, 79, 80, 86, 88, 106, 112, 113, 114, 127, 134, 136, 143, 146
—— cross in, i. 1, 13; ii. 61, 88, 112, 114, 117, 122
Cheeke, Sir John, ii. 91

INDEX.

Chekin, parson. *See* Southwood, Thomas
Chelsea, Middlesex, i. 43, 83
Cheney, Margaret, Lady Bulmer, i. 63, 64
Cheney, Sir Thos. Lord Warden of the Cinque Ports, i. 94, 167
Chersey, Robert, Alderman, ii. 47
Cheshire, i. 93, 156
Chessher, Thomas, his maid murdered, i. 137
Chester, William, draper, ii. 76
Chichester, Bishop of. *See* Day, Heath, and Sampson
———— Chancellor of. *See* Crofte, Dr.
Chidley, Mr. ii. 12
Cholmeley, Sir Roger, Recorder of London, and Chief Baron of the Exchequer, i. 93, 128, 162, 165, 168; ii. 8, 12, 70, 91, 103
Christ Church, Canterbury, ii. 142
Christ Church or Creechurch in London, ii. 16, 42, 130, 147, 178
Christ's Church, Norwich, Abbey of, i. 82
Christ's Hospital, ii. 79, 80, 82, 94, 130
Church, hanged, ii. 20
Church goods, seized, ii. 83
Church, Roman Catholic, i. 79
Cinque Ports, Lord Warden of the, ii. 64, 71, 89; *and See* their names
———— Lords of the, i. 19, 21
Clarence, Duke of. *See* Plantagenet, George
Clarencieux King-at-arms, i. 165, 178; ii. 26
Clayton, Thos. baker, ii. 72, 73
Cleere, Mr. of Norfolk, i. 125
Clement, Dr. ii. 34; his daughter, ii. 34
Clerk, John, Bishop of Bath, i. 99, 103
Clerkenwell, i. 85; ii. 139; Benedictine Nunnery at, i. 105
Clerks, Wardens of the, ii. 49
Cleves, Anne of, Queen of Henry VIII. i. 109-112, 117-119; ii. 103, 138
Cleves, John, Duke of, i. 109, 119
———— William, Duke of, i. 145
Clifford, Edward, i. 85
Clink, the, i. 115
Clinton, Edward de, Earl of Lincoln, Lord High Admiral, i. 117; ii. 65
Cobbler, Captain, i. 56
Cobham, Lord. *See* Brooke, George
Coffin, Mr. i. 69

Coinage, the, i. 15; ii. 48, 50, 54, 58, 59, 102
Cokerell, Dr. i. 63
Colchester, i. 90; ii. 12; Abbot of, 108, 109
Coldharbour, ii. 65
Coleman Street, i. 135, 175; ii. 27
Coligny, Gaspard de, Seigneur de Châtillon. Admiral of France and Ambassador to England, ii. 39
Collins burnt, i. 119
———— Mr. i. 137; ii. 73
Commissioners, Ecclesiastical, or Visitors, seize church goods, ii. 83, 84
Common Prayer, Book of, ii. 9, 78, 79, 97, 145; called the King's Book, ii. 17, 18, 23
Commons' House of Parliament, ii. 82, 114; *and see* Parliament
Connisbie or Conesby, Edmond, i, 84, 116
Constable. Sir Robert, i. 63, 65
———— William. *See* Featherstone, William
Convocation, i. 47, 52, 55, 65, 94, 101, 133, 187; ii. 82, Act of, 52
Cooper. *See* Cowper, John
Cootes, John, Lord Mayor, i. 137, 140
Corbell, near Paris, i. 174
Corbett, Robert, ii. 91
Corier, Monsr. ii. 106
Corn, importation of, i. 147, 156; ii. 37, 45, 47
Cornhill, i. 72, 95, 96, 164, 165, 181, 187; ii 1, 8, 71
Cornwall, co. i. 3; ii. 14, 15, 32
Cottisford (Cottesfurth), S. T. P. ii. 40
Cotton, Sir Richard, ii. 71, 89, 92
Coulogne (Columme), near Calais, i. 61
Council, the King's, or Lords, i. 74, 76, 80, 81, 134-137, 149, 151, 153, 159, 167, 170, 178, 179, 185; ii. 24, 25, 28, 29, 31-36, 42, 48, 50, 57-59, 64-67, 70, 77, 82-89, 96, 98-100, 106, 107, 112, 115-119, 122, 124, 125, 128, 141, 144, 145
———— Clerk of the. *See* Mason, Sir John
Councils, General, i. 52, 53
Counter Prisons, i. 76, 109, 128; ii. 8, 42, 43, 53, 54, 68, 71, 86, 112, 126, 131
Court, the, i. 3, 113, 135, 140, 145; *and see* names of places where resident
Court-at-Street, in the parish of Lympne, Kent, i. 23

152   INDEX.

Courtenay, Edward, afterwards Earl of Devonshire, ii. 95-98, 102, 106, 113, 116, 128
Courtenay, Henry, Earl of Devon and Marquis of Exeter, i. 62, 88, 91, 92, 101, 102 ; his children, 102
Coventry, insurrection in, i. 14
Coverdale, Miles, ii. 14 ; his works to be burnt. i. 169
Cowper or Cooper, John, sheriff, ii. 54, 66
Cox, Dr. Richard, almoner and preceptor of Edward VI. Dean of Westminster, ii. 4, 96, 144
Crane, Mr. ii. 57 ; his wife, *ibid.*
Crane, the, in the Vintry, ii. 33, 63, 109
Cranmer, Thomas, Archbishop of Canterbury, i. 20, 21, 23, 24, 33, 34, 40, 45, 48, 67, 71, 74, 78, 81, 95, 97, 99, 109, 179, 184; ii. 11-13, 14, 16, 17, 20, 24, 34, 37, 45, 46, 47, 89, 103 ; his arraignment, ii. 104; degraded, ii. 133; burnt. ii. 134
Cratwell, the hangman of London hanged, i. 85
Crawford Castle, Captain of. *See* Carmichaell
Cripplegate, i. 2, 161 ; ii. 16, 110, 112, 142
Crofte, Dr. chancellor of Chichester, i. 91, 92
—— Elizabeth, ii. 117
—— Sir James, ii. 115
—— Sir William, ii. 95
Crome (Cromer) Dr. Edward, i. 101, 142, 166, 167, 169
Cromer, Dr. George, archbishop of Armagh, i. 72
Crowe, Giles, i. 150
Croydon (Crowden), in Surrey, ii. 42, 49
Crumwell, Gregory, son of Thos. Lord Crumwell, i. 96, 117
—— Sir Richard, *alias* Williams, nephew of Thos. Lord Crumwell, i. 96, 117, 118, 119
—— Sir Thomas. Lord Crumwell, 1536-40 ; Earl of Essex, 1540 ; attainted and beheaded, June 1540, i. 26, 31, 36, 49, 51, 52, 55, 65, 83, 85-87, 95, 96, 98, 115, 117, 119, 120
Crutched Friars, or Crossed Friars, on Tower Hill, i. 59, 65, 69, 179; *and see* Tower Hill

Culpepper, Thos. i. 73, 118, 131, 132
Cunningham, Wm. Earl of Glencairn, i. 138
Curfew-bell discontinued, ii. 49
Curson, Sir William, a baron of the exchequer, ii. 12
Curteis, Thomas, alderman, i. 170 ; ii. 47, 66

Dacre, William Lord, i. 25
Dacre of the South, Lord.   *See* Fienes, Thomas
Damport, Robert, i. 133
Daniell, John, executed, ii. 136
Danzig (Danske), i. 147, 156 ; ii. 30, 45
D'Arcy, George, Lord, ii. 64, 89
—— Thomas, Lord, i. 57, 62, 65
—— Sir Thomas, Captain of the Guard, ii. 33
Darington and his wife, i. 135
Dartford, i. 110, 122
Daunce, Henry, i. 82, 93
Davenett, Ralph, merchant, ii. 52
Davenport, a Yeoman of the Guard, i. 125
David, King.   *See* Psalms of
Davie, Margaret, boiled in Smithfield, i. 134
—— Mr. ii. 73
Day, Dr. George, Bishop of Chichester, ii. 55, 97
—— John, parson of St. Ethelberga, Bishopsgate Street, ii. 100, 101
—— Thomas, i. 156
Deacon, Richard, i. 150
Dean of the Arches. *See* Quent, Dr.
Dee, Rowland, mercer, ii. 91
Degavaro, Balthazar, ii. 32
—— Charles, ii. 32
Denham, Sir William, i. 133, 137
Denis, Sir Thomas, i. 108 ; his wife, Lady Murffen, *ibid.*
Denybowte, Admiral of France. *See* Annebaut
Deptford, ii. 108
—— Strand, near Greenwich, i. 154, 172
Derby, Earl of. *See* Stanley, Edward
Derbyshire, i. 156 ; ii. 74
Derham (Dorand), Francis i. 131, 132

INDEX. 153

Derike, *alias*, Dedike, or Dethick (John) executed, ii. 135
Desalvaron, Michael, ii. 32
Desalvasto, or Devalesco, Francis, ii. 32
Desmond, Earl of. *See* Fitzgerald, James
Devereux, Lord Ferrers, ii. 103
Devonshire, co. of, ii. 15, 20, 30, 32, 68
——— Earl of. *See* Courtney, Edward
Dieppe (Deepe), i. 157, 171
Dingley, Thos. a knight of Rhodes, i. 101
Divelyn, Bishop of. *See* Dublin.
Dobbs, Richard, Alderman, ii. 55
Domer, Mr. ii. 25
Done-a-Brune. *See* O'Brien, Sir Donough
Dordrecht in Holland, ii. 70
Dormer, Sir Michael, Lord Mayor, i. 133
Dorphin (Dolphin) of France, i. 167, 174
Dorset, Marchioness of, i, 23
Douglas, Archibald, Sixth Earl of Angus, i. 54
——— Lady Margaret marries Lord Thomas Howard, i. 48, 54, 70, 110; ii. 60
Dover, i. 109, 149, 159, 160; ii. 130, 137
——— Castle, i. 109
Downs. the, i. 3
Drake, John, ii. 117
Drought and Pestilence in England, i. 123
Dublin, Archbishop of. *See* Allen, John
Dudley, Lord Ambrose, ii. 91, 104
——— Sir Andrew, ii. 91, 99
——— Edmund, beheaded i. 7
——— Lord Guildford, fourth son of the Duke of Northumberland, and husband of Lady Jane Grey, ii. 85, 91, 104, 111
——— Lord Henry, ii. 91, 104, 135
——— John, Viscount Lisle, Earl of Warwick, Duke of Northumberland, Lord High Admiral, and Lord Great Chamberlain, i. 117, 118, 160, 174, 177, 182; ii. 21, 22, 24, 28, 32, 33, 41, 42, 48, 56, 60, 61, 64, 65, 69, 71, 85, 87, 90, 91, 96, 99, 100, 106
——— Lord Robert, Earl of Leicester, ii. 91, 106
Dungannon (Dunsane), Lord. *See* O'Neill, Matthew
Dunkirk, ii. 141

Dunne, Angel, i. 108
Dunsane, Lord. *See* Dungannon, Lord
Dunstable, ii. 74
Dunstall, Dr. *See* Tunstall, Cuthbert
Durham, mint at, ii. 13
——— Bishop of. *See* Ruthal, Thomas, and Tunstall, Dr. Cuthbert
Durham Place, in the Strand, i, 117; ii. 39, 105
Dutchmen burnt for heresy, i. 28, 90
Dyer, Clement, i. 135
Dyer, Sir James, Speaker of the Commons' House, ii. 82
Dymmock, Sir Edward, i. 183

Easing Spitel, i. 133
Eastcheap, ii. 48
Easterlings, a company of merchants, i. 153
Edinburgh, i. 186
Edling, John, i. 162; his wife, Johan, *ibid*.
Edward VI. born 12 Oct. 1537, i 66-69, 178, *et seq.*; ii. 1-86; his establishment when Prince of Wales at Enfield, i. 140; receives the High Admiral of France, i. 173; proclaimed King, i. 178; his coronation, i. 180, 182; grants a general pardon, ii. 9; establishes uniformity of service in the Church of England, ii. 9; his reception of Mary of Guise, queen of James V. ii. 60; his death, ii. 85, 86, 88; obsequy for, ii. 96, 97; mentions of, ii. 102, 133, 134, 145
Edward the Confessor, his sceptre, i. 46; called St. Edward, i. 66
Egerton, Ralph, of London, i. 123
Egmont, Count (Coutie de Augmonte), ii. 105, 141
Egypt, the Mamaluke Sultan of Egypt defeated by Selim I. i. 11
Elizabeth, Queen of England, daughter of Henry VIII. and Queen Anne Boleyn, born 7 Sept. 1533, i. 22, 23, 68; ii. 88, 92, 94, 103, 113, 141-146; committed to the Tower, ii. 116; received at Court, ii 128; proclaimed Queen, ii. 141, 142; crowned ii. 143
Elizabeth of York, Queen of Henry VII. i. 1; her death, i. 5
Ellerkar (Elderkar), Sir Ralph, i. 60

CAMD. SOC. x

154 INDEX.

Ely Abbey, ii. 128
Ely, Bishop of. *See* Thirlby, Thomas, West, Nicholas
Emperor, the. *See* Maximilian I. 1493-1519, Charles V. 1519-1558.
Empson, Sir Richard, beheaded, i. 7
Enfield, Prince Edward's establishment at, i. 140
England, Church of, i. 65, 185; ii. 86; Henry VIII. takes the title of Supreme Head of, i. 26, 52, 55; uniformity of service in, ii. 9
Erith i. 122
Erskine (Herskin), John, twelfth lord, i. 138
Essex, county of, ii. 15, 18, 19, 61, 92, 127, 134
———— Earl of. *See* Bourchier, Henry; Cromwell, Sir Thomas; Parr, Sir William
Eton College, i. 181
Eure (Evers), Sir Ralph, slain, i. 153
———— Sir William, Lord Eure, slain, i. 153
Evangelists, the, i. 78
Exchequer, the, i. 144, 154, 155, 162, 171, 179
———— Barons of the, i. 109, 179
Exeter, ii. 15, 20, 108
———— Bishop of. *See* Voysey John
———— Marchioness of, i. 23, 68; ii. 94, 98; *and see* Blount, Gertrude
———— Marquis of. *See* Courtenay, Henry
Exmew, Mr. or Exmouth, Thomas de, i. 28

Farmar, Richard, arraigned, i. 119
Farnham, i. 158, 159
Farringdon Without, Ward of, ii. 43
———— Within, Ward of, ii. 47, 50
Fawlkes, Anthony, ii. 79
Featherstone, Richard, i. 120, 121
———— William, *alias* Constable, simulates Edward VI. ii. 129, 133, 134
Feckenham, Dr. John, Dean of St. Paul's, and Abbot of Westminster, ii. 114, 136
Feiry (Farye), John, mercer, sheriff, i. 104
Fenchurch Street, ii. 94
Ferdinand II. King of Spain, father of Queen Catherine, i. 4

Ferrars (Ferris), George, lord of merry disports at the court, i. 135 ; ii. 80
———— Lord. *See* Devereux
Filicirga, Captain, an Italian, ii. 31
Fines, Sir Thomas, Lord Dacre, i. 125, 126
Finsbury Court, ii. 4
———— Fields, i. 159, 162, 175, 186; ii. 54, 55, 110, 139
First Fruits and Tenths, ii. 130
Fish Market in Cheapside, ii. 143
Fish Street, i. 141, 164; ii. 8, 52
Fisher, Henry, ii. 44
———— Dr. John, Bishop of Rochester and Chancellor of Cambridge University, i. 24, 25; his trial and execution, i. 28, 29
Fitzalan, Henry, Lord Maltravers, and Earl of Arundel, i. 154, 177; ii. 33, 62, 79, 89, 90, 91, 92, 94, 105
———— William, Earl of Arundel, i. 21
Fitzgerald, Gerald, ninth Earl of Kildare, dies in the Tower, i. 25, 26, 30, 61; his son. *See* Fitzgerald, Thomas
———— James, fifteenth Earl of Desmond, i. 136
———— (Garratt), Thos. Earl of Kildare, i. 30, 61, 77; made prisoner and committed to the Tower, i. 26
Fitz-James, Richard, Bishop of London, i. 9, 12
Fitz-Roy, Henry, Duke of Richmond, natural son of Henry VIII. i. 41, 45, 53, 54
Fitz-Walter, Lord. *See* Ratcliffe, Thomas
Fitz-Warine (Fitz-Waren), the Lord. *See* Bourchier, John
Fitzwilliam, Sir William, Earl of Southampton, i. 37, 68, 98
Fitzwilliams, William, merchant taylor, i. 5
Flanders, i. 116, 174; ii. 45, 93, 118, 141
Fleet-bridge, in Fleet Street, ii. 68
Fleet prison, i. 152; ii. 56, 66, 115, 145
Fleet Street, London, i. 59, 165, 178
———— ii. 3, 50, 68, 83, 111, 112
Fleetwood, Mr. i. 123
Fleming, Malcolm, third Lord, i. 138, 186
Flodden Field, in which battle James IV. was slain, i. 8
Forman, Sir William, Lord Mayor, i. 98, 99, 152

INDEX. 155

Forrest, Dr. John, i. 78, 79, 80
Fortescue (Foskewe), Sir Adrian, i. 101
Foster Lane, i. 184; ii. 117
Fotheringay Castle, ii. 116
Founsing Besse, ii. 4
Fountains, abbot of. *See* Thurst, William
Fox, Edward, Archdeacon of Leicester and Provost of King's College, made bishop of Hereford, i. 30
——, John, parson of St. Mary Magdalen, i. 185
France, i. 1, 2, 8, 9, 10, 107, 116, 120, 148, 151, 155, 157, 160, 163, 166, 167, 173, 174, 182, 184, 185; ii. 37, 39, 40, 59, 65, 108, 138, 139
——, Admiral of. *See* Annebaut, Claude d'
——, ambassadors from, i. 51, 52, 98, 184
——, king of. *See* Louis XII., Francis I., and Henry II.
Francis I. king of France, i. 10, 14, 32, 60, 66, 98, 99, 120, 142, 143, 156, 157, 160, 165, 167, 171, 173, 174, 183, 184
——, his widow, ii. 141
——, his ambassadors, i. 98, 99
Framlingham in Norfolk, ii. 122
Francke, Edward, executed, i. 2
Frankleyn, William, Dean of Windsor, i. 181
Friars Observants, the, at Greenwich, ii. 128, 134
——, White, Black, and Grey, of London, i. 129
Friday Street, ii. 77
Frith, John, burnt, i. 22
——, his works to be burnt, i. 168

Gadarn Darvell, or Gatheren, David, i. 80
Gage, Sir John, Constable of the Tower, and Chamberlain to Queen Mary, i. 139, 179; ii. 28, 94, 107, 122
Gambolde (Gambo) Sir Peter, ii. 31
Gardiner, Stephen, bishop of Winchester, i. 99, 113, 114, 115, 136, 155; ii. 3, 4, 45, 95, 96, 97, 101, 103, 114, 115, 119, 120, 122, 124-126, 132, 133
Garrard (Garrett and Jerrard) Thos, parson of Honey Lane, i. 114, 121
——, Lord Thomas. *See* Fitzgerald Lord Thomas

Garrard, William, Alderman, ii. 76, 86, 89, 91, 92
Garter Knight-at-Arms, ii. 28, 69, 88
Garter, Order of the, ii. 121
Gatehouse, prison in Westminster, ii. 127
Gates, Henry, ii. 91, 99
——, Sir John, ii. 91, 99, 100
——, William, ii. 21
Gedyworth. *See* Jedworth
Gelderland, i. 136
Geneva, ii. 144
Germany (Dutchland) i. 81, 109; ii. 105, 144, 145
Gibbes, ii. 108
Gibson, Mr. a surgeon, i. 76
Gifford, Sir George, ii. 123
Glastonbury, abbots of, i. 108, 109
Glencairn (Glainekarne, *alias* Lord Kilmayre) Earl of. *See* Cunningham, William
Godsalve, John, i. 129
Godston, Surrey, ii. 49
Goodrick, Dr. Thomas, bishop of Ely, ii. 65, 66, 81; Lord Chancellor, ii. 89
Goodyere, Alderman, ii. 15, 16
Gostife, Mr. the king's sergeant, i. 31
Gracechurch in London, conduit at, i. 2
——, or (Gracious) Street, ii. 8, 94
Grafton, Richard, ii. 52, 84
Graham, John, fourth Earl of Monteith, i. 139
Granado, Jakes, ii. 5
Gravelines in France, ii. 141
Gravesend, i. 110, 159, 172; ii. 107
Gray, Alice, i. 24
——, Mr. i. 116
——, (Gragie) Patrick, fifth Lord, i. 138
Graydon (Greaden), laird of. *See* Ker, Robert
Gray's Inn, i. 57; ii. 77
Great St. Bartholomew's in Smithfield, ii. 134
Great Zacharie, the, of Dieppe, i. 171, 172
Greenwich, i. 2, 4, 10, 13, 17, 18, 23, 25, 35, 37, 44, 59, 110-112, 122, 124, 125, 135, 140, 154, 167, 171, 172; ii. 19, 36, 40, 48, 69, 76, 80, 83, 85, 108, 128, 130, 134, 145, 146
Gresham, Sir John, ii. 8, 27, 43, 55
——, (Gressame), Sir Richard, Lord Mayor, i. 67, 71, 77, 80, 124, 130, 162, 176; ii. 8

INDEX.

Grey (Graie), Lady Elizabeth, i. 78
—— Friars, the, i. 82, 177; ii. 76, 79
—— Henry, Marquis of Dorset and Duke of Suffolk, i. 78, 98; ii. 5, 56, 60, 71, 89, 91, 92, 108, 110-113, 115, 117
—— Thomas, fifth Marquis of Dorset, i. 78
——, Lady Jane, proclaimed Queen, ii. 85, 86, 91, 104, 111
——, Lord John, ii. 5, 28, 32, 110, 117
——, Lord Thomas, ii. 115, 117
——, Lord Leonard, son of the Marquis of Dorset, takes the Earl of Kildare prisoner, i. 30, 125
—, Thomas, Marquis of Dorset, i. 125
—, William, Lord, i. 21; ii. 56, 101, 140
—, William, of Reading, ii. 28, 34
Grindall, Edmond, bishop of London, ii. 146
Grocers' Hall, the, i, 155
Grove, Roger, sheriff, i. 6
Gryg, the false prophet, ii. 42
Grymes, John, sheriff, ii 71, 72, 76
——, Richard, ii. 54, 92
Guard, the, ii. 27, 33
Guildford (Gilford) i. 160
Guildhall in the City, i. 2, 5, 11, 16, 31, 62, 127, 128, 129, 131, 141, 146, 152, 155, 162, 167, 169, 171, 175, 176, 177, 178, 184; ii. 6, 7, 15, 21, 24, 25, 26, 29, 32, 40, 48, 51, 52, 57, 62, 70, 71, 75, 79, 84, 93, 98, 104, 106, 107, 108, 115, 116, 133, 135
—————— Chapel, i. 23, 43, 55, 59, 77
Guisnes (Guynes), i. 142; ii. 101, 140
Gunston, Mr. his sons, i. 126
Gynning, Darby, i. 121

Hackney, Middlesex, i. 51, 162
Hadlam or Adlams, John, i. 167
Hadleigh (Hadley), i. 83
Hadley, parson of. *See* Taylor, Dr.
Haies, Thomas, Chamberlain of the City, ii. 5, 44
Hail, terrible storm of, ii. 70
Haile, John, Vicar of Isleworth, i. 27
Hailes, Abbey of, i. 75
——, blood of, i. 90
Halam, his rebellion, i. 60

Hale, John, Justice, ii. 84
Hales, Christopher, made Master of the Rolls, i. 49
Haliwell. *See* Holywell
Hamburgh (Hambrough), ii. 45
Hamilton (Hamerton), Sir Stephen, i. 63
Hamersmith, ii. 68
Hampton. *See* Southampton
—————— in Wilts, ii. 21
—————— Court, i. 66, 67, 70, 122, 130, 143, 186; ii. 25, 28, 40, 56, 60, 128, 130
Hamylkewe. *See* Ambleteuse
Handsome, Mr. ii. 57
Hanthill. *See* Ampthill
Harbard. *See* Herbert, Sir William
Hare, Sir Nicholas, Speaker of the Parliament, Lord Chancellor, and Master of the Rolls, i. 116; ii. 66, 70, 71, 77, 101
Harford, Thomas, i. 77
Harman (Herman), Thomas, i. 123
Harper, Sir George, ii. 110
—————— Mr. merchant taylor, ii. 73
Harpesfielde, Mr. ii. 105
Harpin, William, i. 176
Harvie, Thomas, a baker, ii. 71, 106
Harvye, a priest of Calais, i. 126
Hastings, Sir Edward, Master of the Horse, ii. 93
—————— Francis, Earl of Huntingdon, ii. 64, 71, 91, 110, 111
Hatfield, ii. 142
Havre-de-Grace, called Newhaven, in Brittany, i. 157
Hawkes (Hikbye), Thomas, burnt, ii. 127
Hawkins, under porter at the Tower, ii. 7
Hawley, Thomas, Clarencieux King-at-Arms, called King of Heralds, i. 68
Hayward or Howard, recantation by, i. 148
Head, a Yeoman of the Guard, ii. 8
Heath, Dr. Nicholas, Bishop of Worcester, Chichester, and Archbishop of York, Lord Chancellor, i. 168; ii. 56, 103, 132; deprived, ii. 145
Hedgehogs, the, i. 157
Hemley, John, priest, i. 169
Hening, Mr. his son, i. 130
Hennage, Sir Thomas, i. 69
Henry VII. i. 1-6; presented with a cap of maintenance, i. 2; died at Rich-

mond, i. 6 ; mentions of, ii. 44, 85, 97; anniversary of, ii. 2, 116
Henry VIII. succeeded to the throne on the death of his father, Henry VII. 22 April, 1509, i. 6-178 ; born at Greenwich, i. 2 ; created Duke of York, *ibid.;* proclaimed King, i. 6 ; married to Katherine of Aragon, i. 6, 35 ; crowned, *ibid.;* death of his first son, Prince Henry. i. 7 ; subsidy granted to, i. 8, 9 ; his daughter Mary born, i. 10 ; his divorce from Katherine, i. 17, 18 ; makes Anne Bolleyn his Queen, i. 17 ; his daughter Elizabeth born, i. 22 ; Supreme Head of the Church of England, i. 26, 52, 55, 60 ; his style and title, i. 26 ; miscarriage of his Queen Anne Boleyn, i. 33 ; called our Sovereign and Emperor, i. 35, 52; divorced from Anne Boleyn. i. 41; Anne's trial and execution, 37-40; marries Jane Seymour, i. 43, 44, 55, 59, 105 ; rejects the authority of the Pope, i. 52 ; rejoicings at the birth of Prince Edward, i. 66 ; presides at the trial of Nicholson for heresy, i. 89 ; marries Anne of Cleves, i. 109-112; marries Katherine Howard, i. 121-124, 130-134; proclaimed King of Ireland, i. 133 ; his title to the realm of Scotland, i. 140 ; marries Katherine Parr, widow of Lord Latimer, i. 143 ; mortgages the Crown lands to the City, i. 148 ; levies a benevolence or forced loan, i. 166 ; his death, i. 178 ; his will, i. 179 ; his burial, i. 181 ; his executors, ii. 41 ; mentions of, ii. 85, 88, 97, 105, 106, 136
────── Prince, infant son of Henry VIII. i. 7
────── natural son of Henry VIII. *See* Fitz-Roy
────── II. King of France, ii. 35, 37, 39, 40, 65, 132, 134, 138, 144, 146 ; ambassadors from, ii. 20, 39, 40 ; ambassadors to, ii. 31
Hepburn (Hayborne), Patrick, i. 139
Heralds, the, ii. 34, 86
Herbert (Harbard), Sir William, Lord Herbert of Caerdiff, and Earl of Pembroke, ii. 56, 61, 65, 71, 88, 89, 99, 110, 111, 119, 120, 138
Hereford, Bishop of. *See* Fox, Edward

Herne, Mrs. i. 128
Heron, Giles, i. 121
Hertford (Hareforde), i. 179
────── Earl of. *See* Seymour, Edward
Hewit, Andrew, burnt, i. 22
Heytesbury (Hatesburie), i. 47
Highgate, ii. 6
High Street, the, of London, i. 139
Hikbye. *See* Hawkes
Hikeman, Thurstan, monk, i. 184, 185
Hill, Sir Rowland, Lord Mayor, i. 127, 135 ; ii. 24-28, 43, 55
Hilsey, John, Prior of the Dominican Friars in London, Bishop of Rochester, i. 30, 34, 74, 90, 104
Hinde, Augustine, sheriff, ii. 53
────── the King's plumber, ii. 67
Hobbie, Sir Philip, ii. 71
Hobson, John, ii. 54
Hodgkin, Dr. Suffragan of London, i. 106
Hodnill in Warwickshire, i. 84
Hog Lane, ii. 69
Holbeach, Henry, Bishop of Rochester, and afterwards of Lincoln, i. 177, 184, 186, 187
Holborn, i. 95, 154, 176 ; ii. 24, 27, 41, 77, 112
Holcroft, Sir Thos. ii. 58
Holgate, Robert, Archbishop of York, i. 184
Holland, a servant of Lord Montacute, i. 91, 92
────── ii. 37, 47, 70
Holles, Sir Wm. Lord Mayor, i. 67, 111
Holmes, Mr. secretary to the Duke of Northumberland, ii. 71
────── Thos. a rebel, ii. 30, 32
Holte, Mr. keeper of Ludgate, ii. 84
Holy Maid of Kent. *See* Barton, Elizabeth
Holywell (Halywell), Benedictine nunnery at, i. 50, 107
Home, Dr. ii. 144, 145
────── (Hune), George, Laird of Ayton, i. 138
Honey Lane, parson of. *See* Garrard, Thos.
Honninges, the, ii. 143
Hooper, John, Bishop of Gloucester and Worcester, ii. 40, 41, 126
Hops, searchers of, ii. 55
Horn, William, i. 121
Horsey, Dr. i. 9

158   INDEX.

Horsleydown, Surrey, i. 176
Houghton, John, late Prior of the Charterhouse in London, i. 27, 185
Howard, Catherine, Queen of Henry VIII. i. 121, 122, 124, 130-134
—— Capt. Charles, i. 142
—— Lord Edmund, i. 122
—— Henry, Earl of Surrey, i. 37, 50, 98, 118, 132 ; his wife, Anne, i. 132
—— Lady Mary, wife of Henry Fitz-Roy, i. 53, 54
—— Michael, i. 150
—— Thomas, Earl of Surrey and third Duke of Norfolk, i. 12, 14, 16, 18, 21, 25, 27, 34, 36, 37, 38, 39, 48, 50, 53, 54, 57, 58, 60, 67, 68, 70, 80, 96, 98, 99, 105, 109, 122, 131-32, 136, 167, 170, 176, 177
—— Thomas, Lord, brother to the Duke of Norfolk, attainted (1536), i. 54 ; his death, i. 70
—— Thomas, Duke of Norfolk, ii. 95, 96, 97, 99, 107, 108, 122
—— William, Lord, i. 21, 132, 133; i. 109, 110, 117, 118 ; his wife, Lady Margaret, i. 132
Hubarthorne (Hobulthorne), Sir Henry, Lord Mayor, i. 175-178, 180, 181; ii. 55, 91
Huett, Mr. Sheriff, ii. 107
Huicke, Dr. ii. 145
Huise, Richard, a tailor, ii. 50
Hull, or Kingston-upon-Hull, i. 60, 65
—— Mayor of, i. 60
Hungary, Queen of, ii. 141
Hungerford, Sir Walter, Lord Hungerford, i. 47, 120
Hunn, Richard, tailor, hanged, i. 9
Hunsdon, Herts, i. 51
Hunt, William, burnt, ii. 127
Huntingdon, Earl of. *See* Hastings, Francis
Huntley, Earl of, Chancellor of Scotland, i. 186
Huntlow or Huntley, Thomas, sheriff, i. 104
Husband, Richard, Keeper of the Counter in Bread Street, ii. 42
Hussey, Sir John, Lord Hussey, i. 62, 65
Hyde, Abbot of. *See* Salcot, John
Hyde Park, ii. 64, 112
Hyll, a weaver, ii. 118
Hynde, Justice, ii. 8

Inner Temple, London, i. 61
Innes of Court, the, i. 180; *and see* their several names
Ipswich, i. 83
Ireland, i. 25, 26, 30, 136, 140, 160, 182 ; ii. 86 ; Henry VIII. proclaimed King of, i. 133
Isabella or Elizabeth, Infanta of Portugal, wife of the Emperor Charles V. i. 97 ; obit. for at St. Paul's, i. 97-99
Isleworth (Thistleworth), Vicar of. *See* Haile, John
Islington, Middlesex, ii. 12
Iwan Wasilejevitch, Emperor of Russia, ii. 137

Jackson, Mr. ii. 73
James IV. of Scotland slain, i. 8
James V. of Scotland, i. 139, 140 ; his Queen delivered of a daughter, i. 140
Jane, Queen of Spain, grandmother of Philip II. ii. 129
Jarvis, Richard, i. 154, 166, 171
Jedworth [Gedyworth], in Scotland, i. 152
Jennings, Barnard, ii. 54
Jerningham, Sir Henry (Sir John), Captain of the Guard, ii. 99, 108
Jerome, William, Vicar of Stepney, i. 114, 120, 121
Jerrard, Thomas. *See* Garrard
Jervaulx (Gervase), Abbot of, i. 63, 64
John III. King of Portugal, ii. 139
Jones, John, i. 93
Joseph, John, Rector of St. Mary-le-Bow, ii. 18
Joye, George, his works to be burnt, i. 169
Juana, Queen of Castile, wife of the Archduke Philip, i. 6
Judd, Sir Andrew, Lord Mayor, ii. 29, 30, 35-43, 60 ; his wife, ii. 44
Julian, an Italian, i. 173, 174
Julius III. Pope, ii. 127

Keith (Kythe), David, i. 139
Kennedy, Gilbert, Earl of Cassilis, i. 138, 186
Kent, county of, i. 125, 150; ii. 15, 18, 49, 107, 111, 112

INDEX.

Kent, Joan of. *See* Butcher
Ker, Robert, (Cary, Dan), Laird of Graydon, i. 138
Kett, Robert, ii. 21, 30
—— William, ii. 30
Keyme. *See* Askew, Anne
—— Thomas, i. 155, 167
Kildare, Earl of. *See* Fitzgerald, Gerald
Kinge hanged, ii. 111
King's Bench, the, i. 11, 119, 125, 126, 132, 155, 162, 179, 181; ii. 12, 13, 36, 96, 112, 117, 129, 130, 145
—————— Chief Justice of. *See* Montague, Sir Edward
—— Book, the, i. 145; *and see* Common Prayer, Book of
—— Bridge, the, at Westminster, i. 99
—— College, Cambridge, ii. 90
—— Head without Newgate, ii. 31
—— Street, Westminster, ii. 131
Kingston on Thames, i. 66, 176; ii. 110, 112
Kingston, Anthony, i. 117
—— Lady, wife of Sir William, i. 38
—— Sir William, Constable of the Tower, i. 36, 37, 94
Kirton, Alderman, ii. 15
Knight, Stephen, ii. 127
Knotting, Mr. ii. 54
Knyvett (Nevill), Sir Anthony, ii. 117
—— Sir Edmond, i. 125
—— Sir Henry, Ambassador to the Emperor, i. 49, 69, 174
—— Sir Thomas, Master of the Horse, blown up in the Regent, i. 7

Lamberd. *See* Nicholson, Sir William
Lambeth, i. 11, 40, 78; ii. 13, 24, 34, 45, 46, 47, 124, 134, 142
Lancashire, i. 156
Lancaster Herald. *See* Myller, Thomas
Langton, Thomas, ii. 46; his widow, ii. 46
Lascelles (Lasell), John, i. 169
Latimer, Dr. Hugh, Bishop of Worcester, i. 30, 35, 17, 64, 71, 72, 78, 79, 80, 101, 103; ii. 103, 131
—— John Nevill, Lord, i. 143
Laurence, Thomas, Prior of Hexham, i. 27

Lawrence, Sir John, priest, ii. 127
—————— Robarte. *See* Laurence, Thomas
Laxton, Sir William, Lord Mayor, i. 151, 161; ii. 23, 43, 55
Leadenhall, i. 11, 12, 164, 165, 175, 178, 181; ii. 71, 94, 107, 112
Lee, Edward, Archbishop of York, i. 20, 21, 45, 48, 57, 97, 99
—— Thomas, i. 31, 124; ii. 54
Leicester, i. 16, 110, 111
—— burial of Cardinal Wolsey in Our Lady Chapel in Leicester Abbey, i. 16
Lent, eating flesh in, ii. 68
Leonard, Lord. *See* Grey
Leslie, George, Earl of Rothes, i. 139
—— John, i. 139
Lever, Sir Thomas. *See* Seymour, Edward, Earl of Herts
Lewes in Sussex, Cluniac Priory at, i. 82
Lewyn, Thomas, i. 163
Lincoln i. 61, 65
—— Bishop of. *See* Longland, John; Watson, Thomas, and White, John
—— Earl of. *See* Pole, John de la
—— Place, or Southampton House in Holborn, ii. 41
Lincolnshire, i. 27, 56, 57, 61, 62, 155, 167; ii. 13
Lincoln's Inn, i. 137, 179
Lisle (Lyeles), Viscount. *See* Plantagenet, Arthur, and Dudley, Sir John
Listre. *See* Lyster, Sir Richard
Litany in English, i. 148
Littleton, Edward, i. 169
Liturgy. *See* Common Prayer, Book of
Locke, Sir William, Sheriff, ii. 9, 27
Lodge, Thomas, Sheriff, ii. 93
Lollards' Tower, i. 9
Lomeley, George, i. 63, 64
London (*passim*); fire in, i. 6; rising of apprentices, i. 11; crafts of, i. 12, 13, 18, 24, 66, 71, 111; ii. 16; reception of Anne Boleyn in, i. 18, 19; plague or death in, i. 56, 145; ii. 5; election of Ralf Warren for Lord Mayor, i. 57, 59; Lord Mayor and Lord Mayor and Aldermen, (*passim*); Cratwell the hangman hanged, i. 85; rejoicings at the birth of Edward VI. i. 66; great muster of citizens, i. 95, 96; chamber of London, i. 59, 134,

178; ii. 12, 16, 53, 57, 72, 73; watch dispensed with, i. 100; alteration in the time for election of sheriffs, i. 103; pageant at the marriage of Anne of Cleves, i. 111, 112; charter of, i. 129; water bailiff of, i. 129; recorder of (*passim*), but *see* Baker, Mr.; Cholmeley, Sir Roger; and Brooke, Robert; markets and prices in, i. 141, 147, 163, 175, 185; ii. 6, 23, 30, 37, 42, 45-47, 66, 68, 70, 80, 81, 105, 143; limitation of the number of dishes at the tables of the Lord Mayor and Aldermen, i. 141; hustings, court of, i. 147; ii. 73; rejoicings for victory in Scotland, i. 147; trained bands of, i. 148; ii. 3, 5; forced loans or benevolences, i. 148, 151; ii. 102, 140, 141; Alderman Rede sent to the war in Scotland for refusing his contribution to the benevolence, i. 151; Court of Aldermen, i. 154, 183; ii. 42, 43, 50-53, 55, 59, 62, 71, 73, 92, 107, 113; companies of the city, i. 156; ii. 16, 20, 25, 35, 57, 58, 70, 74, 92, 95, 100, 107, 141, 145; chamberlain of, i. 156, 160, 175, 182, 183; ii. 5, 25, 44, 45, 55, 60, 72-76, 92; citizen army marches to Farnham for relief of the Isle of Wight, i. 158; reported conspiracy by priests and strangers to fire the city, i. 159; Common Sergeant, ii. 59, 72, and *see* Brooke, Robert; Atkins, Thomas; Guildhall, *see* Guildhall; Christ Church or St. Bartholomew's Hospital given to the city, i. 178; proclamation of martial law in, ii. 15; commons or liverymen of, ii. 16, 44, 45, 48, 51-54, 57, 73-76, 92, 93, 98, 100, 102, 106, 108; preparations for defence of, ii. 16; Bartholomew Fair, ii. 21; liberties of Southwark purchased by the city, ii. 36; Borough, the, added to the city, ii. 40; Common Council of the, ii. 43, 44, 53, 57, 59, 72, 73, 75, 87, 100, 107; council chamber, the, ii. 45, 84, 108, 109; Lord Mayor's Court, the, ii. 54, 59, 84, 108; common crier, ii. 54, 108; sword bearer, ii. 107; town clerk, ii. 59; knight marshal, ii. 33, 108; wards of, ii. 66; the King's place of Bridewell in Fleet Street given to the city as a workhouse for the poor, ii. 83; Reception of Queen

Mary, ii. 93-95; dole money, ii. 97; strangers ejected, ii. 112
—— Bishop of. *See* Bonner, Grindall, Ridley, and Stockesley
—— Bridge, i. 5, 14, 24, 29, 44, 59, 64, 65, 74, 84, 85, 92, 112, 120, 124, 132; ii. 4, 27, 39, 62, 77, 87, 103, 109, 116, 134, 142
—— Stone, i. 76
—— Wall, ii. 26, 142, 174
Long, Sir Richard, i. 69, 125, 129
Long Acre, ii. 63
Longland, John, Bishop of Lincoln and Chancellor of the University of Oxford, i. 34, 99; his chaplain, i. 56
Lopez (Lopers), Ferdinando, ii. 36
Lords, the. *See* Council
Lords' House, ii. 81
Lorraine, Duke of, son of, supposed to have been engaged to Anne of Cleves, i. 119
Lothbury, i. 175
Louis XII. King of France, marries Mary, sister of Henry VIII. i. 9; died *ib.*
Louth (Loothe), vicar of, i. 62
Louvain (Loven), i. 185
Lovell, Lord, i. 2
Lucare, Emanuel, merchant taylor, ii. 115
Ludgate, i. 165, 183; ii. 84, 110-112
Ludlow, i. 5
Lukine, Robert, i. 155
Lutrell, Sir John, ii. 31
Lydall, Mr. ii. 14
Lynsey, John, i. 127
Lyster (Listre), Sir Richard, Lord Chief Baron of the Exchequer, i. 69, 161

McWilliam (Mat Williams), created Earl of Clanricarde, i. 142
Maidstone, i. 16, 74; ii. 107
Maitland, John, of Achin, i. 139
Makerell, Dr. the Prior of Barlings, i. 56, 62
Malbie, Thomas, i. 170
Malines (Macline), i. 174
Mannering, William, i. 93
Manners, Henry, Lord Roos and Earl of Rutland, i. 50; ii. 64; his wife. i. 50

Manners, Thomas, Earl of Rutland, i. 50, 56, 110; his daughter Anne, i. 50
Mannings-hall in Newgate, ii. 134
Margaret, Queen Dowager of Scotland, i. 10, 54
——— sister of Henry II. of France, ii. 146
Mark Lane, i. 172; ii. 94, 95
Markes. *See* Smeton, Mark
Marshalsea, ii. 24, 33, 36, 96, 112, 129, 138, 145
Mary, sister of Henry VIII. married to Louis XII. King of France, afterwards to Charles Brandon, Duke of Suffolk, i. 10; her death, i. 22; her daughter, ii. 85
Mary, Queen of England, daughter of of Henry VIII. and Catharine of Arragon, born 18th February, 1516; i. 10, 70, 154; ii. 85-141; bastardized, i. 24; interview with her father, i. 51; stands godmother to Prince Edward, i. 67; her accession disputed, ii. 85-88; entry into London, ii. 93; her coronation, ii. 103; marries the Prince of Spain, afterwards Philip II. ii. 106, 119-121; restores the mass, ii. 113; titles of their majesties, ii. 121; supposed *enciente*, ii. 124, 128; her death, ii. 141
Mary of Guise, Queen of James V. ii. 59-61
Mary Queen of Scots, daughter of James V. i. 140; ii. 35
Mary Rose. the (king's ship), i. 158
Mason, Sir John, Clerk of the Council and Secretary of State, ii. 31, 71, 88, 89
Maundevild, a Frenchman, i. 118
Maximilian I. Emperor of Germany, 1493-1519, i. 5
Maxwell, Henry, i. 139
——— Robert, Lord, i. 138, 139
May, William, LL.D. Master of Queen's College, Cambridge, and Dean of St. Paul's, ii. 17, 114, 146
Maynarde, John, Sheriff, ii. 76, 80
Medley, George, Chamberlain of the City, ii. 5
Meekins, Richard, i. 126
Mellis, Robert, merchant taylor, ii. 76
Mélun (Millon) in France, i. 174
Merchant Adventurers' Company, ii. 45, 77, 85

Merchant Staplers, the,, ii. 85
——— Taylors' Company, i. 5, 77
Mercers' Company, i. 111, 112, 129, 130; ii. 5, 25, 74, 127; chapel, ii. 143; hall, ii. 127
Merton (Martin) Abbey in Surrey, i. 82
Mewtas, Sir Peter, ii. 129
Middlesex, county, ii. 61, 142
Middleton, Mr. haberdasher, ii. 52, 64; his wife, *ib.*
Mile End, i. 95
Mineries, the, i. 83, 94
Mint in the Tower, ii. 74
Mirfin (Murffen), Thomas, Lord Mayor, i. 108
Mommorth, Humphry, i. 72
Monasteries, suppression of, i. 102, 108, 109, 112, 129
Monford, Sir Symon, beheaded, i. 3; his son, *ib.*
Montacute, Lord. *See* Pole, Henry
Montague, Viscount. *See* Brown, Sir Anthony
Montague, Sir Edward, Lord Montague, Chief Justice of the King's Bench, i. 161, 162, 168; ii. 8, 84, 91, 103
Monteith (Mounteith), Earl of. *See* Graham
——— (Mountayffe) William, Laird of Kerse, i. 139
Montreuil (Muttrell), in Picardy, i. 173, 174
More, Sir Thomas, called young Mr. More, i. 12; made Lord Chancellor, i. 16; imprisoned in the Tower, i. 24, 25; beheaded, i. 29
Moorfields, co. Middlesex, i. 122; ii. 26
Moorgate, ii. 27, 112
Morgan, Sir Richard, Sergeant, ii. 12; made Chief Justice of Common Pleas, ii. 101
Moundaie, Thomas, parson of St. Leonard's, i. 184, 185
Mount Surrey by Norwich, ii. 30
Moyne, Mr. i. 61
Murffen. *See* Mirfin, Thomas
Mycenæ, i. 53
Myles, clerk of St. Botolph's, ii. 119
Myller, Thomas, Lancaster Herald, executed, i. 84

Naples and Jerusalem, king of. *See* Philip II.

Narrow Seas, the, i. 160
Negri, M. Chancelier, ii. 106
Netherlands, the, ii. 133
Nevill, Sir Edward, i. 91, 92
—— Sir John, i. 124
—— Lord Henry, i. 50 ; his wife, i. 50
—— Henry, Earl of Westmorland, ii. 138
—— Ralph, Earl of Westmorland, i. 50 ; his daughter, Lady Dorothy, i. 50 ; his daughter, Lady Margaret, 50
Newbury, Berks, ii. 67
Newgate prison, i. 24, 62, 73, 77, 79, 84, 85, 92, 95, 96, 126, 132, 156, 168, 169, 176, 183 ; ii. 20, 27, 31, 32, 38, 42, 52, 64, 77, 110, 112, 118, 126, 127, 134, 135, 136
—— market, ii. 6, 130
Newcastle or Newhaven, by Boulogne, ii. 22, 31
Newhall iu Essex, ii. 92
Newhaven. *See* Havre-de-Grace
Newnam Bridge. *See* Nieulay
New Testament, translation by Tyndale or Coverdale to be burnt, i. 168
—— —— in French, i. 184
Nice, General Council of, i. 53
Nicholson, Sir William, ii. 88, 89
Nieulay (Newnam Bridge), near Calais, ii. 140
Nitigate, Francis, or Nidigate, Sebastian, i. 28
Norfolk, county, i. 125, 177 ; ii. 15, 21, 30, 87, 122
—— Duchess of, i, 20, 23 ; ii. 94
—— Duke of. *See* Howard, Thomas
Norris, Sir Christopher, i. 96
—— Henry, i. 35, 36 ; beheaded, 39, 40
Norroy King-at-arms, i. 165 ; ii. 26
North, Sir Edward, Lord North, ii. 71 ; his house, ii. 142
North, the, i. 2
Northamptonshire, i. 27, 149
Northumberland Alley, by Aldgate, ii. 105
—— —— Duchess of, ii. 60
—— —— Duke of. *See* Dudley, John
—— —— Earl of. *See* Percy
Norton, John, ii. 111
Norwich, i. 6, 16, 82 ; ii. 19, 21, 22, 30

O'Brien, Sir Donough, created Lord Ibracken, i. 142
—— (Obrune), Murrough, created Earl of Thomond, i. 142
Offley, Thomas, sheriff, ii. 16, 90, 93
Old Bailey, ii. 105, 111, 136
Old Fish Street, i. 141 ; ii. 12, 104
Old Man, the, at Boulogne, i. 157 ; ii. 22
Oliphant (Olivante), Lawrence, third Lord, i. 138
O'Neil, Conan, chief captain of Tyrone, created Earl of Tyrone, i. 136 ; called the Great O'Neil, *ib.*
—— Matthew, or Feardoragh, Lord Dungannon, i. 136
Owen, John, a gunner, ii. 87
Owyn, Richard, ii. 52
Oxford, i. 75 ; ii. 133, 134
——, Lord of. *See* Vere, John de
Oxfordshire, ii. 21

Packington (Paginton), Robert, i. 59
Paget, Sir William, Comptroller of the Household, created Lord Paget, Lord Privy Seal, ii. 31, 32, 62, 69, 89, 90, 132
Pagett, Alderman, i. 134
—— Sir William, Secretary of State, i. 177
Paine, Christopher, i. 127
Palmer, Mr. i. 118
——, Sir Thomas, ii. 57, 91, 99, 101
Pansgrove, Dr. i. 172
Papers, one of the clerks of the, i. 168
Papists, i. 83 ; ii. 34
Pardon churchyard pulled down, ii. 29
Pargitor, Lady, wife of Sir Thomas, i. 73
Paris, City of, i. 157, 174 ; ii. 146
——, university of, i. 107
Parliament, i· 8, 9, 19, 26, 29, 42, 45, 46, 48, 51, 52, 54, 62, 64, 94, 100-102, 105, 120-122, 133-136, 143, 145, 146, 152, 156, 162, 187 ; ii. 2, 5. 9, 10, 18, 29, 30, 32, 66, 68, 81, 82, 103, 105, 114, 115, 123, 125, 131, 140, 143, 145
—— Acts of ii, 35, 69, 79, 88, 97, 102, 105, 123, 145
—— —— Commons House of, i. 187
—— —— Speaker of, i. 116, 187
—— —— Sergeant-at-Arms, i. 135
—— —— Chamber, i. 52, 94, 133, 178, 187

INDEX. 163

Parliament House. i. 135
Parr, Catherine, late Queen, death of, ii. 5
—— Sir Wm. Lord Parr, Earl of Essex and Marquis of Northampton, i. 94, 143-155, 172, 177, 180, 182 ; ii. 19, 32, 33, 64, 71, 90, 91, 97, 99, 107, 145
Parson or Person, Sir Thomas, i. 154
—— Sir William, i. 177
Partridge, Sir Miles, ii. 58, 66, 67
Pary, Mr. ii. 84
Pate, William, of Islington, ii. 12, 13
Paul IV. Pope (Giampietro Caraffa) ii. 130
Paulet, William, Lord St. John, Earl of Wiltshire and Marquis of Winchester, Lord Treasurer, ii. 26, 27, 31, 32, 56, 63, 71, 99, 103, 107
Pavia in Italy, battle of, i. 14
Payne, hanged, ii. 20
Peckham, Sir Edmund. i. 135 ; ii. 84
—— Henry, executed, ii. 136
Peerson, Mr. i. 76
Pembroke, Earl of. *See* Herbert Sir William
—————— Marchioness of. *See* Bulleyn, Anne
Percy, Henry Algernon, slain, i. 2
—— Henry Algernon, Earl of Northumberland, i. 41. 63, 64
—— Sir Thomas, Earl of Northumberland, i. 63, 64, 65 ; ii. 137
Persons, Anthony, a priest, i. 143
Perwyn, Friar, ii. 134
Peter, a Dutchman, ii. 104
—— Sir William, ii. 31
Peterborough, i. 33
Pewterers' Hall, the, i. 170
Philibert, Emanuel, Prince of Piedmont, and Duke of Savoy, ii. 125, 139, 146
Philip, Archduke, King of Castile, driven by tempest into England, i. 6
—— made Knight of the Garter, *ib.*
Philip II. King of Spain and England, ii. 106, 118-121, *et seq.*
Philiper, a yeoman of the guard, i. 126
Philpott, Clement, i. 121
—— John, Archdeacon of Winchester, burnt, ii. 132
Picardy in France, i. 9
Pickering (Pykeringe) John, i, 63
Pigott, William, burnt, ii. 127
Plague in London, ii. 5

Plantagenet, Arthur, i. 21, 61, 121
—— Edward, Earl of Warwick executed, i. 4
—— George, Duke of Clarence, brother of King Edward IV. i. 4
—— Margaret, Countess of Salisbury. i. 102, 124.
Playhouses. *See* Bowling-alleys
Pole, Edmund de la, beheaded, i. 8
—— Sir Geoffrey, i. 91, 92
—— Henry, Lord Montacute, i. 88, 91, 92, 102, 124
—— John de la, Earl of Lincoln, i. 1
—— Cardinal, Reginald, i. 92 ; ii. 123-126, 131 ; made Archbishop of Canterbury, ii. 134, 139 ; his death, ii. 141, 142
Pollard, Mr. the king's Remembrancer, i. 133
—— hanged. ii. 111, 115
Pope, the (Bishop of Rome), i. 12, 30, 34, 35, 52, 53. 72, 73, 79, 80, 81, 89, 92, 99, 100, 104, 148 ; ii. 15, 125, 133 ; *and see* Julius III., Paul IV.
—— Sir Thomas, founder of Trinity College ; Oxford, ii. 8, 27
Poplar, ii. 76
Portman, William, a judge of the King's Bench, i. 181
Portsmouth, ii. 59 ; haven, i. 158
Portsoken, ward of, ii. 15, 16
Portugal (Portingale), ii. 37
—— King of, i, 97
Pott or Potter, Gilbert, ii. 86
Potter, a serving man, i. 93
—— Richard, i. 150
—— William, i. 150
Poulet, Thomas, i. 61
—— Sir William, Lord St. John, Lord Great Master, and afterwards Earl of Wiltshire, i. 69, 94, 177, 180, 183, 186
Poultry, the, ii. 8, 53, 86, 126
Powell, Dr. Edward, i. 121
Poynings, Sir Edward, comptroller of the Household, i. 37
—— Sir Thomas, Lord Poynings, Governor of Boulogne, i. 117, 160
Poynet (Ponett), Dr. bishop of Rochester and afterwards of Winchester, ii. 46, 99
Poyntz (Poynes), Sir Nicolas, ii. 58
Presence, Chamber of, i. 179, 180
Prices of provisions. *See* London

164   INDEX.

Primers, the new, i. 156
Proctor executed, ii. 138
Psalms of David, i. 106, 114
Puttoe, a tanner, ii. 12, 13

Queenhithe, i. 185 ; ii. 8, 67, 105
Quent, Dr. Dean of the Arches, i. 78

Randall, Mr. of the Temple, ii. 67
Rastall (Restwold), Alice, i. 132
Rastall, Mr. ii. 34
Ratcliffe, i. 44; ii. 39
——— Henry, Earl of Sussex, ii. 106, 107, 121
——— or Radcliff Robert, Viscount Fitzwalter and Earl of Sussex, i. 21, 45, 48, 80, 98, 131
——— Thomas, Lord Fitz-Walter, ii. 95
Reading, ii. 28
——— Abbot of, i. 108, 109
Red Bulwark on Tower Hill, i. 179
Redcross street, ii. 118
Red Lion, sign of the, in Lower Thames street, i. 115
Reede, Richard, alderman, sent to the war in Scotland, i. 151, 153, 163
Reformation, progress of, i. 30, 34, 35, 43, 54, 55, 72, 74-6, 78-86, 104; ii. 1, 2, 9, 17, 24, 47, 56, 78, 143
Regent of England, a ship, i. 7
Reigate (Rigate) in Surrey, i. 150 ; ii. 49
Religion, houses of suppressed, ii 145
Reynold, Richard, monk of Sion, i. 27
Rhodes, Isle of, i. 14
——— knights of, i. 101, 126
Rich, Sir Richard Lord Rich, Baron of Leeze, Lord Chancellor, i. 187; ii. 24, 25, 27, 34, 65, 99
Richmond or West Sheen, Surrey, i. 4, 6, 186; ii. 33, 41, 97, 102, 116, 122
——— Carthusian Priory at, i. 25, 104
——— Duchess of, i. 110; ii. 60
——— Duke of. *See* Fitz-Roy, Henry
——— John, Armourer, i. 127, 128, 129; ii. 76
Ridley, Dr. Nicholas, Chaplain to Archbishop Cranmer, Bishop of Rochester, i. 94, 187, and afterwards of London;
ii. 38, 40, 41, 47, 56, 78, 81, 84, 88, 91, 131
Rikethorne, Mr. haberdasher, ii. 72
Rise or Risse, Griffith, beheaded for treason, i. 17
Risebanck near Calais, ii. 140
Robinson, George, warden of the Mercers, i. 130
Roche, Sir William, Lord Mayor, i. 126, 151, 152
Rochester, i, 109; ii. 108
——— Abbey of, i. 109
——— Bridge, ii. 108
——— Castle, ii. 108
——— Bishop of. *See* Poynet, Scory, Holbeach, Ridley, Fisher, and Hilsey
Rochford, Lady, widow of George Viscount, i. 131, 133, 134
——— Lord. *See* Boleyn
Rogers, John, prebendary of St. Pancras in St. Paul's Cathedral, ii. 126
Rome, i. 2, 52, 73, 80
——— bishop of. *See* Pope, the
——— Church of, i. 79, 132
——— St. Peter's at, i. 73
——— Emperor of. *See* Charles V.
Romford (Raynesford), Essex, ii. 19
Rooffe, Thos. i. 83
Roos, Lord. *See* Manners, Henry
Rose tavern, ii. 68
Rossey (William), executed, ii. 135
Rotchmeire, William, i. 123
Rothes, Earl of. *See* Leslie, George
Rouen (Rone), i. 171
Rouge (Rach) Dragon, i. 165
Roy, his works to be burnt, i. 169
Rudd, Mr. a priest, i. 132
Rumpye, La Conte, French carac. i. 157
Russell, Sir John, Lord Russell, Earl of Bedford, Lord Privy Seal, i. 69, 94, 180; ii. 20, 31, 64, 71, 89, 99
Russia, Emperor of. *See* Iwan Wasilejevitch
Ruthal, Thomas, bishop of Durham, i. 12
Rutland, Earl of. *See* Manners
Rynacyacy or Rinatian, James, i. 122
Ryse, an Irishwoman, ii. 68

Sackville, Sir Richard, ii. 145
Sadler, John, alderman, i. 163 ; ii. 52

INDEX. 165

Sadleyr, Sir Ralph, i. 115
St. Alban's, i. 146; ii. 74
─────── Abbot of, i. 99
St. Andrew's Castle, taken by the French, i. 185
St. Andrew's, Holborn, i. 154; ii. 41
St. Angelo, Castle of, i. 73
St. Ann's-in-the-Willows burnt ii. 6
St. Antholin's (Antlins) in Watling Street, i. 132
St. Anthony's, ii. 130
St. Austen's or Augustine's Abbey. *See* Canterbury
St. Bartholomew's, i. 81, 108, 177, 178; ii. 44, 47, 55
St Bennet, Order of Monks, ii. 136
St. Botolph's Church, ii. 68, 94, 118
St. Bride's, Fleet Street, vicar of. *See* Cardmaker
St. David's, bishop of. *See* Barlow, Dr.
St. Edmondsbury, i. 17, 22
St. Elizabeth, Queen of Portugal, i. 97
St. Erconwald's shrine in St. Paul's, i. 98, 106
St. Ethelberga [St. Alborow], Bishopsgate Street, ii. 100, 107
St. Ewin's (Eton's), i. 177
St. Faith's or the Crowds, ii. 101
St. Faustus' Church, in Foster Lane, ii. 117
St. George's Southwark, ii. 44
─────── Fields, i. 158
St. Giles without Cripplegate, i. 161
St. Gregory's church, i. 93
St. Helen's, ii. 36
St. James' Westminster, i. 53, 59, 60, 95, 154 ; ii. 63, 64, 103, 110, 111, 131, 139, 141, 142
─────── Park, i. 95
St. John, Lord. *See* Poulet, Sir William
St. John, Serjeant-of-Arms to the Parliament House, i. 135
St. John's in Smithfield, i. 119
St. John's, Lord of. *See* Weston, Sir William
St. John's Head, sign of, ii. 86
St. Lawrence Lane, ll. 80
St. Leonard's in Foster Lane, i. 184
St. Magnus the Martyr, i. 5, 115, 164, 178; ii. 112
St. Margaret Pattins, i. 81
St. Margaret's Lothbury, i. 175

St. Margaret's Southwark, i. 113; ii. 19, 127, 128
St. Martin's, i. 132
─────── parson of. *See* Wilson
St. Mary-at-Hill by Billingsgate, ii. 72
St. Mary-le-Bow or at Arches, ii. 134
St. Mary Magdalen, i. 113, 185
St. Mary Overy's, Southwark, i. 108, 113; ii. 114, 122, 126, 132, 133
─────── called the largest and fairest church about London, ii. 113
St. Mary's Lock, ii. 87
─────── Spital, i. 114; ii. 2, 68, 82, 144
St. Matthew's, Cheapside, ii. 114
St. Michael's le Querne, i. 164, 172, 181
St. Nicholas Shambles, i. 177 ; ii. 8
─────── Shambles Alley, ii. 105
─────── Old Fish Street, ii. 104
St. Olave's, ii. 13
St. Paul's Cathedral, London, i. 3-5, 8, 12, 14, 17, 22, 31, 32, 47, 52, 59, 64, 66, 71, 82, 84, 94, 97-99, 106, 133, 147, 149, 160, 163, 164, 169, 184, 186, 187 ; ii. 1, 3, 10, 12, 14, 16, 17, 29, 38, 41, 43, 56, 59, 61, 78, 80, 82, 84, 88, 89, 100, 101, 102, 104, 106, 109, 112, 113, 117, 123, 124, 126, 127, 129, 132, 137, 139 ; bishops palace by, i. 172; ii. 60, 61, 96; altar in, ii. 146; chain, i. 93; consistory, ii. 113, 128; church-yard, i. 59, 164; ii. 29, 35, 88, 98, 110, 117, 144, 146; communion table, ii. 47, 79; cross, i. 17, 23, 33-35, 58, 74, 77-79, 90, 92, 93, 104, 106, 115, 142, 152, 167, 169, 170, 175, 177, 184; ii. 1, 4, 6, 10, 12, 13, 14, 18, 24, 35, 40, 78, 88, 97, 99, 100, 114, 117, 122, 124, 128, 129, 130, 144; Dean of. *See* Sampson, Feckenham, and May; reader of. *See* Cardmaker, John; Lollard's Tower, i. 9; Our Lady Chapel, ii. 82; choir or quire, i. 66, 69, 71, 72, 97, 123, 161, 164; ii. 2, 9, 17, 20, 35, 47, 79, 82, 104, 124; school, i. 32, 164, 130; steeple, light in, ii. 104; wharf, ii. 60, 88, 124; bowling alleys and play-houses at, ii. 43
St. Peter's, Cornhill, i. 72, 187
─────── at Rome, i. 73
─────── Westminster. *See* Westminster Abbey
St. Quintin's, in France, ii. 139
St. Saviour's Abbey at Bermondsey, i. 77

166   INDEX.

St. Sepulchre's by Newgate, i. 126, 132; ii. 31, 126
—— vicar of. *See* Rogers, John.
St. Stephen's Church, in Coleman Street, i. 175
St. Swithin's parish, i. 76
St. Thomas-a-Becket, of Canterbury, i. 86, 87, 89
St. Thomas Acars, i. 59, 87, 88,129
St. Thomas's Hospital, ii. 76, 79
St. Thomas Waterings, i. 101, 126 ; ii. 13, 135
St. Uncomber. *See* St. Wylgefortis
St. Wylgefortis (Uncomber), i. 84
Salcot, John, *alias* Capon, DD. Abbot of Hyde and Bishop of Bangor, i. 35, 103 ; Bishop of Salisbury, i. 103
Salisbury, ii. 137
—— Bishop of. *See* Shaxton, Nicholas; Salcot, John
—— Countess of. *See* Plantagenet, Margaret
—— Place, by Bidewell, ii. 105
Salvage, Mr. ii. 145
Sampson, Mr. Parson of All Hallows, ii. 77, 144
—— Richard, Bishop of Chichester, i. 48, 66, 81, 84, 103
Sandy Sykes or Solway Moss, battle of, i. 137
Sandys (Sanders), Dr. Edwin, ii. 91
—— Thomas, Lord, ii. 135 ; his son hanged, ii. 135
—— William, Lord, i. 45
Sarum, use of, ii. 102, 113
Satilian or Chatillon. *See* Coligny, Gaspard de
Saunders, Laurence, ii. 126
—— Ninion, ii. 86
Savoy, Duke of. *See* Philibert, Emanuel
—— the, i. 24; ii. 33, 36, 83
Sawtery, John, i. 155 ; his wife Joan, *ibid.*
Saxony, Vice-Chancellor of. *See* Burgart, Francis
Scarborough Castle, co. York, ii. 138
Scotland, i. 8, 10, 116. 136, 140, 147, 151, 153, 155, 156, 160, 161, 165, 185 ; ii. 3, 5, 24, 31, 35, 59-62, 137, 144
—— King of. *See* James V.
Scots, the, i. 139, 185, 186 ; they enter England, i. 137 ; defeated at Solway Moss, i. 137-40 ; Queens of. *See* Margaret, Mary of Guise, and Mary daughter of James V.
Seaton, Alexander, a Scotchman, i. 132
Selim I. defeats the Mamaluke Sultan of Egypt near Aleppo, i. 11
Sergeants' Feast, the, i. 119 ; ii. 77
Seymour, Sir Edward, Viscount Beauchamp (1536), Earl of Hertford (1537), and Duke of Somerset, Lord Protector, i. 47, 68, 77, 80, 105, 131, 152, 155, 168, 177, 179, 180,182, 183, 185, 186, 187 ; ii. 5, 10, 19, 20, 21, 24-28, 33, 34, 36, 41, 42, 56, 57 ; sent to the Tower, ii. 56 ; his trial and sentence, ii. 62, 63 ; beheaded on Tower Hill, ii. 65 ; his eldest daughter, Anne, marries John Dudley, Viscount Lisle, ii. 41
—— Jane, third wife of Henry VIII. i. 43, 44, 55, 59, 64, 66, 68, 69, 70-72, 105, 182
—— Sir John, i. 43
—— Sir Thomas, Lord Seymour of Sudley, Lord High Admiral, i. 69, 117, 182 ; ii. 5, 7, 10
Shaxton, Nicholas, Bishop of Salisbury, i. 35, 101, 103, 167, 168, 170
Sheen. *See* Richmond
Sheffield, Sir Edmond, Lord Sheffield, i. 182 ; ii. 78
Shelton, Sir John, i. 116
Sherington, Sir William, ii. 7, 30
Shetheur, Sir John, priest, ii. 127, 128
Shingleton, a priest, i. 142
Shooters Hill, i. 110
Shoreditch, London, i. 107
—— Church, ii. 61, 127
Shrewsbury, Earl of. *See* Talbot, Francis and George
Shropshire, ii. 49
Shrouds, or Crowds, the. *See* St. Faith's
Shulnige, Count de. ii. 105
Silvestre, Robert, i. 149
Simnel, Lambert, made prisoner, i. 2
Sinclair (Sinkler), James, i. 138
—— Oliver, i. 138
Sion, i. 81 109,131,133 ; ii. 57, 145
Six Articles, law of the, i. 102, 103, 155
Smeton, Mark (Markes), i. 36, 39, 40
Smith, Dr. i. 184
Smithfield, or East Smithfield, i. 7, 9, 17,

28, 64, 89, 90, 108, 118, 119, 120, 121, 124, 126, 134, 162, 169, 170; ii. 4, 27, 32, 37, 38, 47, 68, 112, 127, 129, 132, 134, 137, 139, 146
——— St. John's in, i. 119
Smyth, Sir Thomas, Secretary of State, ii. 28, 34
Soam, river, ii. 139
Solway Moss, battle of. *See* Sandy Sykes
Somerset county, i. 61 ; ii. 13
——— Duchess of. *See* Stanhope, Anne
——— Duke of. *See* Tudor, Edmund
——— Place, Strand, ii. 125, 142
——— William, Earl of Worcester. ii. 89, 95
Somerville (Semerwell), Hugh, 5th Lord i. 138
Soper Lane, i. 59 ; ii. 27, 112
Soudan, the. *See* Egypt
Southampton, ii. 118
——— or Hampton, Earl of *See* Wriothesley, Sir Thomas ; and Fitzwilliam, William
——— House. *See* Lincoln Place
Southfield in Suffolk, ii. 21
Southwark, i. 59, 108, 118, 119, 129, 176; ii. 12, 13, 18, 19, 21. 28, 36, 40, 42, 43, 44, 46, 55, 71, 76, 79, 109, 110, 112, 114, 122, 126, 129, 133
——— St. George's Bar in, i 12, 118, 119
Southwell, Sir Richard, ii. 27
——— Robert, Master of the Rolls, i. 133
Southwood, Thomas, priest of St. Nicholas, Old Abbey, in Old Fish Street, ii. 104
——— Mr. goldsmith, ii. 72
Spain, i. 13, 99, 116 : ii. 142 ; merchants of, i. 98, 99
——— King of. *See* Ferdinand II. Charles V. and Philip II.
——— Prince of. *See* Philip II.
Spears, pensioners so called, i. 112
Spencer, Mr. of Warwickshire, i. 84 ; his wife, i. 84
Spital, the. *See* St. Mary's Spital
Stafford, Edward, Duke of Buckingham, i. 13, 54
Stafford, Henry, Lord, ii. 138
——— Thomas, beheaded, ii. 138

Standard, the, in Cheapside, i. 11, 178 ; ii. 8, 136
Stanhope, Anne, Duchess of Somerset, ii. 57, 97
——— Sir Michael, ii. 28, 34, 58, 66, 67
Stanley, Edward, Earl of Derby, i. 21, 50 ; ii. 106, 119, 120
——— Sir William, beheaded, i. 3
Stanton, William, ii. 135
Staplers, merchants, i. 149
Star Chamber, the, at Westminster. *See* Westminster
Steelyard, merchants of the, i. 3, 67, 98, 99, 111 ; ii. 30, 47
——— liberties of the, ii. 60
Stepney, i. 95 ; ii. 69 ; vicar of. *See* Jerome, William
Stetchley executed, ii. 138
Stitisborne, Richard, i. 150
Stockesley, John, Bishop of London, i. 17, 46, 47, 59, 80, 81, 94, 97, 99, 105, 106
Stocks market, in London, i. 141, 164 ; ii. 8
Stoke, Battle of, i. 2
Stookes, Dr. *See* Stockesley, John
Story, Dr. Bishop of Rochester, ii. 38, 46, 82, 118, 132
Stourton, Charles, Lord, executed, ii. 137
——— Mr. ii. 22
——— William, Lord, ii. 13, 22
Strand, the, ii. 79, 92, 125, 142
Strangers ejected, ii. 112
Stratford, Essex, i. 12, 83 : ii. 10
——— Langthorne, Cistercian abbey at, i. 82
Stratford-le-Bow, town of, ii. 135
Sturgeon, John, ii. 44, 45
Subsidies, i. 8, 9, 26, 56, 143, 144 ; ii. 9, 10
Suckley, Henry, sheriff, i. 129, 134, 135
Sudley, Lord Seymour of. *See* Seymour
Suffolk, co. i. 83, 108 ; ii. 15, 21, 87, 116
——— Duchess of, i. 110 ; ii. 60, 85
——— Dukes of. *See* Brandon, and Grey, Henry
Suffolk Place, by Charing Cross, ii. 105
Supremacy the Queen's, confirmed by Act of Parliament, ii. 145
Surbot, Ralph, i. 153
Surrey co. i. 150 ; ii. 12, 42, 49
——— Earl of. *See* Howard, Henry and Thomas

168   INDEX.

Sussex co. i. 157
―― Earl of. *See* Ratcliffe, Henry and Robert
Swarte, Martin, i. 2
Swartrotters or Switzers, ii. 139
Sweating Sickness, i. 1 ; ii. 49
Synods, i. 65 ; ii. 131

Tadlow, George, ii. 52
Talbot, Francis, Earl of Shrewsbury, ii. 88, 89
―― George, Earl of Shrewsbury, i. 56, 57
―― Lord, son of the Earl of Shrewsbury, i. 20
Talboys, Elizabeth, Lady, i. 53
Tartarsall, i. 124
Taske and Disme, i. 1
Taylor, Dr. John, Dean of Lincoln and Parson of St. Peter's, Cornhill, i. 72, 187
―― Dr. parson of Hadley, ii. 3, 126
―― Serjeant, i. 135
Tempest, Nicholas, i. 63
Temple, the, ii. 67, 82
―― Bar, i. 12, 59 ; ii. 28, 35, 51, 103, 111, 125
Terouenne (Turwyn) taken by Henry VIII. i. 9
Testament, the, in English, i. 74, and *see* Bible
Testwood, Robert, i. 143
Tewkesbury, Abbot of, i. 99
Thame, ii. 116
Thames, River, i. 18, 24, 44, 49, 57, 99, 100, 122, 129, 146, 157 ; ii. 40, 76 ; frozen over, i. 10, 11, 60 ; pageant on, i. 111, 112
Thames Street, i. 81 ; ii. 8, 65
Thetford, co. Norfolk, i. 54, 70
Thirlby, Thomas, Bishop of Norwich, and Ely, ii. 133, 145
Thistleworth. *See* Isleworth
Thomas, Mr. a baker, ii. 55
―― William, Clerk of the Council, ii. 116
Thorne, i. 124
Three Cranes in the Vintry, i. 146
Throckmorton, John, ii. 135
―― Sir Nicholas, ii. 115
Througher, suit of, ii. 84
Thurst, William, Abbot of Fountains, i. 63

Thynne, Sir John, ii. 28
Tinley's wife, i. 135
Titsey, Surrey, ii. 49
Tompkins, Thomas, burnt, ii. 127
Tong, Dr. the King's Chaplain, ii. 2, 3
Tothill (Towtehill), ii. 110
Tottenham (Totnam), ii. 21
Tournay (Turney), besieged by Henry VIII. i. 9
Tower of London, i. 5, 11, 17-19, 23-30, 36-42, 44, 54, 60. 62, 64, 67, 70, 88, 92, 94, 101, 102, 108, 112, 114, 116, 120-124. 126, 131-135, 138, 139, 146, 162, 168, 169, 172, 173, 177, 179, 180, 182 ; ii. 3, 4, 6, 7, 9, 16, 23, 27, 30, 32, 33, 34, 45, 46, 51, 56, 57, 58, 62, 63, 65, 69, 74, 79, 83, 85, 86, 90, 91, 94-101, 103, 106, 107, 110, 111, 113, 115, 116, 125, 134, 137, 138, 142, 143, 144, 145
―― Constable of. *See* Kingston, Sir William ; Gage, Sir John
―― Lieutenant of. *See* Walsingham, Sir Edward ; Chamberlaine, Sir Leonard
Tower Hill, i. 4, 7, 8, 12, 13, 17, 28, 29, 32, 39, 59, 65, 69, 73, 92, 93, 101, 125, 126, 176, 177, 179 ; ii. 10, 21, 28, 67, 69, 101, 111-113, 115, 136, 138 ; Crutched Friars at, i. 59 ; Abbey of White Monks at, suppressed, i. 94
Tower Wharf, i. 159, 172 ; ii. 33, 90, 95, 130
Towley, John, hanged, ii. 128
Tracye, his works to be burnt, i. 169
Tréport (Trayport), i. 160
Tresham, Sir Thomas, Lord of St. John, ii. 116, 139
Tudor, Edmund, Duke of Somerset, third son of Henry VII. i. 4
Tunstall (Dunstall), Dr. Cuthbert, Bishop of Durham, i. 34, 99, 179 ; ii. 65, 96, 114
Turk, the Great, i. 143 ; *and see* Selim I.
Turke, a fishmonger, i. 115
―― Richard, Alderman, ii. 15, 23, 26
Turner, Edward, ii. 135
―― (Tourner), William, i. 169
Turwyn. *See* Terouenne
Tyburn, i. 14, 17, 24, 27, 28, 29, 39, 60, 62, 64, 65, 77, 84, 85, 92, 101, 121, 123, 124, 126, 132, 135 ; ii. 21, 32, 106, 112, 116, 134, 135, 138

INDEX. 169

Tylney, Catharine, i. 132
—— Malin, i. 132
Tyndale, William, his works, to be burnt, i. 168
Tyrone, Earl of. *See* O'Neil, Conan

Udall or Waddall, Richard, Captain of the Isle of Wight, executed, ii. 135
Underhill, Thomas, i. 142
Universities, the, i. 83
Uses, Statute of, i. 116

Vane (Varne), Sir Ralph, ii. 57, 66, 67
Van Paris, George, a Dutchman, burned in Smithfield, ii. 47
Varne. *See* Vane, Sir Ralph
Venice, ii. 76; secretary of, i. 184
Vere, John de, Earl of Oxford, i. 18, 45, 50, 98, 113
—— sixteenth Earl of Oxford, Lord Great Chamberlain, ii. 19, 71
Vernam or Varney, Francis, ii. 135
Vicar-General. *See* Cromwell, Sir Thomas
Vicars, a Yeoman of the Guard, hanged, ii. 111
Vintry, the, i. 146; ii. 33, 63, 109
Voysey, John, Bishop of Exeter, i. 105
Vrmon, Lord, ii. 107

Walbrook, ii. 33
Walden, co. Bedford, i. 83, 91
Wales, i. 5, 83, 84; ii. 13
—— North, i. 80
Walgrave, Edward, i. 132
Wallop, Sir John, i. 142
Walsingham, Sir Edmond, Lieutenant of the Tower, i. 37
Walsingham, Our Lady of, i. 83
Waltham, ii. 20, 61, 62
—— Abbot of, i. 59
Wanstead in Essex. ii. 93
—— Heath, ii. 95
Wansworth, Vicar of, executed, i. 101
Warbeck, Perkin, i. 3, 4
Wardgate, bridge next the, i. 170
Wardrobe, the, ii. 84
Ware, ii. 90
Warne, John, burnt, ii. 129
Warner, Sir Edward, ii. 107
—— Robert, i. 127

CAMD. SOC.

Warreyn, Sir Ralph, Lord Mayor, i. 57, 59, 146, 147, 176; ii. 8, 27, 43, 55, 87
Warton, Sir Thomas, i. 138
Warwick, Earl of. *See* Plantagenet, Edward, and Dudley, John
Watson, Thomas, B.D. Chaplain to the Bishop of Winchester, Dean of Durham, and Bishop of Lincoln, ii. 99, 144
Weaver, Hugh, i. 153
—— William, i. 160
Webbe, James, ii. 21
Webster, Augustine, Prior of Bevall, i. 27
Weld, Mr. i. 119
Weldon, Mr. Master of the Household, ii. 67, 102
Wentworth, Thomas Lord, Lord Chamberlain, ii. 33, 99, 144
West, Dr. Nicholas, Bishop of Ely, i. 10, 12
—— William, *alias* De la Warr, ii. 135
Westminster, i. 4-11, 15, 19, 25, 26, 29, 32, 36, 42-47, 51, 53, 59, 60, 62, 63, 73, 74, 93, 95, 112, 115, 119, 123-25, 132, 133, 135, 139, 143, 146, 147, 154, 157, 162, 171, 178, 182, 187; ii. 2, 9, 29, 30, 33, 35, 57, 60, 62, 66, 81, 82, 83, 106, 108-114, 116, 117, 123-125, 127, 128, 131, 132, 137, 140; Abbey, or St. Peter's, Church, i. 19-21, 31, 45, 46, 48, 94, 133, 182, 187; ii. 96, 97, 103, 114, 131, 138, 142, 143, 144, 145; Henry VII.'s Chapel in, ii. 97, 142; Abbot of, i. 46, 66; ii. 136; Dean of. *See* Cox Dr. Richard; bridge or staith at, i. 99, 131; Chamber of Presence at, i. 59; ii. 9; Gatehouse prison in, ii. 127; Hall, i. 11, 16, 19-22, 25, 36, 91, 147, 162, 179, 182, 187; ii. 62, 99, 129, 130, 136, 143, 144; King's Bench, the, at. *See* King's Bench; Palace, i. 73, 89, 94, 96, 99, 116, 133, 137, 183, 187; ii. 3, 9, 19, 20, 29, 45, 46, 130, 143; Parliament Chamber at. *See* Parliament; Star Chamber at, i. 74, 116, 130, 139, 152, 153; ii. 33, 115, 128; Tilt-yard at, ii. 113, 131
Westmorland, Earl of. *See* Nevill, Henry and Ralph
Weston, Sir Francis, i. 36; beheaded, 39, 40
—— Michael, i. 150

Z

Weston, Sir William, Lord Prior of St. John of Jerusalem, i. 118
Whalley, Mrs. ii. 58
Whetstone, Thomas, haberdasher, ii. 115
Whight, Mr. ii. 91
White, John, bishop of Lincoln, and of Winchester, ii. 144
—— Nicholas, i. 167, 168, 170
—— Sir Thomas, Lord Mayor, ii. 105
Whitechapel, called Blanck Chappeltone, i. 11, 82; ii. 93
Whitehall, i. 43: ii. 20, 29, 35, 39, 57, 60, 77, 81, 82, 83, 96, 103, 105, 114, 123, 126, 130, 131, 137, 139, 143
Whitrents, William, ii. 136
Whittington's (Wydington) College, i. 184
Wight, Isle of, i. 158; ii. 57
Wilkes, Thomas, sheriff, ii. 51-54
Wilkinson, Mr. the King's sheriff. i. 92
Williams, Sir John, Master of the Jewels, i. 133
—— John, Lord, ii. 116
—— Richard. *See* Crumwell.
Willoughby, Sir William, Lord Willoughby, i. 182
Wilson (Wyllson), Dr. i. 81, 113, 114
Wiltshire, Earl of. *See* Poulet, William; Boleyn, Sir Thomas
Winchester, ii. 118, 132, 133
—— bishop of. *See* Poynet, Gardiner, and White
Windham or Wymondham, in Norfolk, ii. 21, 30
—— Sir Edmund, sheriff of Norfolk, ii. 30
Windsor, i. 1, 6, 57, 58, 65, 70, 71; 143, 160, 181; ii. 25, 27, 121
—— palace at, i. 181
—— Andrews, Lord Windsor, i. 98
—— Dean of. *See* Frankleyn, William
—— Herald, i. 165
Wingfield, Sir Anthony, Captain of the Guard, ii. 27, 33
—— Sir Richard, i. 10, 94
Winstome, Mr. of Newbury, ii. 67
Wishe, John, a founder, i. 183
Wolf, Edward, ii. 28, 34
Wolfe, an Easterling, i. 24
Wolsey, Thomas, Archbishop of York, Cardinal and legate, i. 14; deposed 15; his death at Leicester, 16

Woodshaw's wife, ii. 8
Woodstock, ii. 116
Wood Street, new Counter in, ii. 131
Woodville, Elizabeth, widow of Edward IV. i. 2
Woolwich, ii. 76, 77
Worcester, i. 5
—— Bishop of. *See* Latimer, Dr. Hugh; Bell, Dr. John; Heath, Nicholas; and Hooper
—— Earl of. *See* Somerset William.
Wriothesley, Charles, Windsor Herald, writer of this Chronicle, i. 108; his wife, Alice, *ib.*; his cousin, Sir Thomas, i. 115
—— Henry, son of Lord Wriothesley and 2nd Earl of Southampton, i. 154
—— Sir Thomas, Lord Wriothesley, Lord Chancellor and Earl of Southampton, i. 130, 136, 147, 149, 151-155, 167, 169, 170, 176, 177, 178, 180, 182, 183, 187; ii. 33, 41
—— called my cousin, i. 115
Wyatt, Sir Thomas, ii. 107-113, 115
Wyckliffe, John, his works to be burnt, i. 169
Wyke Castle, laird of. *See* Maitland, John
Wyllford, John, Alderman, ii. 39
Wyneslowe, a rebel, ii. 30, 32
Wyngfield, Sir Anthony, Captain of the Guard and Lieutenant of the Tower, i. 176
Wysedome, Mr. curate of St. Mary the Virgin, Aldermanbury, i. 142

Yewer, Mr. i. 77
York, i. 65, 84, 124, 125
—— Archbishop of. *See* Wolsey, Thomas; Lee, Edw..; Holgate, Robert; and Heath, Dr.
—— Duke of. *See* Henry VIII.
York Place in Westminster, i. 15, 22, 44, 45, 47, 48, 49, 51, 94, 123; ii. 132
Yorke, Sir John, sheriff, ii. 26, 28, 33, 92
Yorkshire, i. 57, 58, 60, 61, 84; ii. 138

Zeeland, ii. 37

WESTMINSTER:
PRINTED BY J. B. NICHOLS AND SONS,
25, PARLIAMENT STREET.